HASKELL OF GETTYSBURG

Frank A. Haskell, courtesy of the State Historical Society of Wisconsin.

HASKELL
OF GETTYSBURG

His Life and Civil War Papers

EDITED BY

Frank L. Byrne and Andrew T. Weaver

The Kent State University Press
Kent, Ohio, and London, England

© 1989 by The Kent State University Press, Kent, Ohio 44242
All rights reserved
Library of Congress Catalog Card Number 88–30599
ISBN 0–87338–386–9
Manufactured in the United States of America

Previously published by the State Historical Society of Wisconsin in 1970.

Library of Congress Cataloging-in-Publication Data

Haskell, Franklin Aretas, 1828–1864.
    Haskell of Gettysburg : his life and Civil War papers / edited by
Frank L. Byrne and Andrew T. Weaver.
        p.   cm.
    Reprint. Originally published: Madison : State Historical Society
of Wisconsin, 1970.
    Includes bibliographical references and index.
    ISBN 0–87338–386–9 (alk. paper) ∞
    1. Haskell, Franklin Aretas, 1828–1864.   2. United States—
History—Civil War, 1861–1865—Personal narratives.   3. Gettysburg,
Battle of, 1863—Personal narratives.   4. Soldiers—Wisconsin—
Biography.   I. Byrne, Frank L. (Frank Loyola), 1928–
II. Weaver, Andrew Thomas, 1890–1965.   III. Title.
E601.H345   1989
973.7′349′0924—dc19
    [B]   88–30599
                                                                        CIP

British Library Cataloging-in-Publication data are available.

In memory of
ANDREW THOMAS WEAVER
who wished to dedicate his book
to his family

CONTENTS

Preface to the Second Edition   ix

Preface to the First Edition   xvii

I
"Ambitious as Lucifer"   1

II
Forging the Iron Brigade   23

III
Awaiting Armageddon   52

IV
Gettysburg   87

V
Afterglow   206

VI
Ambition Fulfilled   241

Index   253

Preface to the Second Edition

A CENTURY AND A QUARTER after the battle of Gettysburg, the Kent State University Press is republishing the classic description of the biggest battle yet fought in North America. Some eighteen years ago, I completed the editing of Frank A. Haskell's eyewitness account of that engagement. Then the principal justification for offering to readers another work on Gettysburg was that no previous publication of Haskell's excellent essay had fully and accurately reproduced the original manuscript. Moreover, Haskell had also left behind letters with valuable material on such other Civil War battles as Second Bull Run, Antietam, Chancellorsville, and Bristoe Station; these together with a biographical sketch would supplement Haskell's most important piece of battle prose. Though at the time of this book's original publication Gettysburg was already the subject of more printed words than any other battle in America's most studied war, interest has continued in the great battle and in the Civil War. Some discussion of how that persistent interest has affected the fame of Gettysburg might be of interest to readers.

Anyone inclined to doubt the continuing American fascination with the Civil War should pay attention to the increase of groups devoted to its reenactment. Since the war's centennial, these organizations have become more numerous and more scholarly in their approach to their avocation. As a result, the one hundred-twenty-fifth anniversary of the Civil War found many men and women prepared not only to reproduce company encampments and drills but even to represent a semblance of a major battle. Because of its size and reputation as a turning point, Gettysburg inevitably became the climax of this move-

ment, attracting some 12,500 reenactors. Their near real combat suggested that North-South rivalries and even interstate
contention (as between North Carolina and Virginia) were still
vigorous. This event and others like it near the original battlefield drew another generation of Americans to study and to
venerate the hallowed ground. Unfortunately the accompanying commercial development and the general growth of population in the eastern United States also has threatened to trans-
form the battlefield itself. One hopes that readers of Frank
Haskell's Civil War papers will be moved to support the organizations struggling to save from despoliation the fields where
he fought.

Meanwhile, scholars have enhanced our understanding of
the Civil War generally and of Gettysburg's role within it. Especially illuminating is Herman Hattaway and Archer Jones's
How the North Won.[1] While no brief summary can do justice
to the richness of its content, the book argues that the war was
decided more by logistics than by tactics. From its viewpoint,
Lee's second invasion of the North in 1863 was really a "raid," a
temporary incursion for mainly defensive objectives, including
relieving Lee's supply problems. The battle of Gettysburg
which was its culmination confronted the Confederates with
the greater challenge because the authors contend that the defense was tactically supreme, as proven by the Second Day and
most especially by Pickett's Charge on the Third Day. Yet even
if the Confederates had somehow won, they could not have destroyed the Federal force. The organization, maneuverability,
and weaponry of Civil War armies were such that even in defeat
they were usually able to retire and fight again. The authors thus
argue at length that no probable outcome of the battle was
likely to have ended the war on Confederate terms. Similarly
improbable of course was the destruction of Lee's army by its

---

[1] Herman Hattaway and Archer Jones, *How the North Won: A Military History of the Civil War* (Urbana, Chicago, London: University of Illinois Press, 1983).

opponent. This provocative thesis calls into question the assumption of Haskell and of most who have written then and since that Gettysburg was a turning point—mayhap *the* turning point of the war.

While not thus questioning the strategic significance of Gettysburg, another book differs from Haskell's understandable focus on the climactic Third Day. Instead, Harry W. Pfanz, *Gettysburg: The Second Day*[2] stresses earlier events. After giving some attention to the Confederate failure to seize Cemetery Hill on the First Day, Pfanz characterizes as decisive the fighting on the Union left on the Second Day. Less critical than Haskell of General Daniel Sickles, he nonetheless shows how Sickles's advance exposed his corps to the attacking Confederates. The repulse of that Confederate assault which Haskell describes more as an observer than as a participant may have been the battle's turning point. There rather than at the Angle on the following day, the Confederate wave may have reached its High Water Mark.

Less distinctive in terms of interpretation, William A. Frassanito, *Gettysburg: A Journey in Time*[3] differs factually at two points from *Haskell of Gettysburg*. With this book Frassanito began to make his reputation as the foremost analyst of Civil War military photographs, comparing contemporary photographs of battlefield sites with modern views of the same locations. In the process, Frassanito corrects many errors in the traditional captioning of scenes of Gettysburg. Thus he shows that the photograph which since 1866 has been identified as "the Base of Little Round Top" actually shows Confederate dead in the Slaughter Pen at the foot of Big Round Top.

[2] Henry W. Pfanz, *Gettysburg: The Second Day* (Chapel Hill: University of North Carolina, 1987).

[3] William A. Frassanito, *Gettysburg: A Journey in Time* (New York: Charles Scribner's Sons, 1975). Another of this author's books with some relationship to Haskell is *Antietam: The Photographic Legacy of America's Bloodiest Day* (New York: Charles Scribner's Sons, 1978).

Another well-known photograph of a dead Confederate soldier believed to have been taken near the Round Tops can be located more precisely in the Devil's Den near Little Round Top. Frassanito also explains that the photographers moved this body some forty yards to create the oft-reproduced view of the dead sharpshooter at his post in the Devil's Den.

While scholarly works like the foregoing are cited in *Haskell of Gettysburg*, I followed the professional historian's practice of making no reference to fiction. Because this edition may reach a popular audience and, more importantly, because fiction can convey important aspects of a battle's emotional and physical reality, it deserves attention here. Surely Stephen Vincent Benét's recollections of a boyhood visit to the Gettysburg battlefield have the power to move us even today while his poetic account of the Confederate charges—perhaps inspired by Haskell's essay—tells well what happened there. Moreover, no more graphic description of Pickett's Charge from the viewpoint of an ordinary North Carolina soldier exists than that contained in Joseph Stanley Pennell's *The History of Rome Hanks and Kindred Matters*. Yet of all the fiction about Gettysburg, the best by all odds is Michael Shaara's Pulitzer Prizewinner, *The Killer Angels*. Shaara uses the novelist's license to invent conversations and to imagine the thoughts of historical personages. Thus he creates strong characterizations while generally remaining true to the probabilities of history. With less of Haskell's sense of the battle's glory, he gives an unforgettable impression of its horror.[4]

Besides providing another sense of reality, fiction also has a unique ability to give a vision of what might have been; Gettysburg's reputation as a turning point has several times inspired writers to exercise that option. By the standards of Hat-

---

[4] Stephen Vincent Benét, *John Brown's Body* (New York: Doubleday Doran and Company, 1928); Joseph Stanley Pennell, *The History of Rome Hanks and Kindred Matters* (New York: Charles Scribner's Sons, 1944, reprinted 1982); Michael Shaara, *The Killer Angels* (New York: David McKay, 1974).

taway and Jones, most exaggerate the battle's significance. In one early example, written in the aftermath of World War I, Winston Churchill argues that Confederate victory would have made possible the ultimate reunification of the English-speaking nations and a more peaceful world. Even grander in scope, MacKinlay Kantor's *If the South Had Won the Civil War* makes the war turn on the accidental death of Grant during the Vicksburg campaign, followed by Confederate victory at Gettysburg (the result of a suddenly decisive Robert E. Lee issuing unambiguous attack orders to Richard Ewell at the end of the First Day!) After the war's end, the United States continues to exist with its new capital in Columbus, Ohio, but the Confederacy later suffers the secession of Texas. On the eve of the Civil War's centennial, the three American nations have agreed to reunite.[5]

The most remarkable example of this speculative genre is Ward Moore's insufficiently known *Bring The Jubilee*. While Moore makes too much hang on the outcome of the battle of Gettsyburg alone, he is successful in creating a plausible mid-twentieth-century world in which the defeated United States is more racist than the victorious South and infinitely more backward in every way. Impoverished Northerners have few choices but to indenture themselves or to join the Confederate Legion in which they can earn valuable Confederate money. Of course the rest of the world is also a different place, as Moore suggests. Among his more amusing touches are references to such publications as the sermons of an "obscure Irish theologian," George B. Shaw, and the classifications of human personalities by the "Swiss police chief, Carl Jung." Moore's central character manages to become a student of the history of Lee's victorious final campaigns. From its beginning to its re-

---

[5] Winston S. Churchill, "If Lee Had Not Won the Battle of Gettysburg," in J. C. Squire, ed., *If: Or, History Rewritten* (New York: Viking, 1931; Port Washington: Kennikat, 1964); MacKinlay Kantor, *If The South Had Won the Civil War* (New York: Bantam Books, 1961).

consideration of Gettysburg, Moore's book inspires thought about the nature of historical causation.[6]

The alternative possibilities that apply to nations at war exist as well for the individual participants; the bullet that killed Frank Haskell was but one of his life's options. The events of the interval since the completion of the original edition of *Haskell of Gettysburg* have stimulated me to further consideration of the effect of war on human lives. The year of the publication of *Haskell* was one in which protests against the Vietnam War at the university at which I teach resulted in four deaths and the alteration of many lives. The greater effects of the war itself are suggested by its principal American monument which consists of an overwhelming list of the individual names of the dead. As a member of the board of the Ohio Society of Military History, I have often visited its museum at Massillon which is wholly devoted to the lives of particular veterans including many Medal of Honor winners—frequently awarded posthumously. I also have coedited the letters of another Civil War colonel, Marcus Spiegel, killed within a year before peace.[7] In his case, it seems likely that his military career might otherwise have culminated in promotion to general followed by success in business and/or politics. What were the probabilities had Frank Haskell survived the Civil War?

One might readily guess that his civilian life would have consisted of routine legal practice. Though he undoubtedly would have retired as a brigadier general, the Haskell who appears in these letters did not have the political capacity to win high office in Wisconsin. It is difficult to imagine him competing successfully with his fellow Iron Brigade veteran, wily Lucius Fairchild, in exploiting for political effect his wounds and military record. Much most likely would have been a decision

[6] Ward Moore, *Bring The Jubilee* (New York: Farrar, Straus & Young; Ballantine, 1953, Avon, 1972).

[7] Frank L. Byrne and Jean Powers Soman, *Your True Marcus: The Civil War Letters of a Jewish Colonel* (Kent: Kent State University Press, 1985).

to stay in the military; in the catch phrase of twentieth-century soldiers, Haskell seemed to have "found a home in the Army." He might have served in the Reconstructed South or in the Indian Wars, probably anonymously in either case unless it had turned out to be the "Haskell" rather than the Fetterman Massacre! Frank Haskell's best chance for limited military distinction might have been a staff appointment with John Gibbon or Winfield Scott Hancock.

Among alternate possibilities, the greatest probable loss to Frank Haskell and to us was the early termination of his career as an author. Like many Civil War soldiers, he had improved his writing by practice and the Gettysburg essay demonstrates that he was consciously honing his skills. Had he lived, he had the ability and the connections with the high command of the Army of the Potomac necessary to write insightfully about the war's last campaigns. Whatever his postwar career, but certainly if he had remained in the army, it is likely that he would have written about his experiences and perhaps have dealt with military aspects about which we still know too little. With the death of Frank Haskell at Cold Harbor, posterity probably lost one of the Civil War's great memorialists. While we may mourn that loss, we may be glad that we again have the papers reproduced in *Haskell of Gettysburg*.

FRANK L. BYRNE

Kent, Ohio

Preface to the First Edition

FRANK HASKELL won his reputation through the battle of Gettysburg. At the supreme crisis of that conflict, he had the courage, the military knowledge, and the luck required to influence its outcome. Others might claim a similar accomplishment. But no one else also wrote a gripping, detailed narrative in which he relived his own experience within the context of the entire battle. Haskell had the time, the literary interest, and the technical skill to write the classic description of Gettysburg. No other participant matched him as a combined actor-author; no other Wisconsin author on any subject during the period surpassed him; and though he was killed less than a year after his great battle, he achieved a kind of immortality. Frank Haskell made it impossible to write or read very much about a turning point of American history without encountering his name.

But how had Haskell's life prepared him to win this distinction? To illuminate his background, this book contains the first detailed biographical sketch of the soldier-author. Moreover, it includes the bulk of his Civil War papers. Thirty-nine of the letters which Haskell wrote to his brothers in Portage, Wisconsin, still survive. While Frank Haskell may have intended several of them for possible publication, they are mainly the private letters of an intelligent staff officer who, like many Civil War soldiers, was convinced of the historical importance of what he was doing. All but one of the Haskell letters are in the Manuscripts Division of the State Historical Society of Wisconsin. Of these, thirty appear in the following chapters. The eight omitted letters, whose dates are indicated at appropriate points, are mostly brief; and all are inconsequential or repetitious in content. Haskell's most famous letter, his narrative of Gettysburg, is in the collection of the Pennsylvania Historical and Museum Commission. As explained below (page 87), this carefully composed masterwork is more an essay than a letter. And though the Gettysburg piece is no stranger to print, this book contains the first scholarly edition of it based upon the original manuscript. All of the letters are uncut and just as Haskell wrote them.

This volume was the dream of Andrew Thomas Weaver, Professor of Speech at the University of Wisconsin. For years his avocation was the study of Frank Haskell. He examined, of course, the Haskell papers and related documents in Pennsylvania and Wisconsin. Following in the footsteps of his hero, he visited Haskell's birthplace, his college, the places associated with him in Wisconsin, and his principal battlefields. He also tracked down and interviewed Haskell's closest living relatives. In 1963 he put his dream on paper and called it "Haskell of Gettysburg." Before he could revise his manuscript, he died in a tragic accident. The State Historical Society of Wisconsin invited me to prepare the work for publication. I have done so, using Professor Weaver's manuscript and materials and the results of my own research. While I have rewritten and revised, I believe that the man contained in these pages is still essentially Andrew T. Weaver's Haskell of Gettysburg.

Wishing to thank all who assisted in his project, Professor Weaver expressed particular appreciation to some who were most helpful. Among them were Harvey Harrison Haskell, Richard Haskell, and Glen H. Noyes, all related to Frank Haskell and all sources of family information. Professor Weaver was grateful to learn the location of the long-overlooked manuscript of the Gettysburg narrative from James B. Stevenson, a relative by marriage of Haskell's and the Chairman of the Pennsylvania Historical and Museum Commission. He wished also to thank these institutional staff members who aided him: Edward Connery Lathem and Ethel Martin of Dartmouth College; Leslie W. Dunlap and James A. Kent of the State University of Iowa; and Helen Northup of the University of Wisconsin. Edwin C. Bearss, William K. Kay, and Jeanne B. Harvey supplied data and assistance for which Professor Weaver was grateful. He acknowledged with thanks the financial support of the Research Committee of the Graduate School, University of Wisconsin, and he especially appreciated the interest of John E. Willard and Vernon Carstensen of that institution. For aid in preparing his manuscript, he thanked Ruth Price and his daughter-in-law, Ruberta Harwell Weaver.

I join Professor Weaver in acknowledging the help of the following people and institutions whose co-operation has been invaluable. The Pennsylvania Historical and Museum Commission generously facilitated our access to Haskell's Gettysburg narrative. Donald H. Kent, S. K. Stevens, and William H. Work of its staff helped both of us. The State Historical Society of Wisconsin provided us with the mass of Haskell letters, and we thank its former director, Leslie H. Fishel, Jr., for his active interest. We are also grateful to Josephine L. Harper, head of the Manuscripts Division, and to Ruth H. Davis, Service Librarian. A grant from the Wisconsin Civil War Centennial Commission, husbanded by the State Historical Society of Wisconsin since 1965, made possible the publication of this volume.

Fortunately for scholarship, historians' wives have traditionally been willing to accept a line of acknowledgement in return for a great deal of help and toleration of inconvenience. While this seemingly inequitable arrangement can not actually pay my debt to my wife, I use it to offer an installment of thanks.

FRANK L. BYRNE

Kent, Ohio

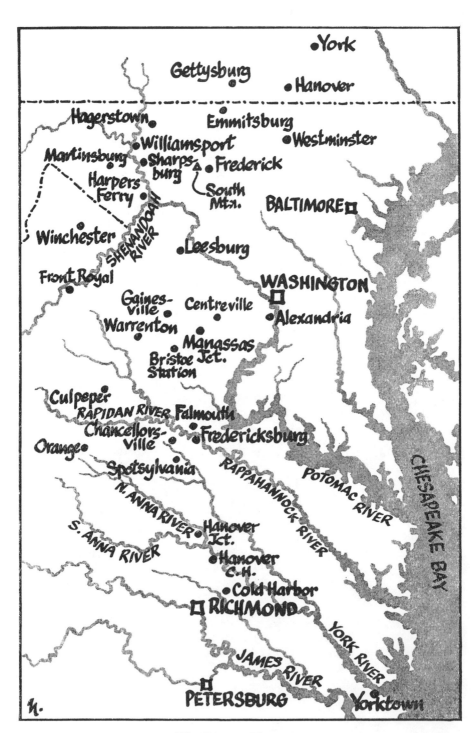

The Eastern Theater

I

"Ambitious as Lucifer"

"HASKELL, FRANKLIN A.," mused Edwin David Sanborn, as he entered the name in his notebook. Sanborn, the distinguished Professor of Latin in Dartmouth College, was evaluating the members of the Class of 1854. While popular with students, who respected his encyclopedic knowlege and teaching ability, the professor was also bluff, outspoken, and extremely critical. In assessing students, he was unsentimentally realistic. He characterized one former undergraduate as "weak in mind, stupid and inefficient—gifted in singing but in nothing else" and another as "A good scholar but a bad man." Thus his appraisal of Haskell was, for Sanborn, a relatively favorable one. "Improved greatly in College—ranked well as a scholar—," Sanborn wrote. Turning then to Haskell's personal character, he added: "—ambitious as Lucifer and possibly mischievous and irregular."[1]

While Sanborn had depicted only Haskell's college past, the mature Frank Haskell would make his professor at least in part a true prophet. Like Lucifer, Sanborn's whilom student would risk his being in his quest for glory. Losing his life, Haskell would win renown that will last as long as men read martial epics.

---

[1] Sanborn's notebook is in the Dartmouth College Archives, Hanover, New Hampshire. For more on him, see Leon Burr Richardson, *History of Dartmouth College* (2 vols., Hanover, N.H., 1932), 2: 567–68.

1

Like most Dartmouth students of his day, Haskell was a true Yankee. Of English stock long settled in America, he was born on July 13, 1828, at East Hill in the town of Tunbridge, Vermont. He was named Franklin Aretas, the latter being his father's Biblical first name. Franklin's mother, the former Anna Folsom, was her husband's second wife. The first, who died in 1816, had borne three children. Aretas and Anna Folsom Haskell had eight more, of whom Franklin was the sixth. To make even more numerous the household in which the boy grew up, his grandfather Job Haskell, the original owner of the family farm, shared the comfortably large frame house. Old Job Haskell was a veteran of repeated enlistments in the New Hampshire soldiery during the Revolutionary War. Since Franklin was nine years old by the time his ninety-three-year-old grandfather died, he might well have heard from the lips of the aged veteran his first tales of war.

Young Franklin grew up in the seasonal routine of the New England farm boy. In spring, he helped his father and brothers to plow the rocky soil. In summer, he tended flocks and herds in the hilly pastures from which he could see the distant Green Mountains. And, after the fall harvest, he attended the district school. While he never received classical secondary schooling at an academy, he occasionally attended a "select school" for a month or two in the fall. Moreover, he was an eager reader, with access to books and with a good memory. Thus, by the time he was seventeen, he was ready to share what his older brother, Harrison S. Haskell, later recalled as "the almost inevitable fate of all New England boys, of any promise": Franklin himself became a school master. For three years, he "taught school winters and wrought upon the farm summers. . . ." By then, in the opinion of his older brother, Franklin Haskell was "an excellent English scholar" in most of the branches required for college entrance, knew some Latin, was well read in history and English literature and, in sum, "was better posted, than most boys of his age and station. . . ."[2]

---

[2] Ira J. Haskell, *Chronicles of the Haskell Family* (Lynn, Mass.,

At the age of twenty, Franklin Haskell placed himself in the hands of his older brother, who did much to cultivate his academic aspirations. Born in 1817, Harrison S. Haskell was the first fruit of his father's conventionally quick remarriage. He too had only a common school education, but he had prepared himself for college, entered the University of Vermont, and graduated in 1845. After beginning to study law in Vermont, he moved in 1846 to Beloit, in Wisconsin Territory, where in a legal office he read enough law to win speedy admission to the bar. In 1847, Harrison S. Haskell established his practice in the frontier settlement of Columbus, Wisconsin, and a year later, like many western lawyers, he also became a land agent. The prospering lawyer took a wife on August 24, 1848, when he married Maria Hawley Pride, a Vermont woman with a young daughter by a previous marriage. Having set up his own household, Harrison Haskell invited his younger brother to join him and to prepare to follow the same path to success.[3]

On September 18, 1848, Franklin Haskell started for the west. Making frequent changes of coach, boat, and train, he traveled by way of Montreal and Toronto to the Great Lakes. On this first break with home, the young man looked eagerly for unfamiliar sights. He chauvinistically contrasted Buffalo with the Canadian towns along the St. Lawrence. "The latter are still, quiet and quite destitute of the bustel [sic] of business; the former, hurrah! boys, hurly burly, go ahead, heavens what a noise." He concluded, "No one needs telling that he

---

1943), *passim;* Andrew T. Weaver's notes on Anna Folsom Haskell's Bible and of a visit to the sites of the Haskell homestead and of Job Haskell's grave, in the Manuscripts Division, State Historical Society of Wisconsin (hereinafter cited as SHSW); [Harrison S. Haskell], Biographical Sketch of Frank A. Haskell, in the Frank A. Haskell Papers, SHSW. All the quoted words are from the last source.

[3] H. S. Haskell, Sketch of F.A. Haskell, in Haskell Mss., and Weaver, notes on Haskell Bible, both in SHSW; entry for H. S. Haskell in U.S., Census Bureau, Manuscript Returns for 1860, Columbia County, Wis., volume, p. 115, SHSW; [C. W. Butterfield], *History of Columbia County, Wisconsin* (Chicago, 1880), 518.

is in the land of Yankees." By lake steamer, he then went to Detroit where he attended the theater, viewed by many of his fellow New Englanders as the antechamber of hell. This descendant of the Puritans was never rigidly puritanical. As Haskell rode on the train west from Detroit, he began to pass less settled lands which offended eyes used to the well-ordered Vermont landscape. He termed the region "one of the meanest (yes, meanest, a better word would be abused) country on the globe. . . ." From the end of track, he took stagecoach and boats to Chicago and then Milwaukee. To the Easterner, his first day's journey in "Wisconsin the land of Badgers" was an unpleasant experience. He rode to Watertown "on board a lumber cart, over sticks, stones, stumps, logs, bogs, mud, mire, muck; jolted, jounced, thrashed, thumped, bruised and very tired. . . ." On the next day, October 6, in a good carriage over a better road, the young traveler finally reached what he satirically called "the urbs, Columbus."[4]

Haskell had become the resident of a raw new settlement. His community was little more than a cluster of buildings recently erected on the rolling land of south-central Wisconsin. True, its settlers were establishing as quickly as possible the institutions of Yankee civilization. Since 1846, the settlement had boasted a schoolhouse—and brother Harrison was Clerk of the School Board. In 1850, those loyal to the traditional New England religious faith established a Congregational Church. Again Harrison S. Haskell was involved, even writing the articles of incorporation. His ubiquity indicated his prominent status in the little village. In his civic-minded, cultivated brother, Franklin Haskell had a strong local sponsor and an able academic counselor.[5]

[4] Frank A. Haskell, Day Book, a brief record of his trips in 1848 and 1850, with some intervening financial accounts, in the Dartmouth Archives. The quoted words are, respectively, from the entries for September 25, 28, and 30 and November [actually October] 5 and 6, 1848.
[5] Butterfield, *History of Columbia County*, 518, 665–69; Weaver, notes of research in Columbus local records, SHSW. No reference has been found to any religious affiliation for Frank Haskell.

Thus Franklin A. Haskell's life at Columbus was less that of a rough frontiersman than of an apprentice professional man. He wore shirts of broadcloth far more often than he donned the cruder flannel, and by the standards of his day he changed them fastidiously often. His work too was mostly clerical. The twenty-one-year-old secured the post of Town Clerk, being appointed to fill a vacancy on October 2, 1849, and winning election in his own right the following spring. On November 20, 1849, he also obtained a position as Superintendent of Schools. His pay for each of his public services was moderate— $1 for each day of active service as Town Clerk, $ .50 for examining a school teacher, $1 for surveying a road—but the totals were enough to be significant: as Town Clerk he made only a minimum of $27.30, but as School Superintendent he earned at least $224.70. He was able to live comfortably and perhaps to save something for college.[6]

Haskell's work left him time to make friends. Of these, according to his brother, his "most intimate friend and companion" was young Edmund Jussen. Like Haskell, Jussen was destined to be a Civil War officer and attorney and ultimately would gain the politically important job of Collector of Internal Revenue at Chicago. Franklin Haskell doubtless also developed some acquaintance with his brother's law partner, Joshua J. Guppy, whose alma mater he decided to attend.[7] Probably most important to the young man, he fell in love. Shortly after he left Columbus, he ". . .dreamed of her in all her lovliness [sic] and girlish simplicity. Would to Heaven the dream were real," he moaned. But his relationship with the unnamed girl faded without trace. Though he would later paint for friends an idealized word picture of his future wife

---

[6] F. A. Haskell, Day Book, in the Dartmouth Archives, contains his laundry list for April 1–July 22, 1850, and also at least part of his accounts as Town Clerk and School Superintendent. For his appointments to these posts, see records in the possession of the Clerk of Columbus Township, Wis.

[7] H. S. Haskell, Sketch of F. A. Haskell, Haskell Mss., SHSW; file on Joshua J. Guppy, W.P.A. Writers' Project Field Notes, SHSW.

and though acquaintances would occasionally link his name with a lady's, Franklin Haskell never married.[8]

Neither friendship nor work took precedence over Haskell's preparation for college. During his two years at Columbus, he read in the law office with some guidance from Harrison Haskell. His brother later admitted that such preparation might well not equal that offered by a classical academy in New England. Self-taught himself, Harrison Haskell argued that his brother had received compensating advantages, had "breathed in, the great spirit of the West," had seen men and things in new ways, "and above all had learned habits of self reliance and perseverance that ever after attended him, and made him succeed in whatever he undertook." Under his brother's tutelage, Franklin Haskell had developed his self-discipline and read enough to enroll in college.[9]

On July 25, 1850, the Yankee from the west left what he called "the old town of my adoption" en route to academe. He stopped at Milwaukee to buy coats, a vest, and gloves suitable for more civilized parts and then he departed by lake steamer. His comments on the trip were more polished than those written two years earlier and reflected his reading. Thus, watching the smoke rising from the steamer's stacks, he remarked, "It floats as smoky and black as did the plumes of Hector: 'His towering helmet black with shading plumes.' " He saw ample evidence of the hazards of steamboat travel, boarding at Erie, Pennsylvania, one boat which had just exploded with heavy human loss. Nevertheless, the hard-driving young man was scornful of slower means of transportation when he took a barge from Erie along what he jokingly called "the 'raging canal' " to the vicinity of Conneautville, Pennsylvania.

---

[8] The quoted words are from F. A. Haskell, Day Book, Dartmouth Archives, July 30, 1850. There is a reference to Haskell's ideal of a wife and another to a rumored engagement in Frank Haskell's autograph album and in correspondence of his classmates. All these items are in the Dartmouth Archives.

[9] H. S. Haskell, Sketch of F. A. Haskell, Haskell Mss., SHSW.

There he visited for nearly two weeks with his half-brother, John Winship Haskell, and with his sister, Olive Folsom Williams. On the morning after his arrival, Franklin Haskell expressed his pleasure at awakening "with a salute from a sister" — his ties with his kin were always close. But on August 12, he bade them farewell with a "Hurrah! for Vt." and a few days later, traveling mostly by train, he was at home.[10]

In September, 1850, Haskell evidently passed the oral examination in Greek, Latin, and mathematics required for admission to Dartmouth College. Located in Hanover, New Hampshire, the institution instructed over two hundred students in several somewhat dilapidated brick and frame buildings. Franklin Haskell had selected a school with a reputation for Congregationalist orthodoxy and with a traditional classical curriculum. Hence he lived a rather Spartan life, with compulsory prayers early and late interspersed with long periods of reading and recitation. He studied much in the ancient languages and in philosophy, a fair amount of mathematics and science, and a smattering of history. Significantly, he also spent considerable time on rhetoric, which gave him much practice in formal writing as well as in oral declamation. According to his brother, Haskell found his first year of the rigorous program to be "exceedingly laborious." Nevertheless, starting below his formally prepared classmates, he steadily improved his academic standing until he ranked among the higher-rated seniors.[11]

In addition to the formal Dartmouth curriculum, Haskell enjoyed other opportunities for self-development. Like most nineteenth-century colleges, Dartmouth had several literary societies which provided a forum for debates, lectures, and the

---

[10] F. A. Haskell, Day Book, Dartmouth Archives. The quoted words are from, respectively, the entries for July 25, 29 and 31, and August 1 and 12, 1850.

[11] Richardson, *History of Dartmouth*, 1: 209–10, 376–77, 393–96, 413–15; 2: 429–45, 479–82; H. S. Haskell, Sketch of F. A. Haskell, Haskell Mss., SHSW.

practice of parliamentary tactics. Haskell joined and participated in the program of the Hermian Society. An additional
educational experience was school-teaching. To enable students to earn money for college, the Dartmouth schedule was
arranged to permit them to spend thirteen or more mid-winter
weeks teaching in district schools. While the effect was doubtless less upon an experienced teacher like Haskell, such teaching probably increased the maturity and self-discipline of most
of the college men. At least so thought one of Haskell's classmates, who later reflected: "It is not any wonder that Haskell
was a better disciplinarian than any other colonel who took
a regiment from Wisconsin during the war. . . ."[12]

Outside as well as inside the schoolroom, Haskell was a conspicuous success. Possibly because at twenty-two he was older
than the average freshman, he quickly became a leader. Near
the end of his first year, when several students were sent home
because of disorders during a railroad excursion, Haskell was
one of the two-man "class committee" which attempted to convince the father of one of those punished that his son had not
been guilty of "acts of gross drunkenness, insult offered to
ladies, and disgraceful obscenity. . . ." By then, Haskell had
shortened his name to Frank,[13] although to his college friends
he was often Billy or Bill. He himself evidently sometimes engaged in collegiate pranks. A classmate later recalled to him
the "codfish that once sent through Old Dartmouth Hall perfumes more redolent."[14] As a senior, Haskell was active in the
many meetings of his class of fifty-seven men and for a time
served as its president. He was prominent in a class movement
to refuse membership in Phi Beta Kappa on the ground that

---

[12] Richardson, *History of Dartmouth,* 1: 244–46, 268–70; 2: 481,
495; items in the Dartmouth Archives, particularly Charles Caver-
no, "Class of 1854: Class History," which contains the quoted
words.

[13] Frank A. Haskell and Reuben D. Mussey to H. Crosby, July
21, 1851, in the Dartmouth Archives.

[14] Frank A. Haskell autograph album, in the Dartmouth Archives.

the local chapter had become more a social than an honorary society. By the time he graduated on July 27, 1854, after a commencement week in which he delivered two orations on literary and artistic topics, Haskell had received training in leadership as well as in scholarship.[15]

Still following the path pioneered by his older brother, Frank Haskell decided to use his education to become a lawyer in the west. In the fall of 1854, he returned to his new home state of Wisconsin. At twenty-six he was no doubt more imposing than the youth who had gone there in 1848. Standing just an inch under six feet tall, he was of erect, almost martial bearing. His face was long, tapering from a large forehead to a somewhat narrow chin. He had hazel eyes under rather heavy brows, a long, straight nose, and a wide mouth. His complexion was fair and his curly hair, which hung partly over his ears and down his neck, was also light; when he experimented with whiskers, a friend termed them pink. As he looked, so he was—a sturdy and promising young man.[16]

Haskell's destination was one of the more challenging arenas for a would-be attorney. In Wisconsin, he settled at Madison, the seat of state and county governments and of local and federal courts. While the city was still new and small — even its boosters hardly dared claim a population much over 5,000 —its unique legal position within the state attracted a numerous and able corps of lawyers whose offices were in the few business blocks which had sprung up on the square around the small stone Capitol. While the more prosperous residents were building homes near the beautiful lakes which girded Madi-

---

[15] "College Record Book, Class of 1854"; a slip in Haskell's writing concerning Phi Beta Kappa; commencement program for 1854, all in the Dartmouth Archives; New York *Tribune,* August 3, 1854; Edward C. Lathem, "Chronicler of Gettysburg," in *Dartmouth Alumni Magazine* (May, 1958), 21–22.

[16] Portraits in *ibid.;* additional physical description in Haskell's file in U.S., War Department, Adjutant General's Office, Compiled Service Records for members of the 6th Wisconsin Infantry, National Archives, Washington, D.C.

son, the city's groves of trees still were more impressive than its relatively few buildings. In this attractive theater of litigation, Haskell made his home.[17]

As was the contemporary practice, especially in the west, the young college graduate prepared to become a lawyer by reading law in an established firm—in effect a form of apprenticeship. The legal partners for whom he worked were distinguished attorneys. Two of them were brothers, Harlow S. and Myron H. Orton. Respectively thirty-seven and forty-four years old, they were originally from upstate New York and were experienced lawyers and office holders. The former brother would one day be dean of the University of Wisconsin law school and a justice of the state supreme court. The third partner, Julius P. Atwood, was about thirty and, like Haskell, was from Vermont, where he had attended a military academy, Norwich University. Under the guidance of these men, on June 30, 1856, Haskell won admission to the bar.[18]

Not long afterward, Haskell became Atwood's junior partner in a new firm. They maintained their office in Bruen's Block, a fine stone building on the Capitol Square, and Haskell boarded nearby at the old American House. In 1859, they took in as senior partner Alexander Lynn Collins, a true Wisconsin legal luminary who had resigned as circuit judge because of ill health. While Collins soon moved to Menasha to join in the speculations of his brother-in-law, ex-governor James

---

[17] William N. Seymour, *Madison Directory and Business Advertiser* (Madison, 1855), 13, 25, 61–63, 125.

[18] H. S. Haskell, Sketch of F. A. Haskell, Haskell Mss., SHSW. For Harlow S. Orton, see *Dictionary of Wisconsin Biography* (Madison, 1960), 272–73 (hereinafter cited as DWB); for Myron H. Orton, see Parker M. Reed, *The Bench and Bar of Wisconsin: History and Biography* (Milwaukee, 1882), 350–51. Atwood served as county judge in 1854, filling a vacancy, and later was an unsuccessful candidate for mayor of Madison and for associate justice of the state supreme court. He subsequently lived in Illinois, Michigan, and the Black Hills of South Dakota, dying at Denver, Colorado, on November 30, 1880. SHSW, *Report and Collections*, Vol. 9 (1880–82), 454.

Duane Doty, his membership in the firm probably helped explain its increasing prominence.[19] Within two years, Collins, Atwood, and Haskell appeared ten times before the Wisconsin Supreme Court.[20] In his years as a Madison lawyer, Haskell fulfilled his initial promise. A contemporary attorney, who regarded Haskell's legal ability as much above the ordinary, later characterized his friend as being "strong, acute, logical, but modest and unpretentious."[21]

While arguing in court and preparing legal briefs, Frank Haskell also practiced more esthetic speaking and writing. He found opportunity for this in the Madison Institute, of which he was president in 1858. The Institute sponsored lectures and maintained a reading room in the same building that housed Haskell's law office. Haskell probably read before the Institute an essay entitled "The American Character" which he wrote in 1858. In it, he demonstrated himself to be optimistic, patriotic, and decidedly unoriginal in thought. But he expressed himself well and gave promise of being able to do justice to a great theme, should one be thrust upon him. Through the Institute, Haskell also developed and intensified friendships. One such was his relationship with Frank H. Firmin, a young lawyer from Massachusetts who also lived at the American House and had his office in Bruen's Block. Haskell would one day find him to be an especially helpful friend.[22]

---

[19] Smith, DuMoulin and Co., comps., *Madison City Directory and Business Mirror. . . , 1858* (Milwaukee, 1858), advertising page for American House and pp. 67, 151; legal advertisement, Madison *Daily Argus and Democrat,* February 3, 1859; biographical sketch of Collins in Wis. Mss., SHSW; Alice E. Smith, *James Duane Doty, Frontier Promoter* (Madison, 1954), 353.

[20] 6 Wis 143, 209, 282; 7 Wis 329, 627; 8 Wis 372; 11 Wis 12, 69; 12 Wis 244; 13 Wis 187.

[21] A. B. Braley to R. D. Mussey, February 8, 1884, in Records of the Class of 1854, Dartmouth Archives.

[22] Seymour, *Madison Directory* (1855), 37–38; Smith, Du Moulin and Co., *Madison Directory, 1858,* 27, 136; original copy of the

Both Haskell and Firmin were members of another Madison civic group, the Governor's Guard. Haskell was among the callers of the meeting which on January 30, 1858, organized this volunteer company of the Wisconsin militia. Among its members, originally eighty-eight in number, were many of Madison's leading young men. At one time there were twenty-five lawyers in the unit. They elected Haskell's partner, Julius P. Atwood, to be their captain because of his military training at Norwich University. On August 25, 1858, when a vacancy occurred for First Corporal, Haskell won that post. The new company, which often drilled weekly and twice weekly, intended to provide a martial display for public events. By the summer of 1858, after great discussion of the details of its uniform, the Guard was clothed in its new finery and able to join in parades. The members enjoyed such marching. As one remarked, "I go in for a reasonable amount of fun, and [the] military has some little fun together with some nonsense in it." The company's many military balls, which Haskell helped to arrange, were a favorite with the little city's social leaders.

In his second year in the Governor's Guard, because of a change in its leadership, Frank Haskell became more prominent. The politically active young men who made up the bulk of the company devoted much time to debates about finances, quibbles about procedure, and threats to resign. For a time, the majority centered its dissatisfaction on Atwood's running of the company. On February 9, 1859, under the leadership of Elisha W. Keyes, a young lawyer who would soon be boss of the Wisconsin Republican party, they replaced Haskell's partner with a man not then a member of the company. The new captain, whom Keyes hoped would unite and rein-

essay in the Dartmouth Archives. Firmin later held local and state offices in Wisconsin and was President of the Madison Plow Company. He then moved to Nebraska and Ohio, dying at Toledo on March 15, 1909. [C.W. Butterfield], *History of Dane County, Wisconsin* (Chicago, 1880), 986; *Madison Democrat*, March 17, 1909.

vigorate the Guard, was George P. Delaplaine, a forty-four-year-old civil engineer, an early settler of Madison and a man of great energy. Haskell was an unsuccessful candidate for First Sergeant; but on April 13, 1859, he won the post in a special election to fill a vacancy. In 1860, when Delaplaine was re-elected, Haskell was the successful contender for the post of First Lieutenant.

As First Sergeant and Lieutenant, he co-operated earnestly with Delaplaine's efforts to improve attendance and performance at drills. The civilian soldiers marched up and down the dusty streets and fired their ancient Springfields at targets along the lake. The men deemed Haskell a hard taskmaster and sometimes reacted in most unmilitary ways. One summer afternoon, Elisha Keyes and a friend simply bolted from Haskell's relentless drill, stacked their muskets at the Armory and "hunted for a cool restful place." The punishment for such defiance was only a fine. Keyes later recalled as Haskell's "peculiar disposition; that he had little sympathy for a raw soldier no matter how much he was suffering from heat dust and thirst when on duty or on the march." Haskell took seriously his role as amateur soldier.[23]

---

[23] The basic sources are Governor's Guard, Madison, Wis., Record Book, in Mss. Div., SHSW, which contains the minutes, and Wis. National Guard, Records of the Governor's Guard, 1858–1861, Ser. 37/4/20, Archives Div., SHSW, which includes two financial registers. The first quotation is from Lucius Fairchild to Libbie [Gordon], February 22, 1859, in the Fairchild Papers, SHSW. See also an announcement of a ball, June 12, 1858, Sarah [Fairchild] to Libbie [Gordon], February 8, 1859, circular letter of George P. Delaplaine, May 25, 1859, in *ibid.* The second quotation is from Elisha W. Keyes, Address on the Governor's Guard delivered March 31, 1910, in the Elisha W. Keyes Papers, SHSW. See also Madison *Daily State Journal,* February 20, 1858, February 15, 1859, April 30, 1895; Madison *Daily Patriot,* February 12, 1859. Keyes, 1828–1910, was a Vermonter who came to Wisconsin as a boy in 1837. He practiced law beginning in 1851 at Madison in partnership with George B. Smith, who defeated Haskell in the mayoralty campaign described below. DWB, 203–04. E. Elmer Ellsworth, organizer of zouaves and one of the first martyr-heroes

While Frank Haskell and his friends found fun in soldiering, there mounted around them the sectional conflict which would turn their game into deadly reality. Haskell was openly committed to the North's sectional party. In 1858 he was a minor contender for the Republican nomination for Police Justice in Madison. A year later, after the Republican City Convention's first choice refused to face certain defeat, Haskell received the Republican mayoralty nomination. He and his friends recognized that his was a forlorn hope. Haskell, who was a delegate to the convention, commented with respect to another nomination that "there was no use denying the fact that republicans were sorely in the minority in Madison. . . ." A Democratic editor, calling Haskell "a young lawyer of many good qualities," patronizingly concluded, "Frank is a very good fellow, but of course will be laid upon the shelf to 'season' a while." In the unenthusiastic balloting of March 7, 1859, Haskell lost to the incumbent Democratic Mayor George B. Smith by a vote of 397 to 961. In 1860, Haskell again was a delegate to the City Convention but not a candidate. That fall the turmoil following his party's first presidential victory ended his political career.[24]

As South Carolina and her Deep Southern neighbors reacted with ordinances of secession to Abraham Lincoln's election, Haskell and his fellow militiamen faced with some uncertainty the possibility of civil war. On January 9, 1861, secessionist batteries at Charleston drove off the *Star of the West,* a federally chartered supply ship en route to Fort Sumter at the mouth of the South Carolina harbor. At a Guard meeting that night, a militant officer, Lieutenant Daniel K.

---

of the Civil War, served briefly in 1858 as drillmaster for a boys' unit of the Governor's Guard. "Colonal Ellsworth's Madison Career" in *Wisconsin Magazine of History,* 1: 89–91 (September, 1917).

[24] Madison *Daily State Journal,* February 22, 1858, March 5, 7, 8, 1859, March 29, 1860. The first quotation is from Madison *Daily Argus and Democrat,* March 5, 1859. The second is from Madison *Daily Patriot,* March 7, 1859.

Tenney, responded to the incident by moving that the company offer its services to the governor to help enforce the laws. Haskell, temporarily acting as chairman, ruled the motion out of order and was sustained. The opponents stressed the absurdity of offering their services to an official who legally could call them out at will. As it turned out, the war excitement declined, the stalemate at Fort Sumter continued, and the Guards kept on drilling and dancing much as usual. Ill-feeling over the episode within the company may have had some influence on the decisions of both Captain Delaplaine and Lieutenant Haskell to decline re-election. This they did in February, despite the protest of a majority of the company meeting and the pleas of various editors, and Julius P. Atwood regained the captaincy. Thus, on April 12, when the Confederate bombardment of Fort Sumter revived the war fever, it was Haskell's partner who finally and dramatically offered the company to the Union.

Like many militiamen, Haskell made his decision to enlist more slowly than legend would have it. On the morning of April 17, Atwood informed Governor Alexander W. Randall that the Governor's Guard had "unanimously" tendered its services, and Randall accepted the company as the first of the 1st Wisconsin Regiment. In fact, however, Haskell, Atwood, and many other Guards did not join their fellows in this unit. Most would go eventually—indeed, by the end of the war, nine of the Guardsmen would be colonels, of whom six received general's rank. But for a time Haskell and others drilled with the Hickory Guards, a new volunteer company heavily laden with state officeholders who obviously did not intend to go to war, and also briefly kept active the remnant of the Governor's Guard. Why did Haskell hesitate after years of drilling? Most probably the ambitious amateur drillmaster awaited a position equal to his expectations.[25]

---

[25] Wis. Governor's Guard, Record Book, SHSW; Keyes, Address on the Governor's Guard, Keyes Papers, SHSW; Madison *Daily Patriot*, January 10, 11, February 25, March 14, 15, 1861; Madison

On June 20, 1861, Haskell accepted a commission as First Lieutenant and Adjutant of the new 6th Wisconsin Infantry Regiment. While his rank was not high, his position on the regimental staff made him the commander's right arm. He would have ample opportunity to use his skill as a drillmaster in helping to instruct both the company officers and their men. Haskell's colonel, Lysander Cutler, was a Yankee from Milwaukee with some experience in the militia and much more as a business executive. A big, grey-bearded man, he looked older than his fifty-four years. His outward sternness hid an inner warmth. With Haskell to supply the technical knowledge, Cutler was well able to turn a thousand civilians, most of them young unmarried country boys, into a disciplined regiment. The 6th Wisconsin's lieutenant colonel, until his resignation in September on grounds of ill health, was Haskell's law partner, Atwood.[26]

Frank Haskell joined his new regiment at Camp Randall, the hastily devised military rendezvous on the State Fair Grounds just outside Madison's settled area. In his fine uniform he overawed new recruits dressed in civilian clothes and wholly ignorant of military life. Captain Rufus R. Dawes, who had raised a company of lumberjacks and others in Juneau County, never forgot the humiliation of his arrival at camp. Haskell, mounted on a fine charger, greeted him with

Wisconsin State Journal, January 15, April 15, 17, 20, 22, 1861; Madison *Daily Argus and Democrat,* February 22, 1861. For a good discussion of the indecision accompanying actual recruitment, see Walter S. Glazer, "Wisconsin Goes To War, April, 1861," in *Wisconsin Magazine of History,* 50: 147–64 (Winter, 1967).

[26] F. A. Haskell file in U.S., War Dept., A.G.O., Compiled Service Records for 6th Wis., National Archives; [Frank A. Flower], *History of Milwaukee* (Chicago, 1881), 789–92; Madison *Wisconsin Daily State Journal,* July 30, 1861; Ezra J. Warner, *Generals in Blue: Lives of the Union Commanders* (Baton Rouge, 1964), 110. In this and in subsequent citations about Wisconsin men, information is derived from Wisconsin, Adjutant General's Office, *Roster of Wisconsin Volunteers, War of the Rebellion, 1861–1865* (2 vols., Madison, 1886).

instructions to march to headquarters with his company in column by platoons, a military mystery to Dawes and his men. The new captain was appreciative of Haskell's kindness that evening in teaching his company some of the rudiments of drill. Still, Dawes thought, "The fun he enjoyed in watching us, amply repaid his service." Under the instruction of Haskell and the other more experienced officers, the 6th Wisconsin was able by the Fourth of July to attract praise, rather than ridicule, for its marching in the local parade.[27]

To the busy Adjutant, life in camp was a pleasure. "I like my new place," he told his older brother, Harrison S. Haskell, on July 7. He was, he boasted, "as hearty as a buck." Frank Haskell was anxious for a visit by his brother, who had moved from Columbus to nearby Portage where he was even more successful. The young officer was also anxious to see another brother, Harvey M. Haskell, and a sister, Alma. Harvey had settled at Reedsburg, where he was banking, and Alma was at the time sharing his bachelor's residence. Aside from a wish for sociability, Haskell had another reason for seeing his family. He explained, ". . . my things I must put in some hands, with directions, in case of my failure to return."[28] The same grim realization of war's consequences was occurring to others. On July 18, two days after the regiment was mustered into

---

[27] Rufus R. Dawes, *Service with the Sixth Wisconsin Volunteers,* ed. by Alan T. Nolan (Madison, 1962), 11–12; Madison *Wisconsin Daily State Journal,* July 5, 1861; Madison *Daily Argus and Democrat,* July 6, 1861. Dawes, an Ohioan who was visiting his father in Wisconsin at the start of the war, finally became colonel of the 6th Wisconsin in 1864 and was brevetted general after his discharge. Alan T. Nolan, *The Iron Brigade: A Military History* (New York, 1961), 14, 276–77.
[28] Frank A. Haskell [to Harrison S. Haskell], July 7, 1861, in Haskell Mss., SHSW. The other contents of this letter are not significant. For Harrison S. Haskell, see U.S., Census Bur., Mss. Returns for 1860, Columbia County, Wis., volume, p. 115, SHSW. For Harvey and Alma Haskell. see *ibid.,* Sauk Co. vol., p. 465, SHSW. By 1863 Harvey also was living in Portage, where he was clerk of the circuit court. Portage *Wisconsin State Register,* April 18, 1863.

the United States service, the soldiers decorated Camp Randall gaily for a supper and dance. A morbidly romantic editor urged, "Go girls! It will be something new, and many of your gallent partners may never return to dance with you again." And so for Haskell and the other Badger recruits war ceased to be a game.[29]

On July 22, 1861, the day after the Union defeat at Bull Run, Haskell's regiment received orders to come to the defense of Washington. Six days later, as a band played and civilians cheered, Frank Haskell watched the troops march to the train. (Dressed in the gray uniforms and blue shirts which Wisconsin issued to its first regiments, they would not be "Boys in Blue" for some weeks. Nor did they receive arms until they reached Maryland.) The Adjutant who had had so much to do with the regiment's training could take comfort in its disciplined marching. By way of Milwaukee, Chicago, and Pittsburgh, Haskell and the 6th Wisconsin rode toward the East. Colonels Cutler and Atwood and some of the other officers brought along their wives and thus postponed the final break with civilian life already made by the bachelor adjutant. A writer who saw Haskell "taking his 'snooze' " in a Pennsylvania field one night commented that "he enters into the spirit of war more decidedly than any man I have seen."[30]

From late summer of 1861 through the spring of 1862, Haskell and his comrades camped at several points in the defenses of Washington. Like the rest of the Army of the Potomac, which General George B. McClellan was remaking after the Bull Run disaster, they drilled, paraded, and drilled. The ambitious former drillmaster of the Governor's Guard had every

---

[29] Madison *Wisconsin Daily State Journal*, July 16, 17, 1861; quotation from *Madison Daily Argus and Democrat*, July 18, 1861.

[30] Madison *Wisconsin Daily State Journal*, July 22, 27, 29, 1861; Madison *Daily Patriot*, July 29, 1861; Michael H. Fitch, *Echoes of the Civil War As I Hear Them*, (New York, 1905), 32. The quotation is from a newspaper clipping in "Correspondence of Wisconsin Volunteers, 1861–65," 1: 238, a series of scrapbooks in SHSW.

opportunity to shine. Captain Rufus Dawes later recalled that Haskell "so elevated his office that some men then thought the Adjutant must at least be next to the Colonel in authority and rank. . . ." Nevertheless, he regarded Haskell as "an object lession in military bearing." In the fall of 1861, Haskell's regiment joined the 2nd and 7th Wisconsin and the 19th Indiana Regiments in a brigade commanded by General Rufus King. A West Point graduate, King had spent much of his career in political journalism. This former editor of the Milwaukee *Sentinel* headed the only all-western brigade in the Union's eastern army. As a member of what became known as the Iron Brigade, Haskell would win a share of its martial fame.[31]

During the long lull in actual fighting, Lieutenant Haskell continued his campaign for higher rank. The Madison lawyer had a host of friends strategically placed to influence the governor, who alone had the power to promote him. On February 8, 1862, they petitioned the new Republican chief executive, Louis P. Harvey, to make Haskell a field-grade officer in the 6th Wisconsin or in any other regiment. Among the signers were state and county officeholders, mostly Republican but with some Democrats, and leading Madison lawyers and businessmen. Harvey responded with a promise to promote Haskell at the first opportunity. A month later, Haskell temporarily secured a higher post, if not an advance in rank. With the elevation of General King to command of the division, Lysander Cutler as senior colonel became temporary head of the brigade. His regimental adjutant became the brigade's adjutant general. Soon after the appointment on May 7 of the brigade's permanent commander, General John Gibbon, Haskell became his aide-de-camp. While still a lieutenant, he continued to win the favor of powerful superiors.[32]

---

[31] Nolan, *Iron Brigade,* 28–42; Dawes, *Service with the Sixth Wisconsin,* 21; DWB, 207.

[32] Petition to Gov. L. P. Harvey, February 8, 1862, in Wis., Executive Dept., Applications for Commissions, 1861–65, Ser. 1/1/5–

In June, 1862, Haskell met unexpected disaster in his quest for promotion. The advancement to a colonelcy in another regiment of Benjamin F. Sweet, Atwood's successor as lieutenant colonel of the 6th Wisconsin, and the consequent promotion of Major Edward S. Bragg created a field-grade opportunity for Haskell. He had the backing of both Gibbon and Cutler, but, unfortunately for Frank Haskell, the latter was a better fighter than a military politician. Cutler first had four captains of equal seniority draw lots to determine precedence. He then attempted to induce a caucus of all his officers to choose his favorite, Haskell, in preference to the winner of the draw, Captain Rufus R. Dawes. The caucus, however, by a vote of 14 to 13, recommended Dawes to be major. With the continued support of Cutler and Bragg, Haskell refused to accept the close result. He and Dawes openly agreed to continue the fight, shook hands on it, and sent their papers to friends in the Wisconsin capital.

There a new governor held sway. Harvey had drowned on April 19 while on a relief expedition to Wisconsin troops, and Lieutenant Governor Edward Salomon had succeeded him. A German-American lawyer from Milwaukee, Salomon was a prewar Democrat whom the Republicans had nominated in an appeal for German votes. By petition and in person, Haskell's politically important friends besieged Salomon. The Milwaukeean resented pressure from this inner circle of Madison politicians. When William F. Vilas, the young Madison attorney to whom Dawes had entrusted his application, called on Salomon to discuss the vacancy in the 6th Wisconsin, the governor at first refused to hear him, saying, "The friends of Mr. Haskell have already harassed me beyond my patience." But, learning that Vilas was on the other side, he listened to Dawes's advocate. Benjamin F. Sweet, the regiment's former

20, Archives Div., SHSW; Frank H. Firmin to Harvey M. Haskell, June 15, 1864, in Haskell Mss., Pennsylvania Historical and Museum Commission; F.A. Haskell file in U.S., War Dept., A.G.O., Compiled Service Records for 6th Wis., National Archives.

lieutenant colonel who had quarreled bitterly with Cutler, then visited the governor to oppose Cutler's protégé. In consequence, Haskell lost the commission to Dawes.[33] Not long afterward, the officers of the 6th Wisconsin backed Haskell to be a field officer in the 23rd Wisconsin, a new regiment being organized by Joshua J. Guppy, Harrison Haskell's former law partner. But though Edmund Jussen, Haskell's old friend from Columbus, secured a commission as field officer in the regiment, Haskell again failed. During the stubbornly independent governorship of Edward Salomon, the Republican from Madison had little chance of promotion.[34]

Perforce remaining a staff officer, Haskell stayed under the influence of John Gibbon. Haskell's general was born in Pennsylvania in 1827 but grew up in North Carolina. A graduate of West Point, he served in the Mexican War and against the Indians. Despite his Southern background, he sided with the United States in the Civil War. Promoted to brigadier general of volunteers in May, 1862, he immediately rose from commanding Battery B, 4th United States Artillery, to the command of the former King's Brigade. In appearance, Gibbon was slightly built. He had deep-set eyes, hair rather closely cropped for his day, a sweeping mustache and a short beard. In outlook, he was a professional soldier who was learning how to adapt rigid discipline to the requirements of an army of civilians. It was he who revised the uniform of his new brigade, requiring the purchase of distinctive black hats, and in a variety of ways built the esprit de corps which would help make it the Iron Brigade.[35]

---

[33] Nolan, *Iron Brigade*, 53, 58; Dawes, *Service with the Sixth Wisconsin*, 49–50; Firmin to H.M. Haskell, June 15, 1864, in Haskell Mss., Pa. Historical and Museum Commission. For Salomon, see DWB, 313–14, and Frank Klement, *Wisconsin and the Civil War* (Madison, 1963), 32–33, 76.

[34] Wis., Exec. Dept., List of Applicants for Military Offices Specially Qualified, Ser. 1/1/5–9, Archives Div., SHSW.

[35] Warner, *Generals in Blue*, 171–72; Nolan, *Iron Brigade*, 51–60.

While Lieutenant Haskell was an amateur soldier, he was proficient enough to be very useful to Gibbon. He soon won not only the general's confidence but also his affection. Haskell in turn acquired from his commander much of the viewpoint of the professional soldier. The lieutenant whose political friends had worked for his promotion would grow to scorn politically appointed officers. Republican Frank Haskell would despise the politicians of his own party who opposed Gibbon's ideal general, Democratic George B. McClellan.[36] The former civilian would develop an ever more sympathetic outlook toward the military. Becoming more deeply immersed in the great war, Frank Haskell at last found a subject able to command his best prose. On Gibbon's staff, he was in a position to see and record the war's more significant episodes. By failing to win quick promotion, he kept the position through which, as an author, he was able to fulfill even a luciferous ambition. □

---

[36] For Gibbon's views on political appointments and McClellan, see John Gibbon, *Personal Recollections of the Civil War* (New York, 1928), 21–24; for Haskell's views, see his letters below.

II

Forging the Iron Brigade

As HASKELL WAITED for promotion, Gibbon's brigade awaited the Confederates in northern Virginia. Together with the rest of General Irvin McDowell's Corps, they had been left to defend Washington when McClellan moved the bulk of his forces by sea to a position east of Richmond. On June 26, the federal authorities incorporated McDowell's Corps into a new Army of Virginia which General John Pope proposed to lead overland toward the Confederate capital. In early August, Gibbon's brigade conducted several small raids, and other portions of Pope's army clashed unsuccessfully with the Confederates at the bloody battle of Cedar Mountain. Meanwhile, McClellan's Peninsular Campaign east of Richmond met defeat at the hands of the new Confederate commander, Robert E. Lee, and McClellan received orders to join Pope. Lee sought to destroy Pope's army before McClellan's arrival. The Confederate chief sent General Thomas J. "Stonewall" Jackson around Pope's flank to attack the Union rear, while Lee followed with the rest of his army. Pope, believing that Jackson was near Centreville, ordered a Union concentration there. On the way, Gibbon's brigade unwittingly stumbled upon Jackson's larger force drawn up on Stony Ridge or Sudley Mountain near the old Bull Run battlefield. The ensuing battle was variously called Gainesville, Groveton, and Brawner Farm.

On August 31, 1862, Haskell wrote a brief note (here omitted) to assure his family that he was uninjured and to tell them of the outcome of the battle. His brother, Harrison S. Haskell, had it published on September 6th in the Portage *Wisconsin State Register*. Frank Haskell then wrote the following, evidently unfinished description of the battle, which seems to have been intended for publication. Although undated by its writer, the back of this sheaf of paper is inscribed September 22, 1862. Similar markings on letters in this collection indicate that this may be either the presumed date of writing or the date of the document's receipt. □

*   *   *   *   *

As the Brigade, at present commanded by Brig. Genl. John Gibbon, formerly by Genl. King, has since the 20th of August been doing some service and been engaged in several battles, it may not be uninteresting to the people of Wisconsin, composed as the Brigade is of the 2nd, 6th and 7th Regiments Wis. Vols. with the 19th Ind. Vols, to learn something of its history during the period mentioned. On the 19th of August the Brigade left its camp upon the bloody battle field of Cedar Mountain, then fresh with the blood of its brothers of the 3d. Wis. and with the rest of the Army of Virginia fell back to the left bank of the Rappahannock, where it arrived on the next day. On the 21st the enemy appeared upon the opposite bank of the river, and during that and the succeeding two days an almost constant artillery skirmish was kept up between us and the enemy, across the river at Rappahannock Station and for some miles above and below.

The Brigade, though much of the time within range of the enemy's guns at this point, suffered but little, the loss being five wounded and seven missing. Of those wounded was Lieut. Oakley, 7th Wis. and the missing Adjt. Dean, 2nd Wis. who we have since learned was taken prisoner unhurt, by the rebel cavalry.[1] On the 23rd of August, learning that the en-

---

[1] Frank W. Oakley of Beloit and Charles K. Dean of Boscobel.

emy was extending himself up the Rappahannock on our right, the Brigade, with other large forces moved up the river to Warrenton, and thence to Sulphur Spring, seven miles from Warrenton, upon the river. At this point on the 26th again a sharp skirmish occurred with the enemy across the river by King's entire Division of Infantry and Artillery. Little damage was done to us, none to the Brigade, but the enemy suffered considerably by our artillery and skirmishers.

On the 27th, learning that the rebel Jackson had come around our right, and was in our rear with a large force, our forces at this point returned in pursuit of him, and for that purpose marched along back upon the Warrenton and Centerville turnpike towards Centerville. On the morning of the 28th Genl. [John F.] Reynolds Division, having the advance, encountered some of the Artillery and Cavalry of the enemy about a mile below Gainesville on the turnpike, and after a slight skirmish, supposing that no large body of them was at this point, passed on towards Centerville.

At a little after noon on the same day Genl. King's Division came up, accompanied by Genl. McDowell, and staff, and halted in the same place where Reynolds had found the enemy. This is a short distance below Gainesville, and where the direct road to Manassas Junction turns off from the turnpike upon which the Division was marching.

Two Brigades of the Division — [General John P.] Hatch's and Gibbon's — filed off upon the Manassas Junction road and were disposed as if the enemy were near, Genl. McDowell believing them to be so; but after such a reconnaisance [sic] as was deemed sufficient, none of them were here found. Genl. King was thereupon ordered to proceed on to Centerville with his Division, Genl. McDowell and staff at the same time proceeding to Manassas Junction. About four o'clock P.M. on the 28th the Division again started for its destination, the Brigades which had moved out upon the Manassas Junction road filing back to the Centerville pike and taking up the line of march, in the order of Brigades, Hatch's, Gibbon's, [General Abner] Doubleday's and [General Marsena R.] Patrick's, the artillery, four batteries being interspersed between the Infantry.

Genl. Hatch, taking the advance, discovered signs of the enemy about one and a half miles after again coming upon the turnpike, and with a section of Artillery and a regiment of Infantry skirmished with them upon the same ground upon the left of the turnpike, where Gibbon's Brigade encountered them as will be described. But Genl. Hatch was of the opinion, when his skirmishers had returned that the enemy was not there in any considerable force, and so without wasting time moved on down the turnpike, Genl. Gibbon and Brigade followed. The turnpike here is quite descending towards Centerville. The country is agricultural, sharply undulating in many places, and is interspersed with tracts of clearing and woods, in about equal proportions. Where Genl. Hatch made his reconnaisance [sic] and skirmished was at the left, the North, of the turnpike, and the ground was a smooth high ridge of cleared land, of several hundred yards in extent, descending into a valley, or ravine upon the North, and falling gradually away towards the East. Beyond this valley, the ground rises rapidly some little distance and is then all along bordered by woods. Between this ground, which was the battle ground, and the turnpike, is a patch of woods, of some four or five hundred yards in extent shaped like the letter "M" the base resting upon the left of the turnpike, and the right hand angle of the "M" extending much farther to the North than the left, and terminating at a point near the ravine.

As the Brigade was passing this tract of woods, the 6th Wis. leading, Genl. Gibbon and staff rode from the head of his column, into an open field to the left of the turnpike and directly below the woods, and from this point directly to the North across the ravine, at some six hundred yards distant he saw the rebels emerging from the woods in their rear, and making rapid movements as if making dispositions against his forces. The General halted his brigade; and first the smoke of a gun, then the hiss of a shell, and its explosion right by him, told unmistakably the character of those who confronted the head of his column. The rebels there and then opened with a full battery upon the column, and their shell came howling in among the ranks of the 6th and 2nd Wis. An order was sent back to the rear of the Brigade and down thundered at a gallop battery 'B' 4th Regular Artillery, Capt. Campbell, with his six splendid brass Napoleon 12 Pdrs.[2] The battery was in position in a twinkling near the crest of the hill below the woods, and from it the wrathful voice of the injured Union was heard among the thickly accumulating rebels around their battery. The fire of the confronting batteries became brisk — the 6th and 2nd Wis. moved up to the support of Campbell's Battery. The firing of an other battery was soon heard by us to the front and left, through the right fork of the woods, but it could not be told whether it was friend or foe. A staff officer soon reported to Genl. Gibbon that it was a section or two, rebel, posted North of the woods, and very near to the spot where Genl. Hatch had made his reconnaisance [sic].

The 2nd Wis. conducted by its brave Col. O'Conner,[3] and the General in person, moved to the left and through this tongue of woods, came into line of battle, swept up over the summit of the hill North of the woods, and moved on in quest of this battery last mentioned. A volley from a rebel regiment of Infantry in support of the battery hissed through the advancing ranks of the 2nd. The 2nd halted but did not recoil an inch, and opened fire. The 19th Ind. Col. Meridith,[4] be-

---

[2] Joseph B. Campbell, formerly second in command of General Gibbon's old battery, had succeeded Gibbon.

[3] Edgar O'Connor, who was mortally wounded in this battle, was born in Ohio in 1833 and came to Wisconsin with his family in 1842. Graduating from West Point, he served in the Regular Army, resigned and was a lawyer in Beloit in 1861. Nolan, *Iron Brigade,* 11, 91.

[4] Solomon Meredith, though without prior military experience, was a Republican politician and a particular favorite of Indiana Governor Oliver P. Morton. After the transfer of Gibbon — and

hind the 2nd in its order in column, was at once ordered up to support the 2nd. The gallant Hoosiers came up at the double quick, formed upon the left of the 2nd, and opened fire. Large forces of the rebel Infantry had now appeared, opposing these two regiments, and the fire of both sides became hot. The 7th Wis. the last regiment in the column of the Brigade, now came cooly, nobly up, and formed upon the right of the 2nd, and at once commenced work. In the mean time Capt. Campbell had silenced the battery that had first opened upon us, and with which he was engaged, and had commenced moving forward to a new position where his shells would smite the rebel Infantry. He took his new position upon the crest of the hill, a number of yards in advance of the old, and in near range of the rebel Infantry, the 6th Wis. at the same time, on the extreme right of our line, moving over the crest and down the slope in front of Campbell, towards the foe, and the 6th and the Battery emulated their neighbors upon the left. As the Brigade was at this time engaged with largely superior numbers of the enemy, at Genl. Gibbon's request Genl. Doubleday promptly sent up two of his regiments, small in numbers, but large in bravery, as reinforcements, and they formed, the 56th Pa. between the 19th Ind. and 2nd Wis. and the 76th N. Y. between the 7th Wis. and the 6th Wis. on its right.[5]

*   *   *   *   *

☐ In his later letter of September 22, 1862, in which he summarizes the campaign, Haskell tells how Gibbon's brigade withdrew after dark from the hard-fought field. It had suffered and it had inflicted casualties of over 33 per cent.[6] Two

---

over Gibbon's opposition — he became commander of the Iron Brigade. *Ibid.*, 20–21, 172–73.

[5] The weight of evidence indicates that both of these regiments sent by Doubleday actually took a position between the 6th and 7th Wisconsin. *Ibid.*, 89, 324.

[6] *Ibid.*, 95–96.

days later, the Black Hat Brigade, as it was coming to be called, lost less heavily when Pope's army attacked Lee's reunited forces in the Second Battle of Bull Run. The defeated Union army retreated into the defenses of Washington and once again became part of General George B. McClellan's Army of the Potomac. On September 6, McClellan began to pursue Lee, who had invaded Maryland. Learning through a fortuitously found copy of Lee's orders that the Confederate leader had divided his forces, McClellan had an opportunity to interpose between and defeat separately the scattered Southern troops. The principal obstacle was the Confederate force holding Turner's Gap on South Mountain, and the brigade took an important part in forcing the gap. In this battle of South Mountain Gibbon's command won the title of the Iron Brigade. Haskell's description, which follows, is more an essay than a personal letter. Like several others in the collection, it lacks a salutation. ☐

* * * * *

Sept. 14, 1862.

This morning at six o'clock the brigade resumed the march from its camp upon the left bank of the Monocacy along the turnpike through Frederick, towards Hagerstown.

The day was fine, — not hot, a little cloudy but with a clear atmosphere near the earth, — and the men were in excellent spirits. Passing through Frederick, the streets of which were all a-bloom with loyal flags, the General made a little speech to the men, which was received with much enthusiasm.[7] As the day wore on we could hear the sound of cannon at long dis-

[7] Gibbon told his men that McClellan had said that two days' hard marching by them would put Lee in a difficult position. Using the psychological techniques with which he had built the brigade's *esprit,* he urged them to jeer at stragglers and claimed that McClellan appreciated his western brigade's fighting qualities. Gibbon, *Personal Recollections,* 74–75.

tance, which told us that we were near the enemy, and as we came in sight of South Mountain, from the eminences we could plainly see the smoke of the batteries, — those of the enemy along the heights, our own, nearer in the best positions they could get. The enemy's batteries had opened upon our advance some miles south of the Mountain, but had been compelled to retire.

After Hooker's corps had passed through Middletown, all of it, except Gibbon's brigade,[8] abandoned the turnpike, and taking a road to the right, it advanced to the foot of the Mountain, and formed in order of battle, constituting with its three divisions, Rickett's, Mead's, and Hatch's, the right of the line.[9] Hooker's left, — Hatch's division — extended to within some six hundred yards of the turnpike. Reno's command[10] constituted our left, and was formed over against Hooker, upon high ground, somewhat nearer the position of the enemy upon the heights than Hooker, with his right resting about a thousand yards left of the turnpike. Our line was thus formed perpendicular to and across the turnpike, the interval between the wings being guarded by numerous batteries placed somewhat in rear of the line, on high ground, on the left of the turnpike commanding the turnpike, and in position to check any demonstration of the rebels in this quarter.

Gibbon[']s brigade was detached from the division and or-

---

[8] Gibbon's brigade was now the 4th Brigade, 1st Division, First Corps. After the second battle of Bull Run, General Joseph Hooker succeeded McDowell as the commander of this corps. A graduate of West Point, Hooker had had a distinguished record in the Mexican War. He had been a brigade and divisional commander in the Army of the Potomac. A newspaper headline had already given him the nickname "Fighting Joe." Warner, *Generals in Blue*, 233–35.

[9] General John P. Hatch had replaced the ailing Rufus King at the head of the 1st division. The other division commanders in the First Corps were Generals James B. Ricketts and George Gordon Meade.

[10] The Ninth Corps of General Jesse L. Reno, who was killed at South Mountain.

dered to report to Genl. Burnside,[11] and remaining in the
turnpike until Hooker was nearly in position, and Reno entirely so, we received orders to form in two lines in double
column closed in mass, and take position on the left of the
turnpike in front of the batteries, in a manner to enable the
fire of the batteries to pass without harm over our heads, —
which order was executed without delay, the first line being
composed of the 7th Wis. on the right, and the 19th Ind. on
the left, and the second line, the 6th Wis on the right, and
the 2nd Wis on the left.

Such were the dispositions at three o'clock, P.M. — There
had been little or no Infantry firing up to this time.

The batteries had at intervals kept up a scattering fire upon
both sides, but with little or no damage upon ours. The enemy was in a very strong position upon the summit of the
Mountain and his movements were much covered by woods,
and the inequalities of the ground.

Genls. McClellan and Burnside, with their staffs were in
rear of our batteries, upon high ground, which overlooked all
of Hooker's movements, and part of Reno's, and the entire
gorge up the turnpike between.

First Reno moved slowly and cautiously forward upon the
enemy, as we could tell by the sound of his guns and skirmishers; — then we saw Hooker throw out his skirmishers, who at
the proper intervals were followed by his deployed lines; and
they moved steadily up the steep mountain side in the direction of the rebels.

The discharges of the batteries attached to these corps respectively became more frequent, — ambulances were put in
readiness for use — depots for the wounded were established,
— all things betokened close action at hand. The brigade was
quiet, with no prospect of immediate work, listening and
looking for what could be heard or seen. The scattering shots

---

[11] Ambrose E. Burnside commanded the First and Ninth Corps,
which then constituted the right wing of McClellan's Army of the
Potomac.

of skirmishers upon the left became more frequent, and more remote, — from shots they deepened to vollies [sic], and from vollies, to a continuous roar, — the batteries got in earnest. Reno was hotly engaged, and was driving the enemy.

Meantime Hooker had disappeared towards the enemy out of our sight, but the roar of his guns, and the frequent wounded returning to the rear told us that he too was doing good work upon the rebels.

Four o'clock came, — the battle roared along the whole line, save the interval across the turnpike between Hooker and Reno. But the enemy must be dislodged here, also. — He must not be allowed to retain his strong-hold, the gorge, and the turnpike leading through it. The turnpike is steep and winds up among the hills. The ground descends from both sides to the turnpike, — is wooded save for a belt from one hundred and fifty to three hundred yards wide upon each side, and is crossed here and there with strong stone fences, and abounds in good natural covers for troops, — altogether an ugly looking place to attack, the enemy's center, and held by artillery and we knew not how much infantry.

So Burnside ordered Gibbon with his brigade and as much of Campbell's battery[12] as he needed, to advance up the turnpike and attack the enemy, dislodge him from the gorge if possible, but at all events to advance far enough to complete our line of battle between Hooker and Reno.

Accordingly a little past four o'clock, P. M. the 7th Wis were moved across to the right of the turnpike and deployed, its left resting upon the turnpike, its front covered by two companies of skirmishers of the 6th Wis. and the remaining eight companies of the 6th were formed in double column at half distance two hundred yards in rear of the colors of the 7th; — a similar disposition was made with the 2nd Wis. and 19th Ind. upon the left of the turnpike, the 19th deployed,

---

[12] Battery B, 4th U.S. Artillery, which had supported Gibbon's brigade in the battle at the Brawner Farm.

and abreast of the 7th, its right resting upon the turnpike, with its front covered by two companies of skirmishers of the 2nd. — Lieut. [James] Stewart's section of the battery was posted upon the turnpike, between the deployed lines. — This was as much artillery as could be here used, on account of the peculiar nature of the ground. —

These dispositions made, Genl. Gibbon ordered his command to move up to the attack. The ground was much obstructed by fences, and orchards in places, and on the right by fields of luxuriant corn, but on they moved, the deployed lines, advancing by the right of companies. The sky which had been somewhat overcast, now cleared up, and his rays came full in the faces of the men, as if he too had an interest in these matters and would see for himself the faces of the "Black Hat" brigade.

Soon we hear a single shot of a skirmisher, — another and another follow, — along the whole line of skirmishers the firing becomes frequent, — we are among the enemy. — The orders from the Genl. [Gibbon] are frequent, "Push forward the skirmishers upon the left!" — "Push on the 7th," — "Push on the 19th." The skirmishers are well engaged, and we advance steadily up the hill, the section of artillery keeping abreast with the first line, but not opening fire, for we receive no fire of artillery from the rebels, and the reserves of his infantry are covered. At length the enemy opens with a section of a battery, from the right of the turnpike, near the summit of the Mountain, upon our infantry, but his shot fly wild, making a good deal of hissing, but doing no harm. Stewart replies to them with his Napoleons, — they shift position to get out of his line of fire, and continue their fire upon the infantry.

At last one of the shells of the enemy explodes in the 2nd Wis. and kills four men and wounds five others, — Capt. Parsons being among the latter.[13] This was all the harm they did

---

[13] William L. Parsons of Racine.

us and very soon afterwards the well directed and persevering fire of Stewart silenced them altogether.

But as the sun disappeared behind the summit of the mountain, the battle meanwhile of Hooker and Reno thundering without abatement and with steady success, we had driven all the enemy's skirmishers home upon their supports and the 7th and the 19th were engaging their lines concealed behind fences and bushes, at close quarters. The fire became sharp, — our skirmishers were recalled and the 2nd was deployed upon the left of the 19th,[14] and the 6th upon the right of the 7th; and in this order, the section still upon the turnpike, but in rear of the infantry, the whole brigade poured in a sharp and well directed fire upon the whole line of the enemy, and as darkness came on drove him to his last stand behind a stone wall near to the summit of the mountain.

Behind this cover the fire of the enemy was sharp and long continued, but men who had fought at Gainesville were not to be deterred in their purpose for victory, even by stone wall breast works, or superior numbers or darkness, or all of these together. We had driven the enemy nearly half a mile; and about this time Genl. Burnside sent word to Genl. Gibbon that Hooker and Reno had been victorious upon the right and left, respectively, — a fact that before had been quite apparent from the direction of their fire, as we heard it, and the continued cheers that greeted our ears from our flanks; so the *Black Hats* redoubled their energy as the darkness increased, determined not to rest until victory to them also, was complete.

The view of this fight after dark was thrilling and grand to a high degree. The opposing lines were very close to each other, — a hundred yards or less, as the advantages of ground induced deviations from straight lines to enable the men to

---

[14] The 2nd Wisconsin actually was deployed upon the *right* of the 19th Indiana, filling the gap between the Hoosiers and the 7th Wisconsin. Nolan, *Iron Brigade*, 123, 125.

get cover, — and the fire of the infantry was incessant. — Flash met flash of the opposing combatants and the frequent vollies roared and reverberated among the hills like continuous thunder; and louder than all the infantry, and with deeper flame, the well handled Napoleons of Stewart belched their iron contents over the heads of our own men, into the ranks of the enemy. All this was going on under the immediate eyes of Genls. McClellan and Burnside.

Flesh and blood could not stand such fire long, — we found our own ammunition nearly expended upon the left, though we had had a hundred rounds to the man, — but at the same time we also discovered that the enemy in the same quarter had become feeble, and his fire scattering and infrequent. Soon it ceased here altogether, — the enemy had been driven from the entire left of the turnpike. The work of the 6th and 7th upon the right was not yet done, but was near completion. The *Butternuts* could not stand these vollies, or the shells; and the 6th, with the left wing engaging them in front, moved up its right wing by the flank, so as to attain a position above, and outflanking, the enemy's left, then wheeling half to the left, both wings poured in a well directed fire, which aided by the front fire of the 7th, soon made an end to the fight. Our ammunition was now all expended save two or three rounds to the man, but if the enemy should appear before more could be had, it was resolved to trust to the bayonet alone. So the line lay down where it had fought, believing the battle over, but in this they were disappointed so far as the 6th were concerned. Soon the enemy in front of the 6th crept up in the darkness, and within a few yards of their line re-opened fire, — the 6th rose up an gave them two vollies, firing by wing, — they were satisfied, — they left without a parting "good night." Then the 6th gave three cheers for the Badger state, — the last shot had been fired, — the victory was won, — the battle was ended between nine and ten o'clock, P. M.

The 6th held their ground during the night — the other three regiments, after the battle was over, were relieved by

Brig. Genl. [Willis A.] Gorman's brigade, and fell back about two hundred yards, for ammunition and repose.

Such is a sketch of the part the Black Hat Brigade took in the battle of *South Mountain,* their third battle. The number of men engaged of the brigade was about one thousand.

We have no means of knowing accurately the force of the enemy opposed to the brigade, but judging from their numbers as we saw them, and from the best data in our possession, there can be not any doubt that their numbers equalled and probably exceeded ours.[15] Their position was much stronger than ours, both from its superior elevation, and from the great number of natural covers and defences, made by stone fences, woods and inequalities of ground. We [being] compelled to be the aggressive party was also under the circumstances to their advantage. And owing to the nature of the ground up this turnpike and through the gorge in the Mountain, the action of the brigade, both as related to them and their enemy, was a distinct battle, neither the brigade nor its opposers, receiving any supports, or reinforcements, or being in a position to receive any without great delay.

The battle of the brigade was distinct, severe, and completely victorious, — a brilliant episode, an important part, in the great battle of South Mountain.

Our loss was, thirty-seven killed; — two hundred and fifty-two, wounded; — and thirty missing, — the missing mostly from the 7th Wis. who soon again turned up — the aggregate loss being three hundred and nineteen.[16] Among the officers

---

[15] While the total Confederate force in the battle of South Mountain was much smaller than that of the United States, General Alfred H. Colquitt's Brigade, which opposed Gibbon's, numbered 1,100 and thus was probably not much smaller than the "Black Hat Brigade." *Ibid.,* 122, 335.

[16] The casualties officially reported totaled 318, including 251 wounded. Gibbon calculated his casualties as constituting 25 per cent of his brigade. These losses surpassed those of any other Union brigade engaged. *Ibid.,* 129.

killed was Capt. Colwell,[17] of the 2nd Wis, a brave and accomplished officer, who fell mortally wounded while conducting his company as skirmishers in the early part of the engagement, and, carried from the field by his men, he died in
about an hour.

We have no means of knowing the loss of the enemy opposed to us. Their killed, left upon the field and burried
[sic] by us, were at least double the number of our own, —
their wounded were many of them carried off in their ambulances.[18]

Col. Fairchild,[19] and Lieut. Cols. Bragg[20] and Allen[21] acted
with conspicuous bravery and skill in the handling of their
respective commands; and their cool and steady, yet quick and
efficient conduct was all the more noticeable, because of its
marked contrast with the bearing of some officers, holding
similar positions, in the midst of similar circumstances.

The General's conduct was as usual. As long as daylight
lasted, stationed upon high ground which overlooked the entire field of opperations [sic], nothing passed without his notice, or direction; — but as usual his tendency was strong to
get up to the front where bullets flew very carelessly.

When darkness came he was near the [artillery] section,

---

[17] Wilson Colwell of La Crosse.

[18] General Daniel H. Hill, Colquitt's superior, later estimated
Colquitt's casualties as totaling 100. *Ibid.*, 129.

[19] Lucius Fairchild of Madison, who had served with Haskell
in the Governor's Guard. He was promoted from the lieutenant-
colonelcy of the 2nd Wisconsin after the death of Colonel O'Connor. Seriously wounded himself at Gettysburg, Fairchild resigned
shortly after his promotion to brigadier general. He subsequently
won three terms as governor of Wisconsin and was commander-in-
chief of the Grand Army of the Republic. Sam Ross, *The Empty
Sleeve: A Biography of Lucius Fairchild* (Madison, 1964), *passim.*

[20] Edward S. Bragg of Fond du Lac commanded the 6th Wisconsin in place of Colonel Cutler, who was still recovering from
a wound received in the battle at the Brawner Farm. Warner,
Generals in Blue, 41–42.

[21] Thomas S. Allen of Mineral Point, 2nd Wisconsin.

sometimes directing its fire, but always doing all that could be done for the brigade.

The work of the day done, the men, such as had retired from the ground where they fought, at rest under the quiet sky, the wounded all carried to the rear and cared for as fast as possible, he too, proud of his *Black Hat* brigade, and they proud of him, on the field among his men lay down to the sleep of the tired soldier and victorious general.

Haskell.

*   *   *   *   *

□ During the night, the Confederates withdrew from South Mountain. Having delayed the Union army for a day, Lee retreated to Antietam Creek near Sharpsburg, Maryland, where he hoped to reunite his still divided forces. Haskell describes the Union pursuit in the following unsigned and evidently incomplete document. While also undated, its reverse is dated as below, probably by Haskell's brother. □

*   *   *   *   *

[September 16, 1862]

On the 15th of September, the day after the batttle of South Mountain, the sun rose bright and clear and soon dispelled the fog that lay over the scene of yesterday's fearful combat. Darkness having come on before this battle was closed, pursuit was for the time impossible; and daylight of the next day alone was sufficient to disclose the completeness of the victory, and the precipitation of the flight of the enemy. McClellan was therefore compelled to spend a portion of the morning of the 15th in ascertaining the situation and purposes of the enemy, which by good fortune he was enabled to do speedily and with a degree of certainty not usual in such matters. The enemy were retiring towards the Potomac, having left all their dead behind, unburied, and great numbers of their wounded, scattered by the road-side where they had been carried during the battle, or collected in barns or houses, for treatment by their medical officers. They retired by the Hagerstown road to Boonsboro, and then, sending forward some cavalry to divert McClellan, their main body took the road to the left to Sharpsburg. McClellan was not diverted by this ruse, but pursued on the road they had taken. Hooker's corps led the pursuit, in the order of divisions as follows: Meade's, Doubleday's, Ricket's [*sic*], and by ten o'clock, A.M. they were on the move. No enemy was seen, save stragglers many of which were picked up by cavalry in the woods and fields, until past noon, when our advance discovered them drawn up in large force upon the high ground upon the right bank of the Antietam, deployed lines of infantry, and batteries in position, as if ready to give us battle. The head of our column halted upon the left bank of the creek, out of range of their guns, and while the rear was coming up some batteries of our Parrott guns were put in position well forward, and thereupon during the remainder of the afternoon, at intervals, a good deal of firing at long range was kept up with batteries of the enemy. We suffered very little, — a few unfortunate mules were, however, knocked over by their shot. As night came, the firing ceased, but their infantry was in position the last that could be seen by day light.

Stationing Pickets.

During the night our pickets and those of the enemy were very near each other upon opposite sides of the Antietam. It was my good fortune to spend the greater part of the night of the 15th in stationing the 19th Ind. on picket.

An order was received by Genl. Gibbon, from Genl. Doubleday,[22] at about ten and one half o'clock at night, after all the

---

[22] Abner Doubleday, often credited with the invention of baseball, was a graduate of West Point. He was reputed to have aimed the first gun fired in defense of Fort Sumter. As a brigade commander, he sent help to Gibbon in the battle at the Brawner Farm. He succeeded John P. Hatch, who was seriously wounded at South

men were asleep, to post one of his regiments as pickets, *"on the right of, and communicating with the pickets of Genl. Richardson's division."*[23] The source whence this luminous and timely order issued was sound asleep long before it was received by Genl. Gibbon, — but an order must be obeyed, and I was charged with the execution of it. Seeking Genl. Doubleday for information as to the whereabouts of Genl. Richardson, the proximity of the enemy, the nature of the ground where the pickets were to be posted, and matters without the knowledge of which it was impossible to post pickets, and waking him with difficulty from his sleep under a tree, I was enlightened and refreshed with the intelligence that of all and singular the matters of which I wished to be informed, the General was himself utterly and profoundly ignorant. But he agreed with me in one proposition, and, as I first broached it to him, a high and brilliant military functionary as he was, his agreement with me was a source of great encouragement to me: — When I said to him that under the circumstances, without any knowledge of the position, ground, or place where to place pickets, it was a difficult matter to post them, he replied — *"yesh, 'tis so"*, and the second hero of Sumpter [*sic*] was again asleep. Then I went and aroused the 19th to go on picket when I should again call for them. — They had little sleep the night before, were weary with the day's march, and were sleeping soundly in their bivouac in a plowed field; — it may well be supposed the order was not agreeable to them, — they swore worse than the "Army in Flanders."[24] — I thought they had reason to, — when we considered that supposing they must go on picket at all, which there was no need

---

Mountain, as commander of the division to which the Iron Brigade belonged. Warner, *Generals in Blue,* 129–30.

[23] Israel B. Richardson, commander of the 1st Division, Second Corps. He died of wounds suffered at Antietam.

[24] " 'Our armies swore terribly in Flanders,' cried my Uncle Toby — 'but nothing to this.' " Laurence Sterne, *Tristram Shandy,* Bk. 3, Ch. 11.

of, as our front was then wholly picketed, they might just as well have been posted before dark. My experiences in finding Richardson's division were rich. I knew nothing positive as to its location, but had heard somebody say in the afternoon that it was away to the left and front of us on the turnpike leading to Sharpsburg, — so afoot and alone I went in search. I succeeded without much difficulty in finding some of his brigades, but to find him or any officer who knew of his pickets was the pinch. "Where is Genl. Richardson?" I would ask of some one loitering by a fire and not yet asleep. — "Right there under that tree," would be the prompt answer. "Do you know, certain?" I would ask; — "O yes, I saw him not ten minutes since, there." I had found him, thank fortune, at last, — but alas! the Genl. was not at the tree. "Do you know Genl. Richardson?" I would ask of a Dutchman up smoking his pipe. "Yes, I know Genl. ——" would be his answer. — "But do you know *Genl. Richardson?*" I would repeat. — "yes, I know Col. ——[."]

Oh, Lord, what should be done? I would arouse a Genl. of brigade and ask him, and he would rub his eyes, and answer, that he was either *over there,* or *over there* (pointing in the opposite direction) or if he was not in either of those places, he did not know where he was.

Good fortune smiled upon me at last, for when I was about to inquire once more; at a place, where no body had directed me resolving then to give the matter up, in despair, an officer sitting up in his blankets asked me if I wished to see Genl. Richardson. I replyed [*sic*] in the affirmative, and he said, "here he is." I soon had the intelligence I needed, — went for the 19th, and by three o'clock had them posted as pickets — according to orders.

The Sixteenth of September

* * * * *

☐ McClellan did not attack on September 16th and thus permitted Lee to reunite most of his army behind Antietam Creek. Even then, the Union men outnumbered the Confederates by about 75,000 to 50,000, an advantage diminished by the unsynchronized execution of the Union attack and by McClellan's unwillingness to commit his large reserve. The Iron Brigade suffered heavily as a result of its participation in the fighting on September 17th, the "bloodiest single day of the war." Nevertheless, as Haskell informed his relatives two days later in a note here omitted, he escaped unharmed. The latter part of the letter below describes the battle of Antietam. ☐

                    *   *   *   *   *

                              Battle Field, Sharpsburg, Md.
                              Sept 22, 1862.

Dear Brothers, and Sisters,[25]

I wish I could write to each of you — both for the love for you all, and because you have all written to me since I have answered, — but I assure you I have much to do. — You have no conception of this life in the field, and my position is full of work. But read all of you what I have to write. I cannot go back over the long period of more than a year, since you have heard much of me. The winter was passed in a tent upon the banks of the Potomac. — I cannot tell you of what we suffered, and how cheerful we all were and how we hoped. I cannot tell you of the spring, no spring to us, and how the Army of the Potomac spread upon a hundred hills upon the ground in March, and how gleamed their one hundred and fifty thousand camp fires. All these have passed to me, and to the country.

_____

[25] Harrison S. Haskell permitted the Portage *Wisconsin State Register*, October 4, 1862, to print much of this letter. Its editor termed it "one of the best letters in relation to the recent battles yet published."

I cannot tell you how we all felt at being left behind when the Army went to the Peninsula and we were left out of the ranks of McClellan, the idol of all the army. — I will not tell of the sickness of five weeks in April and May, and how poor and weak I was, and how much I thought of and longed to see you all, — and how glad I was on the 17th of May to resume my sword and horse again, and in the clear days how like a happy child I was and how the sweet flowers and birds pleased me.

All these have passed away, and the summer with them, but the recollections of them all can never fade from my memory.

With Autumn came the bloody work of battle, — no more of idle marching and returning to no purpose to us, without ever seeing the enemy.

From the 20th of August for the next month, the smoke and roar of cannon and the rattle of musketry was about us continually, almost.

From Rappahannock Station on the Rappahannock to Sulphur Spring near Warrenton, Va., we had constant artillery practice with the enemy, and some encounters with the skirmishers, but we lost but few men, and a good school for us all, to become accustomed to the enemy's shells, and the aspects of battle.

All this schooling we needed, for soon the time for practice came; — on the 28th of August on the turnpike from Warrenton to Centerville, near Gainesville King's Division encountered the right wing of the enemy.

I will not say now where was the fault, but of the Division consisting of four Brigades, two were not engaged at all, and one other but lightly — but Gibbon's, the 2nd, 6th, and 7th Wis. and 19th Ind. which the Rebels have named the black-hat Brigade — they wear black felt army hats — went in to fight, — this was their first hard battle. As the sun was going down upon this pleasant August day their line was formed and they stood face to face with three times their number, no where a hundred yards distant, and in some [places] not more than twenty, and for nearly an hour and a half, until darkness came upon the earth, the little hill whereon they stood was a roaring hell of fire. Retiring never an inch, with no confusion, now standing up, now flat upon the earth, now swaying backwards or forwards to get advantage of ground, the devoted 1800 blazed with fire. Line after line of the rebels confronted them and was swept away, or broke in confusion. Fresh regiments would again appear, upon the ground their discomfited ranks had left, and with a cheer would rush on for a charge upon the "Black Hats", but their rebel cheer was drowned in one three times louder by the Badger boys, and their lines met the fate of its predecessors. No battle was ever so fierce before, — no men ever did better than did the men of Gibbon's Brigade. With the darkness came cessation of the Rebel fire, — and then and not till then ours ceased. — We had yielded not an inch and our pickets covered our advanced lines. Then came the taking off the dead and wounded. — Then we learned the extent of our loss.

Now was the hardest part of the battle — to learn who of our friends were killed or wounded. 771 of the Brigade had fallen, dead or wounded.[26] I cannot give the names of any — you have read them in the papers. — At a little past midnight, we were ordered to leave the scene of our terrible battle, and having cared for the wounded as well as we could, and taking as many as the ambulances would hold with us we silently took up the line of march for Manassas Junction. As the day light came on the next morning, none of us could look upon our thinned ranks, so full the night before, now so shattered, without tears. And the faces of these brave boys, and the morning sun disclosed them, no pen can describe. The men were cheerful, quiet, and orderly. The dust and blackness of battle were upon their clothes, and in their hair, and on their skin, but you saw none of these, — you saw only their eyes, and the

---

[26] Gibbon reported 672 dead and wounded, with 79 missing; total casualties of 751. Nolan, *Iron Brigade*, 95.

shadows of the "light of battle," and the furrows plowed upon cheeks that were smooth a day before, and now not half filled up. I could not look upon them without tears, and could have hugged the necks of them all.

But the work of the Brigade was not yet accomplished. — On and on we moved. — As usual under McDowell, we march one hour to retrace our steps the next, and so back we came and lay down on the after-noon of the 29th of August on the edge of the battle then going on at the old field of Bull Run. We lay right among the graves of the year before, — but these did not interest us — we had seen so many that were new. The Brigade was not engaged on the 29th, at all, but with the 30th came the main battle, and in we went again. — The men of the Brigade behaved admirably — as we knew they would, but our loss was a little less than two hundred in killed and wounded.[27] We participated in this second defeat at Bull Run — The first was due to McDowell's incapacity — the second to his and Pope's together. They both enjoyed the cordial hatred of all their men — and I think both deserved it. On the night of the 30th after the battle the army fell back to Centerville, and Gibbon's Brigade, with Campbell's (formerly Gibbon's) Battery, Co "B" 4th Artillery, was the rear guard of the whole army. This is no small honor, and you may set it down as a fact, the lying newspapers to the contrary notwithstanding.

After the Bull Run defeat, the Rebels pushed for Maryland — poor lying Pope was played out, the man alone who is fit for the place, and whom the country has more abused than any one else in it, *McClellan,* took the Army. The Rebels must take their polluting feet from loyal soil. A General now leads the Army. The troops are drawn across the Potomac and sent after the Rebels in Maryland.

On the 12th of Sept. our advance came up with them at Frederick, and skirmished. They retired, — the pursuit is kept

---

[27] Gibbon's report indicates 102 dead and wounded and 41 missing; total casualties of 143. *Ibid.,* 110

up on the 13th with artillery and cavalry skirmishing, they constantly retiring on the Hagerstown turnpike. On the 14th, Sunday, they had retired to the summit of a hill, or rather ridge of hills north of Frederick, known as South Mountain up through a deep gorge of which the turnpike winds, and on this mountain they made a stand. McClellan attacked them, first with artillery, early on Sunday morning, with Infantry later in the day. Our forces here I suppose exceeded 30,000 — that of the enemy was from 30,000 to 40,000.[28] By one or two o'clock P.M. the battle had become general, Reno first attacking on the left, and Hooker on the right, — the turnpike was the center, and was guarded on our side by our numerous batteries. — At about 4 o'clock P.M. Gibbon's Brigade, which belongs to the bully Joe Hooker's corps, but was that day detached, got orders from Genl. Burnside to move up the turnpike towards the gorge, and attack the enemy and dislodge them. This was the hard place of the whole line, but this Brigade never falters, and amid Hooker's thunder upon the right, and Reno's upon the left, the "Black Hats" moved steadily on to their work.

At the sun an hour high, in the after-noon, with its rays streaming full in their faces, they were engaged with the enemy's infantry largely their superiors in numbers and posted behind stone walls and in woods, the rebel batteries mean time hurling shell among us, to which our own artillery replied with interest. — The Rebel Artillery was silenced, the Brigade drove all before it up the gorge, as darkness came on, and we heard first the cheers of Reno, then of Hooker, upon our left and right, telling us that all but the center was won. Wisconsin though commencing last, and with its work not done, could not fail to do that work well before it slept.

So above the roar of battle went up the cheers of the Wis-

[28] The United States effectives engaged in this battle were probably 28,480 but the Confederates numbered only 17,852. Mark M. Boatner III, *The Civil War Dictionary* (New York, 1959), 20.

consin men, in response to those of their friends upon the right and left, and with the coming on of night they redoubled their work. At about ten P.M. the battle closed — the enemy was dislodged from the gorge, and the Brigade rested upon their arms, — the 6th where they fought, — the others relieved by fresh troops who came and took their places, and they fell back a few yards, first for more ammunition, then for sleep. — And victory was won along the whole line, and the Rebels were in confusion and retreat upon the other side of the mountain.

Their loss is estimated at 15000 [*sic*] in this battle of *South Mountain*. Our loss in the whole I do not know, but it was not nearly, not one half as large as that of the enemy. In our Brigade the loss was 319 in killed and wounded.[29]

On the 15th we pursued, and overtaking the enemy across *Antietam* creek, we skirmished with them, as we did also on the 16th, they still retiring, but slowly and fighting as they retired. But our forces were now collected, — the enemy must be swept from Maryland, or captured, — and so on the 17th, at Sharpsburg, a little after daylight the great battle of the war, so far, opened, by Hooker's attack upon the Rebel left. Hooker was on our extreme right, and King's (now Doubleday's) Division was our [Hooker's] extreme right. Our Brigade moved out to battle at a little after sun-rise, and before we had moved a hundred yards towards the enemy, their second shell, — the first just passed above our heads, — dropped and exploded in the 6th Wis. and killed or wounded thirteen men and officers, — Capt. D. K. Noyes being among the latter. He has had his right foot amputated, saving the heel and ankle joint, is doing well, and undoubtedly will recover.[30] We moved on to battle, and soon the whole ground shook at the discharges of artillery and infantry. Gainesville, Bull Run, South Mountain

---

[29] The total Confederates casualties were 2685, while those of the Union were 1813. *Ibid.* As indicated above, the officially reported Iron Brigade loss was 318, including 30 missing.

[30] David K. Noyes of Baraboo, 6th Wis.

were good respectable battles, but in the intensity and energy of the fight and the roar of firearms, they were but skirmishes in comparison to this of Sharpsburg. The battle raged all day, with short intervals during which changes were being made in the dispositions of troops. At night we were in occupation of almost all we had gained of ground — this was a good deal. —

The enemy's dead and wounded were nearly all in our lines. — The slaughter upon both sides is enormous. All hands agree that before they had never seen such a fearful battle. The loss of the Brigade was in killed and wounded 380, 47½ per cent of the men engaged.[31] The victory was complete, but not decisive. The 18th was consumed in maneuvering and ascertaining the positions of the enemy, and on that night he skedaddled out of Maryland, leaving his dead unburied, his wounded uncared for, and a large amount of arms, and some guns, in our hands. About twenty stands of colors were captured by us, — two by the 6th Wis. The flag of the 6th received four bullets in the flag staff, and some fifteen in the fly, — that of the 2nd Wis. three bullets in the staff and more than twenty in the fly. We are now near the field. — I hope you may never have occasion to see such a sight as it is. I will not attempt to tell you of it.

But amid such scenes we are all cheerful, the men were never more so, — victory in two hard, great battles, and the rebels out of Maryland make us glad.

Through all these four battles which I have hinted [sic] at I have been, and am unharmed. I cannot tell how any one could have survived, — but we are alive, and I have the belief that He who controls the destinies of nations and men, has saved me, and will, unharmed, in many more battles. I have not been afraid of any thing in battle. One does not mind the bullets and shells much, but only looks to the men and the

---

[31] The Brigade's reported casualties totaled 348, including 5 missing, equaling 42 per cent of the 800 engaged. Nolan, *Iron Brigade*, 142.

enemy, to see that all is right. I saw many incidents of battle, that would interest you, but cannot now tell them.

One however I will tell. On the 17th, about 10 o'clock A.M. I was sent to Genl. Hooker with a message.[32] — I had to ride through a hail-storm of bullets, from the enemy not a hundred yards off, and was upon the gallop upon my pet horse, "Joe," a fine creature, fleet as a deer, and brave as a lion, who had carried me in all the battles, when a musket bullet hit him full in the side, he jumped in to the air, — the blood spurted several yards from the wound, and he staggered to fall. I dismounted and patted his neck to take leave of the faithful creature. — He leaned his head against me like a child, — but I must leave him — I started, and he whinnied after me and tried to follow. — I went to him and again stroked his neck and patted him, — He seemed to know as much as a man, — I again started to leave him. — He again tried to follow, but his poor legs could carry him no more, — he whinnied for me, feebly, and fell, and was dead in a minute, — I could not help a tear for him. Capt. Bachelle[33] of the 6th Wis. had a pet Newfoundland dog, that he had raised, and which was always with him. — Master and dog both fell dead together upon the field, shot with bullets.

I find my letter is getting long, — it may not interest you but these matters do me, and you must excuse me. — One word more: — you must have faith in McClellan, and in the ultimate success of the war — and know that we are all ready when the call comes, to give our lives for the country.

I am one of Genl. Gibbon's Aides, — have been since June 17th. — He is a most excellent officer and is beloved and re-

---

[32] Gibbon commended Haskell for this episode in his report of the battle. U.S., War Department, *The War of the Rebellion: A Compilation of the Official Records of the Union and Confederate Armies* (128 vols., Washington, 1880–1901), Series 1, Vol. 19, Part 1, p. 249. Hereinafter cited as *OR*.

[33] Werner Von Bachellé of Milwaukee.

spected by his whole command. — You ask me what my chances of promotion are. — I answer, they are nothing. — If I could myself win some great battle, alone, and then could blow in the papers, and pay news papers to blow for me, and then was besides a d —— d politician, I suppose I could be promoted. — I have been recommended for a field office by Genls. King and Gibbon, have been urged by Col. Cutler — and my friends at home have besought the Gov. — but I suppose I am too good an officer. — The Hebrew mullet [Governor Edward Salomon] will not appoint me. I have got done asking for promotion. — I should like it. — I think I deserve it, — but I shall not get it. — In all the battles, I have had the honorable mention of my General for good conduct.

Frank A. Haskell

[Postscript:]

To you, Maria,[34] I am under special obligations for your good letter. — I[t] came to me away down in Virginia, and on the day when for the first time I had been shot at by the rebels. — We had had a skirmish, and a hard wet day's work and it did me a world of good to read your good, kind letter. — Write to me again, will you not? Write to me at Washington, D.C., How are you, Martha?[35] — Harrison says you want to come to the war. — no, no. — This war is a horrid thing. — You just stay right at home, make some shirts for wounded soldiers, — and if I do not come home again, shead [sic] one tear for me, and you need to do nothing more for the war, — only you must believe in Genl. McClellan. I heard that Harvey was coming to the war. — No boy, you must not think of it, — you could not begin to stand it, — The losses by sickness, are far more than those by bullets. One must be of iron to stand

---

[34] Mrs. Harrison S. Haskell.
[35] Martha Pride, Maria Haskell's daughter by a previous marriage.

it, — I am three fourths iron, and the rest is oak. Cannot you send me something? Send me something and I will kiss it, and wear it in my *weskit* pocket. Much love to all of you,

                                                    Frank

                    *   *   *   *   *

☐ The few weeks of campaigning which ended at Antietam reduced the Iron Brigade from some four thousand men to less than the 6th Wisconsin's original enrollment of a thousand. In Haskell's old regiment, too, only a fourth of the soldiers whom he had helped to train remained in the ranks.[36] Among the effects of the casualties was the promotion of some of the survivors. On November 5, the molder of the Iron Brigade, John Gibbon, replaced a wounded general as commander of the 2nd Division of the First Corps and Haskell, his aide, also stepped up to greater responsibility. Conversely, failure to destroy Lee's army after Antietam or to pursue it rapidly caused the removal of General George B. McClellan as leader of the Army of the Potomac. On December 13, 1862, his successor, General Ambrose E. Burnside, hurled his men in a futile assault on a powerful Confederate position at Fredericksburg, Virginia. General Gibbon was among the host of wounded. Haskell escaped injury and, during the ensuing winter lull, returned to Wisconsin for a visit. ☐

---

[36] Nolan, *Iron Brigade,* 160, 161.

III

Awaiting Armageddon

IN AMPLE TIME for the start of the spring campaign of 1863, Frank Haskell rejoined the recovered General Gibbon, returned with him to camp nearly opposite Fredericksburg and awaited a new assignment in the Army of the Potomac. That seemingly luckless army had a new commander, Joseph Hooker, in place of defeated Ambrose Burnside, whom Hooker had actively undermined. Hooker was at first popular, but Haskell and much of the rest of his men came to dislike and distrust their commander when he led them to disaster in the Chancellorsville campaign. Haskell's unit did not accompany Hooker's main force in this attempt to turn the left flank of the Confederate army entrenched at Fredericksburg. However, Haskell witnessed and well describes the secondary attack across the battlefield of the previous December, a fight which he calls the second battle of Fredericksburg. The young lieutenant also mirrors the demoralization fostered by the widespread hostility to Hooker and his clique. □

* * * * *

Near Falmouth, Va.
March 24, 1863.

Arrived at Washington on the eve of the 21st, Saturday, and then and there found Genl. Gibbon, and Staff, *"all nice and lovely."* My journey thither was devoid of incident, and every thing else save *joggle* and sleep.

52

We all came here from Washington, yesterday P.M. — arrived at 6 ½ P.M. — and slept in a tent again.

The last night before that I was in the field I slept in the open air on the 13th of Dec. after the battle — the tent is an improvement.

I take things easily, now where I left them in the fall. — As I stand here to-day, the last three months appear a dream of an hour.

All about me is as it was an hour ago, — the same spot, — the same aspect of nature, — the same bustle of the camp and faces of men. *"Sech* is life!"

Heigh-ho, — what next? We do not know what will be the General's command but probably shall know to-day or to-morrow.

I have but time to write but a word, as I smoke one of the cigars that Maria gave me at starting. I am much disappointed at the lateness of the season here. — It is not farther advanced than Wisconsin.

Adieu,
Frank A. Haskell.

P.S. I shall not write once in two weeks. — I told Maria I would, but I was only in fun. — It is but just now that I should let you know the truth. — I shall be well during the next four weeks, so do not be alarmed if you do not hear from me. — I will tell you however, as soon as I know where we are to be, so that you can write to me.

F————

*   *   *   *   *

Near Falmouth, Virginia,
March 31st 1863.

I am well. — With this brief announcement, allow me to express the hope that this sample of chirography, may, — I can seem to see it on its "winding way", let it wind — come to your hands, you all mean while, and at the time of the reception hereof, being vouchsafed the thing, or condition

which is expressed in the first three words above: — in brief,
I hope you are the same.

But to change this interesting subject, we remain *in statu*
[*sic*] *quo*, here at the Head Quarters of the Army of the Poto-
moc, unassigned to duty, waiting, watching, and hoping, for
"something to turn up."[1] We, however, expect, but a day or
two more will elapse ere the General will have a Division.

Last night and this morning it has snowed three or four
inches, and the weather has been execrable, raining or snow-
ing half of the time, since I have been here. The mud has no
bottom, — the army cannot move for some days yet at all events,
— the newspapers to the contrary, notwithstanding. The army
is in excellent condition so far as the health and spirits of the
men are concerned. I believe we shall strike some good blows
when the time comes.

We can see the tents and camps of the enemy for miles, thick
upon the other side of the Rappahannock, — we will disturb
them soon however, and give their vile bodies to the buzzards
and crows.

It would give you a disagreeable feeling could you see the
camps of the armies here at present.

Where less than a year ago was one of the loveliest vallies
[*sic*] human eyes ever saw, with farms, and houses, hill and
dale, woodland and meadow, all populous with the images of
God, now is a desolate and unsightly waste, without trees,
fences, or population, and few houses — these deserted and
nearly ruined — but bristling with two mighty armies, thirst-
ing to cut each other's throats! Thank God that the desolation of War comes no nearer to you.

You may consider it bad enough to have friends in the con-
test, who are liable to be hustled into some ditch on an occasion
any day, — but you yet have a shelter, a house not desecrated
by the merciless hand of your enemies.

Humanity bleeds at this war, — but, but, — who made it?

---

[1] Micawber in Charles Dickens, *David Copperfield.*

Who trampled the ensign of Peace and Security in the dust?

By God's help they shall pay the penalty for their sin. May I be one of the instruments of their desolation, and punishment, and to bring it about, that the places that know them shall know them no more forever, and to teach such as they how sacred a thing is the Constitution, and how terrible is the wrath of the offended Republic.

I could not be out of such a war as this.

Frank A. Haskell.

*   *   *   *   *

Camp of 2nd Div. 2nd Corps
Near Falmouth, Va.
April 3d, 1863.

On the 1st day of this month the General, was assigned to the command of this Division, the 2nd, of the 2nd Army Corps of the Army of the Potomac. The Division has the reputation of being one of the best in the service, — has fifteen regiments of Infantry and two batteries of Artillery, and an aggregate present strength for duty of about 6000 men.

It was first commanded by Genl. Stone, — when he was arrested,[2] its next commander was Genl. Sedgwick[3] — who after the battle of Antietam, being assigned to a Corps, was succeeded by Genl. [Oliver Otis] Howard, who commanded at Fredericksburg, and is now just assigned to the command of the eleventh Corps, [Franz] Sigel's old command, — and Genl. Gibbon succeeds him. The appearance of the Division is remarkably good, — the troops are from Maine, Mass., Minnesota, Michi-

---

[2] General Charles P. Stone, made the scapegoat for the Union defeat at Ball's Bluff, was removed from command and imprisoned without charge for six months. William B. Hesseltine and Hazel C. Wolf, *The Blue and the Gray on the Nile* (Chicago, 1961), 4–7.

[3] John Sedgwick was a West Point graduate and veteran of service against Indians and Mexicans. Commanding units during the eastern campaigns of 1862, he was several times wounded. He was killed at the battle of the Wilderness. Warner, *Generals in Blue,* 430–31.

gan, New York and Pa., — the majority from the two latter
states. This Corps is commanded by Genl. [Darius N.] Couch,
— and was formerly commanded by Genl. [Edwin V.] Sumner,
— and this Division is the one that ran so at Antietam, concerning which I told you when at home.[4] — That is the only
bad thing that I hear about them. They fought well at Fredericksburg, and lost 850, in all, — about half as many as Gibbon's old Div. at the same battle. — All our old staff are not
here, — at present only the two other Aids and myself, — but
some of the rest are expected. The General is well pleased with
his new command, — better than with his last, for it is larger,
and under better discipline. I am agreeably situated, and it
seems good once more to have something to do. The Genl.
has reviewed the 1st Brigade to day and to-morrow and Monday he will review the other two.

Our review to-day was on the same ground where on the
18th of April last year, one of King's brigades had a skirmish
with the enemy when we first came to Fredericksburg, and
where Genl. Gibbon, then a Captain in command of a Battery, fired the first hostile shot that he ever fired in his life.
— From the command of less than a hundred men, he has
come to his present command in less than a year.

There is nothing in general new here, — it has not stormed

---

[4] At the battle of Antietam, Gibbon's Iron Brigade had helped
to block the disorderly retreat of Sedgwick's division. Nolan, Iron
Brigade, 143. In arguing for Haskell's promotion, Haskell's brother
later claimed that on this occasion Gibbon's aide had also acted
as "a volunteer aid to Genl. Sumner" in stemming the rout and
thus doing much to gain the victory. Presumably basing his account on the conversation referred to in this letter, Harrison S.
Haskell claimed that Sumner sent Frank Haskell to rally a New
York regiment which had fled as a unit and that his brother,
seizing their battle flag, had led the New Yorkers "directly into
the thickest of the fight. . . ." H.S. Haskell to Gov. Lewis, January 30, 1864, in Wisconsin Executive Department, Applications
for Commissions, 1861–65, Series 1/1/5–20, Archives Division,
SHSW. Sumner made no reference to Haskell in his report on
Antietam. OR, Ser. I, Vol. 19, Pt. 1, pp. 275–77.

for two or three days, — the mud is drying up. Please direct to me officially, "Head Quarters 2nd Division, 2nd Corps, Army of Potomac, Washington, D.C.," and this I hope you may do soon.

With much love to you all, I close.

Frank A. Haskell.

*   *   *   *   *

Near Falmouth, Va.
April 8, 1863.

Still here. — Day before yesterday Uncle Abraham [Lincoln] and Mrs. Abraham came down here from Washington, and *he* reviewed 15,000 Cavalry of this Army, and *she,* lovely female, as she is, sat in a six horse carriage and looked on. Sweet creature, she, very. "Oh for a lodge" &c.[5]

The above number is a great many horses, to be all in one string. You may never see so many together, and I never expect to again. To day we have had a grand Review, by the same personage, of Four Corps d'Armie [sic], the 2nd, Genl. Couch, the 3rd, Genl. [Daniel E.] Sickles, — the 5th, Genl. Meade, — and the 6th, Genl. Sedgwick, — in all some 60,000 Infantry — a small part of the Army. A nice little show, that. They [sic] men looked well, and are in good fighting order.

Let auspicious Heaven give us good weather, and smile upon the cause of the Republic, and these same boys, that I saw today, may do something in a few days for the country.

They could do a devil of a sight of mischief, if turned loose with their guns, among the rebels. There are a great many of them that would shoot.

---

[5] *Oh, for a lodge in some vast wilderness,*
Some boundless contiguity of shade,
Where rumor of oppression and deceit,
Of unsuccessful or successful war,
May never reach me more! . . .
WILLIAM COWPER, *The Task,* Book II.
Haskell's ardor for McClellan, whom Lincoln had removed, may help account for the hostility toward the President.

The weather is still very cold here, and snow still lies around in heavy drifts, in many places, — and the sweet and comely face of the President and his lovely spouse, coming here, do not seem to have changed it at all for the better.

Fresh milk, and unhatched eggs, I am sure, could not stand before that same face of our respected Chief Magistrate, — but the weather can, — and does not seem to mind him at all. It is strange that such is the fact, though, — for I consider that *face* far ahead of the *face* of nature, or old *preface,* himself.

Nothing more now. We are all well. — Hope you are, — Eh?

Why don't you write? Maria, do not sell all of the tomatoes; — save some for me. I'll send for them by-and by, — and some of the blackberry. My love to you and my Niece [Martha Pride].

Frank A. Haskell.

*   *   *   *   *

Near Falmouth, Va.
April 14, 1863.

The eve of great events. — The clouds are gathered in the horizon, — the wind pipes and whispers, — dull thunder from afar strikes upon the listening ear. — Ere this reaches you, probably — no, I will not speculate upon probabilities. — None of us can know the future — It will be revealed to us soon enough.

The army is in magnificent condition, — If it cannot do well, what hope can the country have? I think, under Heaven, we may trust to the results, and that all will be well. According to present prospects, it may be some time ere I can write you again. I cannot write all I know, but you will probably learn by other means, before you could learn from this.

I have no faith in our attempts at Charleston. — I look for the defeat of our expedition there. — I may be mistaken, but I see no chance there at present.[6]

---

[6] Haskell refers to the unsuccessful attack by ironclads on Charleston on April 7, 1863.

We have had good weather for nearly a week, and the roads are quite good. — We hope that Spring has indeed come.

Our camp is in the midst of a little pine grove, on a steep knoll, or hill, — to-day we have got us all — the staff — good new clean tents, and are as comfortable as we could desire to be in the field. This morning we had a regular *"matinee"* by the birds, in the trees all around us. The robin, blue-bird, sparrow, (as in New England) and many varieties of warblers, were there, and we "listened to the mocking bird," in fact.[7]

Oh! come again bright morning, with songs of birds, and after the battle, come brighter morning of peace, — peace to the army, and the country restored!

I close this to go to sleep — good sleep, for the work of to-morrow.

Good night,
Frank A. Haskell.

*   *   *   *   *

Near Falmouth, Va.
April 23, 1863.

In statu [*sic*] *quo.* The "storm in the South, that darkened the day," when I wrote before, was no storm at all. Some rain fell — a flood, — the river rose eight feet. — So, in consequence of this *storm* of rain, the army did not *storm* at all. That is the way it goes in the field! Expectation raised to the highest pitch — the next moment it is flat. Can you wonder at the *character* romances give the soldier? In this moment he may be in the midst of friends, endearments, fun, what you will, — the next, with the shortest notice, he is in the midst of a shower of enemy's bullets, and a hundred times confronts death.

God is over us all; but the soldier should be a *good* man, — brave, earnest, ever ready, — then what matter the accidents of time and place!

---

[7] Septimus Winner's song, "Listen to the Mocking Bird," was popular during the war.

But to proceed, — rain and a flood stopped the move a week ago, — then came a week of good weather, — a move is planned, — last night and to day it rains in torrents, and the Rappahannock forces [?] again. — When we shall move, none can tell.

Old time rolls on, — to-day, we are where we were a year ago, — I am, only then I was sick — now I am well.

The flame of the peach-trees reddens the land, and the cherry buds hint at white. The air is soft, with not a taint of ice in it. Spring, and life, and health are with us, — but what of all these! We have had them oft before. — They are all good, but I want something more, — a great, terrible, thundering battle, not for the fight, but for victory, — and victory not for fame, but for peace.

When will it come! — I am sick of reading the lying newspapers, — sick of the flourish and blowing for trifling and purposeless events.

With fervent longings that "something may turn up," yet without that lively faith that animated the breast, and directed the life of my friend Micawber, I abide my time.

Nothing to write. — The hum-drum of camp is as it was a thousand years ago, and every year since then. — By the way, would it not be a good idea for some of you to write to me?

Adieu,

Frank A. Haskell,

P.S. Tell Mrs. Arnold[8] that long ago the letter she handed me went across our lines, and is doubtless ere this in the hands she designed it for, — and that for so good a woman as she is, and one that I like so well and esteem so much, I should be glad to do such or any other favor at any time.

Give my love to Mrs. Julia.

* * * * *

---

[8] Neither Mrs. Arnold, for whom Haskell had evidently sent a letter to someone in the South, nor Mrs. Julia, mentioned below, have been identified; but they were doubtless acquaintances in Wisconsin.

Near Falmouth, Va.
April 29, 1863.

This letter may not be *"put on its final passage"* for some days, but possibly some of the things transpiring may be of interest to you, though you should not receive this for some time. I hinted a move in my last. —[9] It commenced yesterday or before. The 11th, 12th, 5th, and 2nd, Corps, all but our Division, have moved to the river some miles above Falmouth, we suppose with purpose to cross and attack the enemy upon his left flank. The 1st, 3d, and 6th Corps have moved to the river some few miles below Fredericksburg, and at least one Division ([General William T. H.] Brooks') of the 6th Corps has crossed and gained a footing upon the other side, at the same place where [General William B.] Franklin crossed for the battle in December, — our old ground. Of course I do not know the intentions, but I judge that it is Genl. Hooker's plan to make a demonstration upon the enemy below the town and the old battle field of the 13th of Dec., — cross with a large force above and attack the enemy on his left, or in rear, and then when we shall have come well upon him in this manner, upon his left, our left shall simultaneously attack him furiously upon his right, and so — *the thing will become general,* a big fight and I believe that we shall lick the rascals.

Our army is about 150,000 effective force, — so you see it can be made a big thing, if all goes well.[10] — I am very sanguine of our success. This crossing of the Division I mentioned, took place this morning — possibly much more has taken place today than I know, but I intend to tell you *all I know* — and the enemy were taken entirely by surprise, and some fifty of them captured. — A few companies first pushed over in boats, so rapidly that the enemy's outposts could not assemble to repel

[9] An unimportant note dated April 27, 1863 (here omitted).
[10] Haskell's analysis of Hooker's strategy was generally accurate, but the Third Corps soon joined the main force moving around Lee's left. The total Union strength was about 134,000 to some 61,000 for the Confederates.

them. Our division which has been all the time heretofore stationed near Falmouth and nearer the river than any other force, right in sight of the enemy, has not yet been moved. — We are between the movements that I have described.

The enemy are in some force in plain sight of us across the river in and around Fredericksburg, and to-day seem somewhat uneasy, moving troops, and filling their rifle pits, — and once in a while, through the day, the sound of a great gun has come booming upon our ears, telling of to-morrow's storm. The weather is excellent for our purposes.

Who can tell what will happen before to-morrow's sundown? I think this is the eve of the greatest battle upon this continent, and oh! God, shall we be victorious?

To-night I heard a Solitary Thrush sing her sweet melancholy song, to the coming darkness, as I have a thousand times when a child — the clouds float fleecy and gently across the face of the mild-eyed moon — perfumes from new blossoms come into my tent, upon the soft air, — the poor unpoetical frogs are piping with might and main from every book and puddle, and the Whip-poor-Will complains. —

There is not one whisper or hint of battle in all these! No, no, let the army sleep! — sound slumber, and rosy dreams, such as these gentle voices of nature bid.

To-morow battle and blood, — the country, perhaps, saved or lost!

Good night,
Frank A. Haskell.

*   *   *   *   *

Near Falmouth, Va.
April 30, 1863.

Our division has not moved yet — we have orders to be ready to move at daybreak, to-morrow. — The great battle has not been fought to-day, but the plot thickens. —

Our right is moving around the flank of the enemy, — our left confronts his right, and all this after-noon, the rough edges of the armies have rubbed against each other and at every touch they strike fire. I can just hear the booming sound of hostile cannon away down upon our left now, though it is after dark. This after-noon we could see the pale dun smoke of gunpowder in the same region, rising up and vanishing in the pure air.

Genl. Hooker has to-day published a congratulatory order to the Army, wherein he assures them that the enemy must flee in haste, or come out from his works and fight to be destroyed.[11] God grant this may be true. All looks favorable as could be desired so far. The weather is excellent, mild, not too hot, not dusty, not muddy under foot.

Wish me a good night, and success to-morrow. — I wish the same to you.

Haskell.

*　*　*　*　*

Near Falmouth, Va.
May 1, 1863.

May day! and the army has been "a-maying," too, — not with girls and laughter, but with rebels by thousands in battle ar-ry, and the thunder of great guns, — not for flowers, with fresh perfumes, but for the flash of rifled guns, and the smell of smoke, and the bayonet's gleam.

A lovely day indeed! — The 1st of May was never fairer! Let me tell.

Our division has not moved, but all day long we have been ready.

The 3d. (Sickles'), 5th. (Meade's), 11th. (Howard's), 12th. ([General Henry W.] Slocum's) and two divisions of the 2nd (Couch's) Army Corps have gained the other side of the river — some 80,000 men I suppose[12] — and extend from the U.S. ford, which is some eight or ten miles above Falmouth, to a

---

[11] For this very optimistic document, see *OR*, Ser. 1, Vol. 25, Pt. 1, p. 171.

[12] Nearer to 70,000 men were in this force.

point on the Fredericksburg and Orange C. H. road some ten miles from the former town; — and they have been drawing in upon the rebels, and we think have had a big fight — not the great final — but the commencement of it. As the respective armies are placed, the rebel left is between the camp of our division, and the forces that I have mentioned of our own. At about noon to-day the thunder of the artillery commenced away over opposite us some miles from the river, — at first so far away that we could scarcely hear it — then it came nearer, — we knew the *"fighting Joe Hooker"* was there in person, — and from these two facts we judge, that all is going well with us. — Then we learn that the enemy has withdrawn some of his pickets opposite our division to-day, those farthest up the river and nearest to our forces that are on the other side of the river. — This shows that he is a little *shaky* there and we call it a good sign for us. — Then at three or four o'clock this P.M. over 200 gray backed prisoners are conducted through our camp from the scene of the operations mentioned, a Colonel among them, — good again, say we. — And, last, after sun-down, as dark was coming on, a furious cannonade is heard up the river, and on the other side, so near that we could hear the bursting of the shells, which continued until eight o'clock, a few minutes ago, since I commenced this letter, and we judge the shells we hear are ours, — good again — this shows that our boys are coming down the river upon the enemy's left flank.

These things, our successes, I mean, are only conjectural you must remember, but still I think we are not mistaken. But oh! you may be sure, we are anxious, though!

What if we should be beaten after all! Ah! poor country! Would not all weep for her? If my poor life can be of any avail to avert such a calamity, I would gladly give it, — every drop of my blood as if it were water.

I have been upon the jump all day, for Capt. [J. P.] Wood, the Adjt. Genl. is sick, and off duty, so I have his work and my own to do. Orders to write, — dispatches to send — outposts to visit — quick, quick, — one minute lost may lose a battle!

But I shall lie down in my tent, in my blankets, tired, but with a light, hopeful heart, and I trust to good sleep.

A band is now serenading the General, playing the "Mocking Bird," for something he has been doing in the Division to-day, and so while music may soothe to sleep, I will make disposition to entertain the Gentle Goddess.

Good night, Haskell.

*   *   *   *   *

□ Unknown to hopeful Frank Haskell, Hooker's flanking movement had already become mired. After successfully crossing the Rappahannock and Rapidan Rivers with his massive force, Hooker hesitated at the crossroads of Chancellorsville. Lee, seeing his danger, left some 10,000 men to hold the works at Fredericksburg and led the bulk of his outnumbered army against Hooker. Losing confidence in himself, the Union commander went over to the defensive. As Haskell was writing the following letter, the Confederates had surprised and were routing Howard's Eleventh Corps. Meanwhile, the strong Union forces still near Fredericksburg were mounting assaults against the Confederate positions there. □

*   *   *   *   *

Near Falmouth, Va.
May 2, 1863.

At ten o'clock, last night one of the brigades (2nd) of this division marched to Banks' Ford a point some four miles further up the Rappahannock, — the other two brigades have not moved.

The morning was ushered in by a heavy cannonading up the river by apparently the same forces that closed last evening, that I last mentioned in my note of yesterday, — This subsided by eight o'clock, A.M. and was followed by a similar performance upon the extreme left of our line where the 1st

(Reynolds') and 6th (Sedgwick's) Corps are, which however did not last long. There was quiet in the artillery, and a dearth of news until noon. Then marching troops appeared coming through our camp from the left. They proved to be the 1st Corps, and from them we learned some news. — The 1st division of that Corps had crossed the river some six or eight miles below Fredericksburg, and an order was sent for them to recross to the left bank last night which they did not receive until after day light this morning. And while they were recrossing this morning the enemy's batteries opened upon them and were replied to by ours — this was the noise we heard upon the left. We received very little damage in the recrossing, however.

This recrossing on our part, you will know, was no *"skedaddle"* — but a part of the plan: — a feint of an attack upon our extreme left, was all that was intended then. The first Corps was marching to-day to rejoin our forces upon our right, already crossed.

You will remember that the 1st division that I have mentioned above is King's, (now [General James S.] Wadsworth's) old division and contains the old *"Iron Brigade,"* which won new laurels on the occasion the river was crossed a day or two since. — I really did not ask what day it was, but day before yesterday, 30th. April, I believe.[13] — I have seen the dear old brigade to-day, and what I am to tell, I learned from the officers of my acquaintance, so you may rely upon what they said. They were all in fine spirits and the General and I went down to see them as they passed our camp, and invited several of the officers, Genl. Cutler, Cols. Bragg, and Fairchild, among others, up to our quarters, — *"Mount Zion"* by name.

This was what the brigade did in crossing the river. You may know, the river is rapid and on the right bank at the point of crossing, was lined with rifle pits, and ditches full of the enemy — The old brigade always has the hard fighting to

---

[13] This battle at Fitzhugh's Crossing took place on April 29.

do — and the present instance was no exception to the general rule. Boats had been hauled down the river by night at many places. — The brigade crept up to the river, — in the day time — and the enemy from his pits opened fire upon them, which was returned, and in the midst of this sharp fire going on from the tops of the opposite banks, the Sixth Wis. — my glorious old Sixth, — salied [sic] down to the water's edge, the whole regiment, now some 350 muskets, shoved off the boats, manned them, and pulled for the rebel shore amidst a hail storm of bullets. The men kept as close down as possible, all but the rowers, over they pulled rapidly, the rest of the brigade cheered like great guns upon the bank.

They landed, — sprang up the bank in the very teeth of the rebels, formed at the summit, and *pitched in*. A Louisianna [sic] regiment is said to have made most remarkable time to the rear when confronted by these Badger devils, — but not so fast but that, besides their dead and wounded, that far outnumbered ours, the Sixth captured over 200 prisoners, more than half as many as there was of themselves.[14]

The rest of the brigade followed the Sixth rapidly, and in turn the other brigades of the division. The whole thing was so rapid and bold, that the grey rascals did not know what to do, and the success was capital.

Officers, not belonging to the brigade, describe this exploit of crossing the river as very brilliant indeed, and I have heard two Generals of the other divisions bragging to-day of what the Sixth did there. The loss of the brigade was smaller than could have been expected: — its rapid daring was its safety. The number of killed and wounded I did not learn exactly, but in the brigade it was under 60 in all, of whom 3 were killed and 13 wounded in the Sixth,[15] — one of these latter

[14] The 24th Michigan of the Iron Brigade shared equally with the 6th Wisconsin the responsibility for the assault. The commander of the First Corps, John F. Reynolds, claimed only to have taken more than ninety prisoners. Nolan, *Iron Brigade*, 212–14, 354.

[15] The total casualties in the brigade were 57. *Ibid.*, 214. Has-

was Capt. Plummer, Co "C" by a bullet through the hand. Private *Law* of the Sixth, who always used to cook for Col. Cutler and I, and then when I came with Genl. Gibbon, did the like in the brigade head quarters, had his right arm shot off, and, amputation near the shoulder.[16]

Among the killed were Capt. Gordon, and Lieut. Topping, of the 7th Wis. and from the same regiment were wounded Major Finicum, slightly, and Lieut Ryan, mortally. These officers, who were killed, did not cross the river, but fell upon the left bank. Capt. Gordon I was intimate with, and he was an excellent officer. His residence was Beloit.[17]

So much for *the* brigade. It would have done you good to have seen them to-day. There were never better soldiers.

After the withdrawal of the 1st Corps from the left, to-day, there are none but the 6th (Sedgwick's) left there. This Corps is all upon the right bank of the river, and at five o'clock P.M. we had official information, that Sedgwick was pursuing the retreating enemy across the old battle field of the 13th of December. The retreat we saw from our head quarters, with our glasses. — The signal Officers announce, that they counted 12 regiments of Infantry, 70 baggage wagons, and some artillery and cavalry, of the enemy, in full retreat before Sedgwick. We could not tell their numbers but it did our hearts good to see the scamps fugitive over the same heights that blazed with their cannon for our destruction on the 13th of December. They fled across the same ground where Gibbon's division fought, and they were posted, in the battle of Fredericksburg.

This evening the heights in rear of Fredericksburg, where

---

kell's report of the 6th Wisconsin's losses is exact. *OR,* Ser. 1, Vol. 25, Pt. 1, p. 272.

[16] Thomas W. Plummer of Prairie du Chien and Ransom Lawe of Appleton.

[17] Alexander Gordon, Jr., William O. Topping of Hazel Green, and Mark Finnicum of Fennimore. William W. Ryan of Decorah, Iowa, survived his wound.

was their strong-hold in December, and where we have seen their camps all this spring, are all a-glow with bright large fires, and we have no doubt they are burning their camps, preparatory to a retreat.

To morrow we expect to be in Fredericksburg, and that nothing but ditches and filth will be there to attest their late occupation.

We have heard very little news to-day, from our main army on the right, but we think it is all well there. There has been much cannonading in that direction through the day, but we have to infer the results. It has been reported to us that our cavalry have cut the enemy's railroad communication in his rear, but we do not know this.

May God speed the right.

Haskell.

*   *   *   *   *

Opposite Fredericksburg, Va.
May 3, 1863.

I have been in a great battle to-day, and am well and unhurt.

It is Sunday evening, and although I did not close my eyes in sleep last night, and have not slept six hours in three days, and have had excessively hard work for the body, and anxiety of the mind for the last twenty-four hours, and have not tasted food but once in that time, and that about half an hour since, yet I can scarcely make up my mind to go to sleep — I am too glad. I want to shout for joy all night — Fredericksburg, and the terrible works and heights behind have been stormed by us and carried.

Three cheers. Hurrah! — hurrah! — hurrah!

I am too shattered in mind and body to be able to write well but will try, in accordance with my usage of the last few days, to give you some notion of the events of the day.

Last night, at eleven o'clock, Genl. Gibbon received orders "to take and hold Fredericksburg." Two Brigades only were now with him, of his Division, the 1st and 3rd. You will recollect how matters stood last evening as I described them.

The order received, was communicated to the troops at once, — at two o'clock this morning, the two Brigades were in position opposite Fredericksburg, on the bank of the river, ready to effect a crossing, — the pontoons were upon the bank, ready to commence their being made into a bridge.

It was a lovely night — not a cloud in the sky, and the moon, near the full, from the soft, hazy air shone down upon the ripples of the river, and the silent, lightless town, beautiful as a dream.

You will recollect my anticipations of to-day, as I expressed them yesterday.

The work of making the bridge commenced, — the handling of the boats and timber made ominous sounds in the still air. The men were pushing the first boats into the water, — the General and Staff were upon the bank near the workmen, watching the progress of matters. — Not a sound had come from the sombre town, — not a twinkle of light, when all at once, a small stream of flaky fire, a sharp report, and the hiss of a bullet, startled the senses, — then a volley, of like appearance, and from the same source, spattered in among us from across the river, — these bullets, coming close to one, and unexpectedly, rather startle at night!

The mules brayed and ran, — the men sprang together, in sudden fright, but in a moment all was order again; and our guns hurling in a couple of shells upon the spot whence the fire came, which went over hissing, and crashed with a great roar among the buildings, silence followed and the work went on.

At sunrise, — not before, the bridge was complete, with no more interruption to its construction. As the last planks were being laid, and the storming party were fixing their bayonets, and shaking themselves together in order to rush over, guns began to thunder in the town and below, — musketry to rattle, and from the direction of the sound and the shells we knew that Sedgwick was at them from below. Cheers

followed the volleys, — our cheers, we knew them, — and as
our party were starting to cross, in the lower part of the town
we could see the welcome blue coats coming to meet us. Over
we went, over the bridge, and met Sedgwick's men, — the enemy ran from the rear of town and hid in the earthworks, and
by the time the sun was half an hour up, Fredericksburg was
ours.

The great voices of those guns, as they echoed and rolled
among the hills, and hurled their screeching messengers among
our enemys [sic], were grand music to our ears. We thought
of the 13th of December, and the thousands of our dead there,
whose bodies then upon the winter sod had been stripped
by an inhuman enemy. The time had come now, we thought,
for vengeance, and these thunders were its voice. Our crossing the river was a triumphal procession.

At six o'clock this morning we were in order, in the town,
connecting with Sedgwick's right.

Sedgwick and Genl. Gibbon consulted together, and resolved upon the following plan to take the heights in rear of
the town.

Sedgwick was to open with his Artillery, on the left, to
draw the enemy's fire and Gibbon with his brigades and two
other regiments, was to storm the works, on the right, and
above the town, and having gained them at a point and broken
the enemy, Sedgwick would advance and follow up the attack.

Sedgwick had 20,000 men with a good deal of Artillery, —
Gibbon had 4000, with three batteries. — These numbers are
approximately correct.

But in making the dispositions for these movements it was
found there was a deep canal full of water, which Gibbon
could not cross, between him and the enemy. The plan had
to be changed, — and during the consultation of the Generals,
incident, Gibbon's men suffered severely by the enemy's Artillery. But the men behaved well. Finally Gibbon was to
open with his batteries and make a demonstration of advancing, in order to concentrate the enemy before him, while Sedg-

wick would storm the enemy's right, and have commenced to
repulse them. Gibbon would withdraw from the front, and
their left, and cooperate with Sedgwick, by storming immediately upon his right. — This plan was executed. At nine o'clock,
A.M., at the signal Gibbon opened with his batteries, and began to move his troops.

The enemy replied to him, withdrawing their fire from
Sedgwick. — The plan worked to a charm. Sedgwick's men
rushed upon the enemy's right splendidly, — his guns mean
time turned upon us. —

Up went the stormers. — The rebel rifle pits flashed and
puffed their smoke along the crests, terribly — but Sedgwick's
men could not be stopped, — they were for blood. Soon we
saw the enemy begin to break upon his right, and run from
his earth in utter confusion. — Our men could see it, and they
roared in cheers.

A determined cheer is a fearful thing to its foes. — The
enemy showed signs of fear along his whole line as they heard
our roar. — Now was the time for Gibbon's men. They withdrew from their positions by regiments and rushed up the
hillsides with Sedgwick's at the enemy. At this moment the
battle was wild beyond description. Cannon thundered, —
shells and shot howled and shrieked, — bullets hissed, — men
roared and rushed, — and so amid the smoke of sulphur, the
bloody drama went on.

The battle rage was on our men, — fear and confusion were
upon the enemy. — He fled, shattered and in utter rout. Before ten o'clock A.M. the dread heights were ours, and cheer
upon cheer, great shouts of the heroes, rent the sky.

The army paused to reform, and then commenced the pursuit. — We followed them with shells, from every hill, and with
bullets when ever we could get near enough, — and so kept
on for some three miles. — But fear is swifter than courage,
and so, as we had no cavalry to pursue them with, and the
country was favorable for flight, their main bodies escaped.
I suppose they had from 12,000 to 15000 men. We captured

many prisoners — I suppose 1000, — but do not know. —

Genl. Sedgwick estimates his loss at 5000. — Gibbon's is quite heavy, but I cannot estimate it. — I think the enemy's loss equals ours. We took seven of the enemy's guns that I know of, — probably some more, and a good many small arms, abandoned in the hurry of flight. — Such is a hurried sketch of the 2nd battle of Fredericksburg, — it was sharp, brilliant, and victorious.[18]

We remember the 13th of December with sorrow, — but we shall recall the 3d of May, with feelings that will partly efface it, at least.

At noon Genl. Gibbon's division paused in pursuit, — what was done by Sedgwick in this after-noon I do not know, — and, as Gibbon was ordered to *"take and hold"* Fredericksburg, — the first part of the order being now executed, it remained for him but to execute the last, so he returned, and made dispositions at the town accordingly. In coming back over the heights we had so lately won, we were overwhelmed with astonishment at the view of their strength — saddened and sorrowful at the sight of the dead, and shattered humanity that strewed them over.

Haskell.

* * * * *

Opposite Fredericksburg, Va.
May 4, 1863.

Early this morning the aspect of affairs in this part of the Army was much changed.

During the night we had heard that Genl. Sedgwick's advance on the Orange Court-House road, whereon he was with

---

[18] In this battle, Sedgwick's force of about 25,600 drove from the heights some 11,600 Confederates commanded by Jubal A. Early. Kenneth P. Williams, *Lincoln Finds a General: A Military Study of the Civil War* (5 vols., New York, 1949–59), 2: 595. Haskell overestimates the Union losses. Sedgwick claimed to have lost 4590 in the battles at Fredericksburg and on the following day at Salem Church. Gibbon lost only 110 men during both days' operations. *OR*, Ser. 1, Vol. 25, Pt. 1, p. 191.

his Corps yesterday when we left him at noon, had been checked, some miles further on by the enemy, covered in the woods. His purpose was to have joined Hooker at Chancellorsville that day, driving the enemy before him.

Genl. Sedgwick had also intimated that he feared the enemy was being reinforced from the South, and designed an attack upon his left, this morning.

Should this be the case, his position would be critical.

To render myself intelligible in this present posture of affairs, I perhaps need to explain some matters.

Taking Fredericksburg as a point to start from, up the Rappahannock four miles is Banks' Ford, and six miles further is United States' Ford. — Chancellorsville is some four or five miles from this latter Ford, on the South side of the river, and some fourteen miles from Fredericksburg by way of the Orange Court-House road. Hooker with the whole army, except Sedgwick's Corps, and Gibbon's Division, is between United States Ford and Chancellorsville, his right near the latter place, and his left resting on the former. The larger portion of the enemy is massed in front of Hooker: — all of his force now present, probably, except that opposite us yesterday which I estimated too low in my last. Such appeared to be the state of affairs, last evening and this morning, which had been developing for several days. Could Sedgwick rout the force before him, or drive them in upon the rest of the enemy before Hooker, and then attack them in rear or upon the flank, while Hooker at the same time should advance upon their front, good results were hoped for.

But as I have said Sedgwick was checked last evening, not having advanced more than half way from Fredericksburg to Chancellorsville.

You must remember that this part of the country is very rough and wooded — full of ravines and steeps — much better adapted to defense than attack.

To explain further which, should have been written last

night in my letter of yesterday, when Gibbon's Division returned from the pursuit yesterday, to take position at Fredericksburg, according to instructions he had received, and to meet the views of his superiors in command, as well as to carry out his own, he dispersed one of his Brigades in the town, throwing outposts around the town to the river both above and below, and withdrew the rest of his command to the left bank of the river. All these formidable works that we gained yesterday were abandoned or, rather, vacated by us, — no enemy but the dead being in there, — by nightfall of yesterday.

You perhaps, when you read along further, will criticise, possibly *s-w-e-a-r* a little, when you think all this matter over, and the results, — but our dispositions were all right, nevertheless, in view of our forces, our purposes, and our knowledge at the time.

Now I may proceed with the events of to-day, and, I trust, be understood.

At sunrise we had heard no more from Sedgwick — no firing in his direction — he must, therefore, be where he was last evening.

Were his apprehensions that I have mentioned in the first part of this letter, well founded? We shall see.

All our glasses were in requisition and in use upon available look outs, as soon as light to-day, watching the "Telegraph Road", which is the direct road from Richmond to Fredericksburg, and scanning all points and objects toward the South.

We did not wait long in suspense, — our worst fears were soon realized. The "Telegraph Road" is full of the gray-backed devils, — on they come rapidly, regiment after regiment, pouring in like a torrent towards Fredericksburg, — they appear in the first works on the left of the town, — they cheer, — they rush along to the right into the vacant strongholds — one after another, — the whole heights swarm with

them, — at six o'clock in the morning these works are full
again. — Longstreet is there with, it is said, 40,000 men.[19]

What will now become of Sedgwick and his some 15,000 or
16,000 men, checked in his advance, this force in his rear,
fresh, and they can easily come around his left flank? Sedgwick's men are weary with two days' battle already! Must
this gallant Corps be annihilated? Does the enemy know
Sedgwick's force? and will they rush upon him at once? Is
he aware of his peril, and can he make dispositions in time to
face his new adversary? Can he not retire to Banks' Ford, now
upon his right flank, some four or five miles distant, and put
the river between him and the overwhelming numbers of his
foes? These were some of our anxious inquiries all the morning, for our fears were not for ourselves, as it soon became apparent that Longstreet was not after our little force, but was
for larger game. The day wore on — we learned that Sedgwick had opened his communication with Banks' Ford, — we
heard no guns in that direction. After all we might be mistaken in the strength of Longstreet's forces. From the signal
stations we learned that Sedgwick had made new dispositions
to meet his enemy and showed him a steady front.

Perhaps this Mr. Longstreet does not dare to attack Uncle
John Sedgwick, after all. By the middle of the afternoon we
began to breathe a good deal easier, and thought it might come
out right after all. Perhaps Hooker has learned of these matters and has managed to send reinforcements.

Two hours before sundown some movement was visible
among the rebels, nearest us, — they seem to be coming up
out of the places where they have been lying, in ravines, —

---

[19] General James Longstreet was not on the field; neither had reinforcements arrived for Lee's army. Instead Lee, having defeated
part of Hooker's force and intimidated the rest into remaining on
the defensive, was making an attempt to destroy Sedgwick's Corps.
As part of this operation, troops of Early's Division reoccupied the
works at Fredericksburg. Douglas Southall Freeman, *Lee's Lieutenants: A Study in Command* (3 vols., New York, 1944), 2: 626–30.

away on the farthest heights that are visible troops are moving about rapidly. What is up?

Our batteries throw over from the left bank of the river some shells, from the twenty pound Parrott guns, which burst splendidly among the rebels, and we can see them run. Their officers rally them, and get them in order and they move away towards Sedgwick's position.

We hear infantry firing in that direction, first scattering shots, — but they become more frequent — We can see the smoke of guns away up where we know our men must be, and hear their reports. Yes at last we can see a part of Sedgwick's line of battle not yet engaged however.

The musketry and artillery discharges have become a constant roar, — a thunder storm of sound. Smoke rises and envelopes all the region, swelling highest over the batteries, and pierced at intervals by their long streams of fire.

Oh! that is a terrible battle! The smoke extends further and further towards Sedgwick's rear, — the batteries retire in that direction. — It must be that Sedgwick is being beaten. Then we see just before dark a long line of the enemy advance over the hills, and sweep under fire in the same direction that Sedgwick retires.

Darkness comes on — the battle continues until it is fully dark, and at last the firing ceases. Sedgwick, we judge, must be badly beaten.

Haskell.

*   *   *   *   *

"Phillips House,"
Near Falmouth Va.
May 5, 1863.

I must resume my thread of events where I left it yesterday. — I believe I had Sedgwick *"licked"* last night at the close of my letter, by Longstreet.

— You must make some allowances, for my letters, if there are some things in a subsequent one that contradict the former, when you remember under what circumstances they are written.

I give my impressions, at the close of the day, of the events that come within my own observation, or that I learn from others whom I believe; but sometimes my observations, and sometimes my information, prove incorrect. I write however, for facts, only these things which are so, — my report of feelings and rumors, you will take for what they are worth. But this work in the field, in the midst of such things as have been going on around me for the past few days, is terrible to bear.

It is not so much the work one has to do, and the deprivation of sleep and food, as the fearful anxiety, that wears upon one, anxiety for the great result. And I had rather be in such a battle as that of yesterday, than out of it where I must necessarily be the sport, to a degree, of surmises, and conjectures.

But these startling events thick around one, so long continued, confound.

Dates become confused, and the checkered web of this great drama, unfolds like a dream.

To resume, Sedgwick was repulsed yesterday by an overwhelming force, but his men behaved heroically, under their noble commander, and last night he withdrew his command to this side of the river at Banks' Ford, without demoralization, without the loss of any guns, or prisoners who were not wounded. Some few ambulances, I hear were lost, but no other portion of his train. Of course his killed and some of his wounded fell into the enemy's hands.

But his loss all things considered was light. The men behaved well, and kept in order, and by their firmness, and the skillful use of his artillery, which was far superior to that of the enemy, he effected a masterly retreat in the presence of, and from the attack of three times his number of men fresh on the field, where he had fought two days before, and brought his command to a place of safety.

There has been a slip somewhere — This force of Longstreet never ought to have been allowed to come up, in this way.

As to Genl. Gibbon's command, this morning, at an early hour, he had orders to withdraw to this side of the [river] the brigade in Fredericksburg, and take up the bridges. We expected this yesterday afternoon, and then took the precaution to remove from the town all our wounded in the battle of Sunday, and all trains and supplies. To remove the Infantry was a comparatively easy operation. Our Artillery was posted on this side of the river to command the crossing, and then quietly, the Brigade, regiment after regiment retired and crossed the bridge, — the enemy followed, skirmishing with our outposts, — but little harm was done us, and, by six o'clock this morning we had vacated that shell-battered town, and taken up our bridges.

We then took up positions on this side to watch the enemy, and repel him, should he attempt to cross — He was in full occupation in fifteen minutes after we had left the town.

This after-noon it has rained a flood, — and the river is rising rapidly —

What will be the effect of this upon Hooker, and his force? Are you not apprehensive? This is an evening of painful suspense. — To morrow will develop important news.

Let me recapitulate, and tell you the position of the army at sundown to-day. — Gibbon's Division is upon the North bank of the river, near Fredericksburg. — Sedgwick's Corps is upon the same side, at Banks' Ford. — Hooker with all the rest of the Army of the Potomac is across the river, that is, on the South side, his left at United States' Ford. — We have much Artillery in position up and down the left bank of the river, to resist the enemy should he attempt to cross.

The enemy is still before Hooker with his main force, — but has a heavy force on the right bank of the river, opposite Sedgwick, and he occupies in force the works in rear of Fredericksburg, opposite us.

I can scarcely sleep to night, I am so full of apprehensions.
Haskell.

*   *   *   *   *

"Phillips House"
Near Fredericksburg, Va.
May 6, 1863.

Last night it rained in torrents for some hours, — a thunder-
storm, — and raised the river to a flood.

During the night that portion of the army with Hooker
recrossed the river, to this side, and to-day, the several Corps
are ordered to resume the same positions they have held during
the Winter. At eleven o'clock last night, the trains and Artillery, were all across; the Infantry, by this morning. And all
day long the troops have been pouring along to their old camps
again.

I was no prophet a few days since, when I said the great
battle of the war was about to take place. — It was not. There
have been some brilliant, thrilling episodes, but no great epic
of arms in the past few days. The capture of Fredericksburg
and the heights was magnificent, — and I hear of some splendid fighting on the same day, — May 3d — and brilliant successes of the 2nd and 3d Corps, near Chancellorsville.[20]

The 11th Corps on the same day is said by all to have behaved very badly. These Dutchmen, and Schurz's Division[21]
particularly, ran, many of them, before they had delivered a
shot.[22] In Sedgwick's battle of the 4th of May we suffered the

---

[20] Despite hard fighting, these corps won no "brilliant successes"
in this Union defeat. Haskell underestimates the scale of the battle. The United States forces lost 16,804 in the Chancellorsville
campaign; the Confederates lost 13,156 — including "Stonewall"
Jackson. Freeman, *Lee's Lieutenants*, 2: 644.

[21] Carl Schurz fled Germany after involvement in the unsuccessful Revolution of 1848. Settling at Watertown, Wisconsin, he
participated in Republican politics. His influence with German-
Americans won him a general's commission. DWB, 320.

[22] Haskell reflects the prevailing prejudice against immigrants

severest repulse that I have heard of, though the conduct of the Corps was admirable.

Our losses have not been heavy, considering the numbers engaged, and the amount of fighting done. The estimate that I mentioned of Sedgwick's loss on Sunday was too large. — His Adjt. Genl. to-day tells me that the losses of the Corps on Sunday and Monday will not, he thinks, exceed 4000. — This is probably half the loss of the whole army.[23] The "Iron Brigade" has had no more fighting or losses than I mentioned in my letter a few days ago. — I do not know the losses of the 3d and 5th Wis., or if they have had any. — The 5th, Col Tom. Allen, is with Sedgwick, and lost none on Sunday, — so I learned from him that day, after the battle.[24] The enemy's losses in killed and wounded by Sedgwick, in his fights all together, are not probably as heavy as our own, — they are no heavier at all events, — but it is said on all hands that elsewhere, except before Sedgwick, his losses in killed and wounded must be much greater than ours, — he has repeatedly advanced to attack us, but has been repulsed with great loss on almost every occasion. — Our Artillery is said to have cut him frightfully. We have captured prisoners of the enemy almost as numerous as all our own losses put together.

Some where from 6000 to 10,000 have been captured by us. — We have lost but very few prisoners. What I have said above of losses, & c. is intended to cover all the period of time,

---

which induced many native Americans to make the heavily German Eleventh Corps bear the onus of the defeat. Badly positioned by Hooker and by its commander, General O. O. Howard, it had received the full force of the unexpected Confederate flank attack on May 2nd (not May 3rd). Some units were routed but others fought hard, considering the circumstances, and suffered heavy losses. Bruce Catton, *Glory Road: The Bloody Route from Fredericksburg to Gettysburg* (New York, 1954), 188–206.

[23] See earlier notes for correct figures.

[24] The 3rd Wisconsin lost a total of 101 men, while the 5th Wisconsin's total casualties were 193. *OR*, Ser. 1, Vol. 25, Pt. 1, pp. 184, 191.

since the advance of the army, to the recrossing of the river again.

What did Hooker come back for? I do not know. Was it that his rations and ammunition were almost out, and the river was becoming a flood to destroy his communications, and cut off his supplies? Were the rebels being rapidly reinforced, so as to become too numerous for him? The rebels did not drive him back. The Army has not been defeated. Revolve these matters as you please. — I have told you all I know about them.[25]

I pause to breathe — The great battle has not been fought yet. When will it be?

Will the country get "blue" over these matters of the last ten days? It should not.

Well, how do you all do? Maria, I have to thank you for your real good letter without any date to it, which I received a day or two since, and will write you one in reply as soon as I have had some rest. You must excuse me until I get this horrible nightmare off of me. Will you not? It was real kind of you though to write such a good letter to me, and I appreciate your kindness.

"My niece" shall have a letter, too, in the course of a few days, for she too, has written me, that I have not answered. But I want to write to my good Mother at home and I resolved to do so as soon as I had been in one more battle; so now I shall write that letter, too, as soon as I am "settled".

I do not owe H.S. a letter I think.

Now as it rains horribly, and I think I shall not be disturbed, to-night at all, let me say good night.

Frank A. Haskell.

*   *   *   *   *

---

[25] Hooker had lost his confidence and had ceased his advance against Lee's flank. He had then failed to take advantage of Lee's dividing of the Confederate army and had never effectively coordinated the operations of his overwhelming Union force. Freeman, *Lee's Lieutenants,* 2: 644–47.

Near Falmouth, Va. May 12, 1863.
Back here to the same old place. — Perhaps we shall go into winter quarters here. As to the movements of the Army I can write you nothing new. You can take the statements of my letters, and I can now add nothing to them relative to recent movements.

I cannot think of any thing in them that I would correct, — even later occurrences have confirmed the truth of most of the conjectures of the letters.

By the way, I wonder if you have received all the letters I wrote? I wrote one *every day* from the commencement, to the close, of the late movements. I do not know how many, but the dates will show if you have them all. Please keep these letters, if you have them — Some day I may wish to see them.

The same queries as to why Gnl. Hooker recrossed the river, that were mentioned in my last, are still running through the Army. Nobody can answer them that I have heard of.

Gnl. Hooker has published an order to the Army wherein he congratulates them upon the *success* of the late operations. Do you see it? Oh, if this were any less than a war for the life of the Republic, it would be the most magnificent *farce* that ever was enacted.[26]

A great battle is fought and thousands of our brave men give up their lives in it, as they suppose, for the country; yet, if one may judge from the public prints, and the utterances of our chief men, civil and military, the only earthly use or purpose of all this effusion of blood is to show which is the greatest General and which has committed the more blunders, McClellan, or Hooker or Burnside, or some one else! Even some of the news-papers will discuss the question as to which party, Republicans or Democrats, lost most men in a given battle, and claim it for a victory if their party lost least.

Can it be that this nation is to be smitten and crushed to

---

[26] For this order, see *OR*, Ser. 1, Vol. 25, Pt. 1, p. 171.

death for its sins and folly? I sometimes think it is. The tone
of the newspapers, and their utter disregard to truth, in all
matters — matters here I know about, and know how false
they are, — the ethics of that congress, that would publish, or
would tolerate such a report as that of the "Committee on the
Conduct of the War",[27] the conduct of high civil officers in
making promotions in the army, and generally in the management of affairs, and the lack of success that attends our arms
alarm me. This last is but the consequence of the others, but,
when will it stop? If God would but smite the wicked, with
quick destruction, and the fools would die suddenly, and then
we could have just one man, unselfish, honest, and zealous in
his country's cause, I would hope. — I must say, now, however, that I sometimes have *grave fears*.

I perhaps could not make you believe all these matters, —
but I tell you some of them are to me *monstrous*. That report which I mentioned is awful, wicked, and what is worse,
the country does not seem to know it.

Dan. Sickles is a Major Genl. and commands a Corps in
this Army. Was he ever a soldier? Was he ever a man? Did
he not have criminal intercourse with the mother of his wife
for years before his marriage? Did he not shoot Key many
months after the knowledge of the crime of his wife, and then
take that wife back to his bed?[28]

---

[27] A joint committee of Congress set up to investigate the causes
of Union defeats. Dominated by Radical Republicans, it devoted
special attention to Democratic generals suspected of disloyalty or
lack of vigor. In a report published in April, 1863, it bitterly ar-
raigned Haskell's favorite, McClellan — partly on the basis of
testimony by Hooker. T. Harry Williams, *Lincoln and the Radi-
cals* (Madison, 1941), 62–65, 246–50.

[28] Before the war, Daniel E. Sickles was a New York Democratic
politician associated with Tammany Hall. The rumor that he had
intercourse with his future mother-in-law was only part of the
scandal that trailed after him. In 1859, while a congressman at
Washington, he killed Philip Barton Key, son of the author of the
"Star Spangled Banner" and his wife's lover. Winning acquittal

So the men sing in his hearing, sing in the air of a negro song:

"Sickles killed a man
"Sickles killed a man
"What was it for I ban"[29]

Bah, bah! I am talking too much. (This ink spreads all over things) I'll stop. Of course the President is a good man, and "fighting Joe Hooker" will win. Who doubts it? — who can?

Well, well, it's a hot day, and now that the army is back here, and Wood[30] is well again so I do not have to be Adjt. Gnl., if I did not write I should be doing nothing.

You may rely upon one thing, however, that the army, the men, and subordinate officers are all right. There never was a better army in the world than this is now, — in fine spirits and condition. — The army is capable of doing any thing that reason or duty would require — so it is to-day.

There was no running, but magnificent fighting on this late occasion, by all but the Dutch.

The army has unbounded confidence in "fighting Joe Hooker." (?) We are all sorry that Mrs. *Salm Salm* has left the army. She is a beautiful woman and the presence of *ladies* is so charming in the camp, to chasten the morals and manners of the men.[31]

---

through precedent-setting pleas of temporary insanity and the "unwritten law," he went on to become one of the more notorious of the "political generals." W.A. Swanberg, *Sickles The Incredible* (New York, 1956), *passim*.

[29] The last word cannot be read with certainty.

[30] J.P. Wood, Gibbon's Assistant Adjutant General, who had been ill.

[31] Princess Salm-Salm was a former circus rider who, under the name of Agnes Leclerq, married Prince Felix Salm-Salm in 1862. This soldier of fortune commanded the 8th New York in the strongly German Eleventh Corps. Critics often regarded Mrs. Salm-Salm as a conspicuous part of the dissolute atmosphere which they alleged prevailed at Army Headquarters during Hooker's tenure. Boatner, *Civil War Dictionary*, 717–18; Swanberg, *Sickles*, 170–76. The term "hooker" to denote a prostitute is said to have

The *ladies* of the "Sanitary Commission" are good and wonderfully sanitary in their influence, — soothing after the fatigues of battle, in their attentions to the wounded: — but
then many of these have not youth and grace of person. Eh?[32]

> "Ah God, for a man with heart, head, hand
> Like some of the simple great ones gone
> Forever and ever by.
> One still strong man in a blatant land
> Whatever they call him, what care I?
> Aristocrat, democrat, autocrat, — one
> Who can rule and dare not lie."[33]

Haskell.

---

been derived from the *"ladies"* whom Haskell so scorns. Warner,
Generals In Blue, 235.

[32] The United States Sanitary Commission, a nongovernmental
organization devoted to improving the soldiers' health, sent female
nurses to help at the hospitals.

[33] Alfred, Lord Tennyson, *Maud*, X, 5.

IV

<hr>

Gettysburg

FRANK HASKELL'S DISCOURAGEMENT after the defeat at Chancellorsville and his disgust at his commander were the mirror images of the Confederates' elation and confidence. Taking the offensive, the Southerners planned an invasion of Maryland and Pennsylvania. On June 3, 1863, Lee began withdrawing troops from his positions near Fredericksburg and marching them to the west and north. Hooker, suspicious of the Confederate activity, ordered probing operations which culminated on June 9 in a pitched battle with the Confederate cavalry at Brandy Station. Haskell reported hearsay concerning these actions in brief letters of June 5 and 11, 1863 (here omitted). With the rest of the Army of the Potomac, Haskell then followed Lee's force to the crossroads town of Gettysburg, fought the epic battle he had been awaiting, and helped pursue the defeated Confederates back across the Potomac.

In the following letters, Haskell describes the Gettysburg campaign from the viewpoint of a staff officer who was in the best position to observe the climactic events. While he gives significant details in several briefer letters, he discusses the entire campaign in the oft-quoted "letter," dated July 16, 1863, which must properly be termed an essay. Despite its date, references in Haskell's later letters make it evident that he did not then send it and was probably still working on it months later. It differs in format and in length from Haskell's other Civil War letters. Written on one side of note-

87

book-type paper, its very neatness suggests slowness of composition and the possibility that this was a revised copy. Its author, two of whose war letters had already appeared in print, may well have contemplated ultimate publication. Among the hints of this are his deliberate omission of the name of the major whom he accuses of lack of courage during Pickett's Charge, and his later references to his intention of writing a history of the war. Thus the Gettysburg essay may be viewed as the carefully matured fruit of Haskell's growing ability as a writer of military prose. □

*   *   *   *   *

Westminster, Md.
July 5, 1863

I can write you but a hasty note now — but must say to you that I am unharmed, after the terrific battles of the 2nd and 3d of July, at Gettysburg.

I cannot go into particulars, — the battle has been desperate, — you need not fear the result, but thank God for it.

On the 2nd I had the horse I rode, shot with three bullets, — on the 3d, another horse I then rode was shot with three bullets and a piece of shell.

But now more than ever before I think I am not to be harmed in the battles, for on the 3d a bullet struck my saddle, and glanced going through my pants, drawers, but stopped at the skin above my right knee, and gave me but a *bruise*.

This place is 24 miles from the field, whither I came with the Genl. after the fight of the 3d, and shall return there today. I shall be able to be in the saddle again in a day or two.

Genl. Gibbon is severely wounded in the left shoulder with a bullet, — and will be off duty for some months, — but his wound is not at all dangerous.

He has consented that I may go back to the field, and back I shall go where duty and inclination call me.

Congratulate me upon my part in the great battle of Gettysburg.

I will give you a full description of it in a few days. Direct your letters as usual.

Much love to you all.

Frank A. Haskell.

*   *   *   *   *

Jones' Cross Roads
6 Miles from Sharpsburgh [sic]
Md. July 13, 1863.

I can write but a line for we are actually working all the time, and tired to death. — But I am *"well and hope these few lines will reach you the same."*

I rode back to Gettysburgh [sic] the day I wrote you last, in an Ambulance, and on the 7th resumed duty at Div. Head Quarters as an Aide with Genl. Harrow, who now commands.

On the 11th I was directed to report to Genl. Hays, Comding. 2nd Corps,[1] and am now acting as his Aide, as I probably shall until Genl. Gibbon is well again. So much for me.

The Rebels are between Hagerstown and Williamsport and our Army is drawing in about them, and another great battle will occur in a few days at farthest, I think. May God again give us the victory!

I want to describe to you sometime — I can't at present — the great battle of Gettysburg. Antietam was but a skirmish in comparison.

The 2nd Corps — this Corps — had the honor of meeting the main shock of the rebel attack, and scattering their column like sheep — but our loss was terrible — about 4300 in killed, and wounded, and we have but a few more than that left.

But we paid them for all this *more than twice over,* though. Their dead in our Corps front that we buried, were over 2000. Only think of such slaughter! — And in a few days it will be

---

[1] William Harrow and William Hays had replaced, respectively, Gibbon and Winfield Scott Hancock, both of whom had been wounded at Gettysburg.

repeated ! ! Heaven help us! I suppose Martha thinks it about time for me to answer her letters — Do you, Martha? Well, I will, but how can I now or any time, the last month?

I had a good letter from Betsy Ann[2] but a few days ago. — Why don't Harvey write me.

Now I wish I had some of your good *Carrot* and *Tomatoes*. Dont you?

Well, well. — May be I will come home after the battle. Do you want to see me?

Good-bye,

Frank A. Haskell

*   *   *   *   *

At the Head Quarters 2nd *Corps d'Armie* [*sic*]
Army of the Potomac, near Harper's Ferry,
July 16, 1863.

The great battle of Gettysburg is now an event of the past.[3] The composition and strength of the armies, their leaders, the strategy, the tactics, the result, of that field are to-day by the side of those of Waterloo, — matters of history. A few days ago these things were otherwise. This great event did

---

[2] A then unmarried sister living at the Haskell family home in Vermont.

[3] Unlike the other Haskell letters which have found a home in Wisconsin, the original of this most famous of his writings is in the collections of the Pennsylvania Bureau of Archives and History of the Pennsylvania Historical and Museum Commission in Harrisburg. It bears several corrections and notations in another hand, probably made by Haskell's brother in preparing it for its first printing. These have been omitted, so that the letter here appears exactly as Haskell wrote it. This edition of the letter thus differs in many minor ways from previous publications based on the first printing. Of these earlier editions, that published by the Wisconsin History Commission in 1908 and 1910 (hereinafter referred to as WHC) is most often cited. The footnotes to this chapter will indicate words of the original letter entirely omitted by WHC and the relatively few variant readings which significantly affect the meaning. For the complete publishing history of the Gettysburg letter or essay, see the concluding chapter.

not so "cast its shadow before," as to moderate the hot sunshine that streamed upon our preceding march, or to relieve
our minds of all apprehension of the result of the second
great Rebel invasion of the soil North of the Potomac.

No, — not many days since, at times we were filled with
fears and forebodings. The people of the country, I suppose,
shared the anxieties of the army, somewhat in common with
us, but they could not have felt them as keenly as we did.
We were upon the immediate theatre of events as they occurred from day to day, and were of them. — We were the
army whose province it should be to meet this invasion and
repel it; — on us was the immediate responsibility for results,
most momentous for good or ill, but yet in the future. And so
in addition to the solicitude of all good patriots, we felt that
our own honor as men and as an army, as well as the safety
of the Capitol and the country, were at stake.

And what if that invasion should be successful, and in the
coming battle, the Army of the Potomac should be overpowered? Would it not be? When our army was much larger
than at present, — had rested all Winter, — and, nearly perfect in all its departments and arrangements, was the most
splendid army this continent ever saw, only a part of the Rebel
force, which it now had to contend with, had defeated it, —
its leader, rather, — at Chancellorsville! Now the Rebel had
his whole force assembled, — he was flushed with recent victory, — was arrogant in his career of unopposed invasion, —
at a favorable season of the year. His daring plans, made by
no unskilled head, to transfer the war from his own to his enemy's ground, were being successful, — he had gone days' march
from his front before Hooker moved or was aware of his
departure. Then I believe the army in general, both officers
and men, had no confidence in Hooker, in either his honesty
or ability.

Did they not charge him personally with the defeat at Chancellorsville? Were they not still burning with indignation
against him for that disgrace? And now again under his lead-

ership they were marching against the enemy! And they knew of nothing, short of the Providence of God, that could, or would, remove him. For many reasons, during the marches prior to the battle we were anxious, and at times heavy at heart.

But the Army of the Potomac was no band of school girls. They were not the men likely to be crushed or utterly discouraged by any mere circumstances in which they might find themselves placed. They had lost some battles, — they had gained some. They knew what defeat was, and what was victory. But here is the greatest praise that I can bestow upon them, or upon any army: with the elation of victory, or the depression of defeat, amidst the hardest toils of the campaign, under unwelcome leadership, at all times, and under all circumstances, they were a reliable army still. The Army of the Potomac would do as it was told, always.

Well clothed and well fed, — there never could be any ground for complaint on these heads, — but a mighty work was before them. Onward they moved, — night and day were blended — over many a weary mile, through dust and through mud, in the broiling sunshine, in the flooding rain, over steeps, through defiles, across rivers, over last year's battle fields, where the skeletons of our dead brethren by hundreds lay bare and bleaching, weary, without sleep for days, tormented with the newspapers and their rumors that the enemy was in Philadelphia, in Baltimore, — in all places where he was not, — yet these men could still be relied upon, I believed, when the day of conflict should come. *"Haec olim meminisse juvabit!"*[4] We did not then know this. I mention them now that you may see that in those times we had several matters to think about, and to do, that were not as pleasant as sleeping upon a bank of violets in the shade.

In moving from near Falmouth, Va. the army was formed

---

[4] "Sometime it will please us to remember these things." Vergil's *Aeneid*.

in several columns, and took several roads. The 2nd Corps, the rear of the whole, was the last to move, and left Falmouth at day-break on the 15th of June, and pursued its march through Aquia, Dumfries, Wolf Run Shoales, Centerville, Gainesville, Thoroughfare Gap, — this last we left on the 25th, marching back to Haymarket, where we had a skirmish with the Cavalry, and Horse Artillery of the enemy, — Gum Spring, crossing the Potomac at Edwards' Ferry, thence through Poolesville, Frederick, Liberty, and Union Town. We marched from near Frederick to Union Town, a distance of thirty-two miles, from eight o'clock A.M. to nine P.M. on the 28th. — I think this is the longest march accomplished in so short a time, by a Corps during the war. — On the 28th while we were near this latter place, we breathed a full breath of joy and of hope. — The Providence of God had been with us, — we ought not to have doubted it — Genl. Meade commanded the Army of the Potomac.

Not a favorable time, one would be apt to suppose, to change the General of a large army, on the eve of battle, the result of which might be to destroy the government and country! — But it should have been done long before, — at all events, any change could not have been for the worse, and the Administration, therefore, hazarded little, in making it now. From this moment my own mind was easy concerning results. I now felt that we had a clear-headed, honest soldier to command the army, who would do his best always, — that there would be no repetition of Chancellorsville. Meade was not as much known in the army as many of the other Corps commanders, — but the officers who knew, all thought highly of him, a man of great modesty, with none of those qualities, which are noisy and assuming, and hankering for cheap newspaper fame, — not at all of the "gallant" Sickles stamp. I happened to know much of Genl. Meade. — He and Genl. Gibbon had always been very intimate, and I had seen much of him. — I think my own notions concerning Genl. Meade at this time, were shared quite generally by the army. — At all events all who knew him shared them.[5]

By this time, by reports that were not mere rumors we began to hear frequently of the enemy, and of his proximity. His Cavalry was all about us, making little raids here and there, capturing now and then a few of our wagons, and stealing a good many horses, but doing us really the least amount possible of harm, for we were not by these means impeded at all, and this Cavalry gave no information at all to Lee, that he could rely upon, of the movements of the Army of the Potomac. The Infantry of the enemy was at this time in the neighborhoods of Hagerstown, Chambersburg, and some had been at Gettysburg, — possibly, was there now.[6] Gettysburg was a point of strategic importance, — a great many roads, some ten or twelve at least, concentrated there, so the army could easily converge to, or, should a further march be necessary, diverge from, this point. Gnl. Meade therefore resolved to try to seize Gettysburg, and accordingly gave the necessary orders for the concentration of his different collums [sic] there.[7] Under the new auspices the army brightened, and moved on with a more elastic step towards the yet undefined field of conflict.

---

[5] George Gordon Meade, a West Pointer, had been an engineer for most of his prewar career. A brigade commander during the Peninsular Campaign, he rose to lead successively a division and the Fifth Corps. On June 28, 1863, following Hooker's resignation, Meade took command of the Army of the Potomac. Warner, *Generals in Blue,* 315–17. For a good discussion of the Lincoln administration's reasons for removing Hooker at this crucial time, see T. Harry Williams, *Lincoln and His Generals* (New York, 1952), 255–60. For a fine portrait of Meade as a leader, see Edwin B. Coddington, *The Gettysburg Campaign: A Study in Command* (New York, 1968), 209–14. This masterful work supplies a wealth of material relevant to the Haskell letter.

[6] While the bulk of the Confederate army was at Chambersburg on June 28, its Second Corps was further into Pennsylvania, at Carlisle and York.

[7] Meade's order for an advance toward Gettysburg was issued on June 30, to be executed on July 1. It did not call for the con-

The 1st Corps, Gnl. Reynolds,[8] already having the advance, was ordered to push forward rapidly, and take and hold the town, if he could. The rest of the Army would assemble to his support. Buford's Cavalry cooperated with this Corps, and on the morning of the 1st of July found the enemy near Gettysburg, and to the West, and promptly engaged him.[9] The 1st Corps, having bivouaced [sic] the night before South of the town, came up rapidly to Buford's support, and immediately a sharp battle was opened with the advance of the enemy. The 1st Division[,] Gnl. [James S.] Wadsworth[,] was the first of the Infantry to become engaged, but the other two, commanded respectively by Generals [John C.] Robinson and [Abner] Doubleday, were close at hand, and forming the line of battle to the West and North-West of the town, at a mean distance of about a mile away, the battle continued for some hours, with various success, which was on the whole with us until near noon. At this time a lull occurred, which was occupied by both sides in supervising and reestablishing the hastily formed lines of the morning. New Divisions of the enemy were constantly arriving and taking up positions, for this purpose marching in upon the various roads that terminate at the town, from the West and North. The position of the 1st Corps was then becoming perilous in the extreme, but it was improved at a little before noon by the arrival upon the field of two Divisions of the 11th Corps, Gnl. Howard,[10] these

---

centration of the entire Union army there. Coddington, *Gettysburg*, 237, 671.

[8] John F. Reynolds, a graduate of West Point with a distinguished record before and during the war. At this time he was in command of the left wing of Meade's army. Warner, *Generals in Blue*, 396–97.

[9] General John Buford's cavalry division had reached Gettysburg on June 30, had blocked a Confederate raid on the town, and thus was positioned to hold back the Confederate advance on July 1 until Reynolds came up.

[10] Oliver Otis Howard, a Maine Yankee and a West Pointer, held a number of commands in both the eastern and western theaters of the Civil War. He lost an arm in the Peninsular Cam-

Divisions commanded respectively by Generals [Carl] Schurz and [Francis C.] Barlow, who by order posted their commands to the right of the 1st Corps, with their right retired, forming an angle with the line of the 1st Corps. Between three and four o'clock in the after-noon the enemy, now in overwhelming force, resumed the battle, with spirit. The portion of the 11th Corps, making but feeble opposition to the advancing enemy soon began to fall back, — Gnl. Barlow was badly wounded, — and their retreat quickly degenerated into a disgraceful rout and panic.[11]

Back in disorganized masses they fled into the town, hotly pursued, and in houses,[12] in barns, in yards and cellars, throwing away their arms, they sought to hide like rabits [sic], and were there captured, unresisting, by hundreds.[13]

The 1st Corps, deprived of this support, if support it could be called, outflanked upon either hand, and engaged in front was compelled to yield the field. Making its last stand upon what is called, "Seminary Ridge," not far from the town, it fell back in considerable confusion, through the South-West part of the town, making brave resistance, however, but with considerable loss. The enemy did not see fit to follow, or to

---

paign. Howard was widely and not always favorably known for his display of piety. During Reconstruction, he headed the Freedmen's Bureau and helped to found Howard University. Warner, *Generals in Blue*, 237–39.

[11] The latter part of this sentence, beginning with "Gnl.," does not appear in the Wisconsin History Commission edition (WHC).

[12] "Lanes" in WHC.

[13] As in his account of Chancellorsville, Haskell reflects the native American's prejudice against the mostly German Eleventh Corps. It was true that this unit retreated in disorganization and lost many prisoners. But it had been badly positioned and was taken partly in the flank. Contrary to Haskell's statement below, the First Corps retreated through Gettysburg at about the same time, contributing to the confusion in the streets. Coddington, *Gettysburg*, 295–306. For a temperate, well-reasoned critique of Haskell's strictures, written by a German-born officer of the 26th Wisconsin, see an undated nineteen-page document by Frederick C. Winkler in his papers, SHSW.

attempt to, further than the town, and so the fight of the 1st of July closed here. I suppose our losses during the day would exceed four thousand, of whom a large number were prisoners.[14] Such usually is the kind of loss sustained by the 11th Corps. You will remember that the old "Iron Brigade" is in the 1st Corps, and consequently shared this fight, and I hear their conduct praised on all hands.[15]

In the 2nd Wis. Col. Fairchild lost his left arm; Lit. Col. Stevens was mortally wounded, and Major Mansfield was wounded; Lieut. Col. Callis, of the 7th Wis. and Lit. Col. Dudley, of the 19th Ind, were badly, dangerously, wounded, the latter by the loss of his right leg, above the knee.[16]

I saw *"John Burns,"* the only citizen of Gettysburg who fought in the battle, and I asked him what troops he fought with. He said: "O, I pitched in with them Wisconsin fellers." I asked what sort of men they were and he answered: "They fit terribly, — the Rebs couldn't make any thing of them fellers."

And so the brave compliment the brave. This man was touched by three bullets from the enemy, but not seriously wounded.[17]

---

[14] Total Union casualties were about 8500, with about 5500 in the First Corps alone. Of these, the Confederates captured 3655. *Ibid.,* 305, 307, 309.

[15] Gettysburg wiped out Haskell's old unit as an effective brigade. It suffered casualties totaling 1212 and comprising 65 per cent of its strength. Haskell's original regiment, the 6th Wisconsin, lost least and yet its casualties were 48 per cent of its remaining force. Nolan, *Iron Brigade,* 256.

[16] Lucius Fairchild had been promoted to command his regiment. The others mentioned were George H. Stevens of Fox Lake; John Mansfield, Portage; John B. Callis, Lancaster; William W. Dudley of Richmond, Indiana.

[17] Burns, a civilian then over seventy years old, was an aged veteran, probably of the War of 1812. Captured by the Confederates, he escaped punishment for fighting out of uniform, was thanked for his service in General Doubleday's report, and lived until 1872 as one of the almost legendary figures of the battle. Boatner, *Civil War Dictionary,* 107; Nolan, *Iron Brigade,* 242–43, 245.

But the loss of the enemy to day was severe also, — probably in killed and wounded, as heavy as our own, but not so great in prisoners.

Of these latter the "Iron Brigade" captured almost an entire Miss. Brigade, however.[18] ·

Of the events so far, of the 1st of July, I do not speak from personal knowledge. I shall now tell my introduction to these events.

At eleven o'clock, A. M. on that day, the 2nd Corps was halted at Taneytown, which is thirteen miles from Gettysburg, South; and there awaiting orders, the men were allowed to make coffee and rest. At between one and two o'clock in the after-noon, a message was brought to Genl. Gibbon requiring his immediate presence at the Head Quarters of Gnl. Hancock, who commanded the Corps.[19] I went with Gnl. Gibbon, and we rode at a rapid gallop, to Gnl. Hancock.

At Genl. Hancock's Head Quarters the following was learned: the 1st Corps had met the enemy at Gettysburg, and had possession of the town, — Gnl. Reynolds was badly, it was feared mortally, wounded, — the fight of the 1st Corps still continued — by Gnl. Meade's order, Gnl. Hancock was to hurry forward

---

[18] The Confederate casualties totaled about 7112, almost 1400 less than those of the United States. But, since the Southerners lost only about 931 prisoners, their total of killed and wounded surpassed the comparable Northern total by over 1300. Computed from Coddington, *Gettysburg*, 305, 307, 309. The 6th Wisconsin, aided by other units, captured two to three hundred men, comprising all of the 2nd Mississippi Regiment and parts of the 42nd Mississippi and 55th North Carolina. *Ibid.*, 272.

[19] The former commander of the Second Corps, Darius N. Couch, had been relieved at his own request on May 22, 1863, because he no longer wished to serve under Hooker, whom he blamed for the Chancellorsville defeat. His successor, Winfield Scott Hancock, was a graduate of the United States Military Academy with much military experience, including service in the Mexican War. Generally regarded as one of the more able of the Union's subordinate commanders, he continued in the army after the war. In 1880, he ran unsuccessfully for President as a Democrat. Warner, *Generals in Blue*, 202–04.

and take command upon the field of all troops there or which should arrive, there, — the 11th Corps was near Gettysburg when the messenger who told of the fight, left there, and the 3d Corps was marching up, by order, on the Emmitsburg Road, — Gnl. Gibbon, — he was not the ranking officer of the 2nd Corps, after Hancock, — was ordered to assume the command of the 2nd Corps.[20]

All this was sudden, and for that reason at least, exciting; but there were other elements in this information, that aroused our profoundest interest. The great battle that we had so anxiously looked for during so many days, had at length opened, — it was a relief, in some sense, to have these accidents of time and place established — what would be the result? Might not the enemy fall upon and destroy the 1st Corps before succor could arrive?

Gnl. Hancock with his personal Staff at about two o'clock P.M. galloped off towards Gettysburg, — Gnl. Gibbon took his place in command of the Corps, appointing me his Acting Assistant Adjutant General. The 2nd Corps took arms at once, and moved rapidly towards the field. It was not long before we began to hear the dull booming of the guns; and as we advanced, from many an eminence or opening among the trees we could look out upon the white battery smoke puffing up from the distant field of blood and drifting up to the clouds. At these sights and sounds the men looked more serious than before and were more silent, but they marched faster, and straggled less. At about five o'clock, P.M. as we were riding along at the head of the colum [sic], we met an Ambulance, accompanied by two or three mounted officers.

---

[20] The War Department order appointing Meade to the command of the Army of the Potomac authorized him to assign officers without regard to seniority. Hence these appointments of Hancock and Gibbon, in whom he had special confidence, to command their seniors. But Meade instructed Hancock to turn over command of the troops gathered at Gettysburg to General Henry W. Slocum as senior corps commander when the latter arrived with the Twelfth Corps. Coddington, *Gettysburg*, 215, 284-85, 313, 708.

— We knew them to be staff officers of Gnl. Reynolds. — Their faces told plainly enough what load the vehicle carried — it was the dead body of Gnl. Reynolds. Very early in the action, while seeing personally to the formation of his lines under fire, he was shot through the head by a musket or rifle bullet, and killed almost instantly. His death at this time affected us much, for he was one of the *soldier* Generals of the army, — a man whose soul was in his country's work, which he did with a soldier's high honor and fidelity.

I remember seeing him often at the 1st battle of Fredericksburg, — he then commanded the 1st Corps — and while Meade's and Gibbon's Divisions were assaulting the enemy's works, he was the very beau ideal of the gallant general. Mounted upon a superb black horse, with his head thrown back and his great black eyes flashing fire, he was every where upon the field, seeing all things and giving commands in person. He died as many a friend, and many a foe, to the country have died in this war.

Just as the dusk of evening fell, from Gnl. Meade the 2nd Corps had orders to halt where the head of the colum [*sic*] then was and to go into position for the night. The 2nd Division (Gibbon's) was accordingly put in position upon the left of the (Taney town) road, its left near the South-Eastern base of "Round Top" — of which mountain more anon — and the right near the road; the 3d Division was posted upon the right of the road, abreast of the 2nd; and the 1st Division in rear of these two, — all facing towards Gettysburg.

Arms were stacked and the men lay down to sleep, alas! many of them their last but the great final sleep upon the earth.

Late in the after-noon as we came near the field, from some slightly wounded men we met and occasional stragglers from the scene of operations in front, we got many rumors, and much disjointed information, of battle, of lakes of blood, of rout and panic and undescribable disaster, from all of which the narrators were just fortunate enough to have barely es-

caped, the sole survivors. These stragglers are always terrible
liars!

About nine o'clock in the evening, while I was yet engaged
in showing the troops their positions, I met Gnl. Hancock,
then on his way from the front to Genl. Meade, who was
back towards Taney town; and he, for the purpose of having
me advise Genl. Gibbon, for his information, gave me quite
a detailed account of the situation of matters at Gettysburg,
and of what had transpired subsequently to his arrival there.

He had arrived and assumed command, there just when the
troops of the 1st and 11th Corps, after their repulse, were
coming in confusion through the town. Hancock is just the
man for such an emergency as this. Upon horseback, I think
he was the most magnificent looking general in the whole
Army of the Potomac, at that time. With a large, well-shaped
person, always dressed with elegance,[21] even upon that field
of confusion, he would look as if he was *"monarch of all he
surveyed,"* and few of his subjects would dare to question his
right to command, or do aught else but to obey. His quick
eye, in a flash, saw what was to be done; and his voice and
his royal right hand at once commenced to do it. Genl. Howard
had put one of his Divisions — Steinwher's [sic] — [22] — with
some Batteries, in position, upon a commanding eminence,
at the "Cemetery," which, as a reserve had not participated
in the fight of the day; and this Division was now of course
steady. Around this Division the fugitives were stopped, and
the shattered Brigades and Regiments, as they returned, were
formed upon either flank, and faced towards the enemy again.
A show of order at least speedily came from chaos, — the rout
was at an end, — the 1st and 11th Corps, were in line of

---

[21] Hancock's dress attracted the attention of other contemporaries. Colonel Theodore Lyman of Meade's staff remarked that
Hancock "always wears a clean *white* shirt (where he gets them nobody knows). . . ." *Ibid.,* 700.

[22] General Adolph W. A. F. Von Steinwehr's 2nd Division of
Howard's Eleventh Corps.

battle, again — not very systematically formed, perhaps, — in
a splendid position, and in a condition to offer resistance,
should the enemy be willing to try them. These formations
were all accomplished long before night. Then some considerable portion of the 3d Corps, Gnl. Sickles, came up by the
Emmitsburg Road, and was formed to the left of the Taney
town Road, on an extension of the line that I have mentioned;
and all the 12th Corps, Gnl. Slocum,[23] arriving before night,
the Divisions were put in position, to the right of the troops
already there, to the East of the Baltimore Pike. The enemy
was in the town, and behind it, and to the East and West,
and appeared to be in strong force, and was jubilant over his
day's success. Such was the posture of affairs as evening came
on of the 1st of July. Gnl. Hancock was hopeful, and in the
best of spirits; and from him I also learned that the reason of
halting the 2nd Corps in its present position, was, that it was
not then known where for the coming fight the lines of battle would be formed, — up near the town, where the troops
then were, or further back, towards Taney town. He would
give his views upon this subject to Gnl. Meade, which were
in favor of the line near the town, — the one that was subsequently adopted, — and Gnl. Meade would determine.

The night before a great pitched battle, would not ordin-
arily, I suppose, be a time for much sleep to Generals and
their staff officers. We needed it enough, — but there was
work to be done. — This war makes strange confusion of night
and day! I did not sleep at all that night. It would, perhaps,
be expected, on the eve of such great events, that one should
have some peculiar sort of feelings, something extraordinary,
some great arousing and excitement of the sensibilities and
faculties, commensurate with the event itself; — this certainly

---

[23] Henry W. Slocum, a West Pointer from New York, left the
army to practice law. Returning to the service in 1861, he participated in the major eastern battles through Gettysburg and later
fought in the west. He subsequently won three terms in Congress. Warner, *Generals in Blue*, 451–53.

would be very poetical and pretty, but so far as I was concerned, and I think I can speak for the army in this matter, there was nothing of the kind. Men who had volunteered to fight the battles of the country, had met the enemy in many battles, and had been constantly before them, as had the Army of the Potomac, were too old soldiers, and long ago too well had weighed chances and probabilities, to be so disturbed now. No, I believe the army slept soundly that night, and well; and I am glad the men did, for they needed it.

At midnight Genl. Meade and Staff rode by Gnl. Gibbon's Head Quarters, on their way to the field; and in conversation with Gnl. Gibbon, Gnl. Meade announced that he had decided to assemble the whole army before Gettysburg, and offer the enemy battle there. The 2nd Corps would move at the earliest day light, to take up its position.

At three o'clock, A.M. of the 2nd of July the sleepy soldiers of the Corps were aroused, — before six the Corps was up to the field, and halted temporarily by the side of the Taney town Road upon which it had marched, while some movements of other troops were being made, to enable it to take position in the order of battle. The morning was thick, and sultry, the sky overcast with low, vapory clouds. As we approached all was astir upon the crests near the Cemetery, and the work of preparation was speedily going on. Men looked like giants there in the mist, and the guns of the frowning Batteries so big, that it was a relief to know that they were our friends.

Without a topographical map, some description of the ground and localities is necessary to a clear understanding of the battle. With the sketch [not found] that I have rudely drawn, without scale or compass, I hope you may understand my description. The line of battle as it was established, on the evening of the 1st, and morning of the 2nd of July was in the form of the letter, "U," the troops facing outwards, and the "Cemetery," which is at the point of the sharpest curvature of the line, being due South of the town of Gettysburg. "Round Top," the extreme left of the line, is a small, woody, rocky elevation, a very little West of South of the town, and nearly two miles from it.

The sides of this are in places very steep, and its rocky summit is almost inaccessible. A short distance North of this is a smaller elevation called "Little Round Top." On the very top of "Little Round Top," we had heavy rifled guns in position during the battle. Near the right of the line is a small woody eminence, named "Culp's Hill." Three roads come up to the town from the South, which near the town are quite straight, and at the town the external ones unite, forming an angle of about sixty, or more degrees. Of these, the farthest to the East is the "Baltimore Pike," which passes by the East entrance to the Cemetery; the farthest to the West is the "Emmitsburg Road," which is wholly outside of our line of battle, but near the Cemetery, is within a hundred yards of it; the "Taney town Road" is between these, running nearly due North and South, by the Eastern base of "Round Top," by the Western side of the Cemetery, and uniting with the Emmitsburg Road between the Cemetery and the town. High ground near the Cemetery, is named "Cemetery Ridge."

The 11th Corps[,] Gnl. Howard[,] was posted at the Cemetery, some of its Batteries and troops, actually among the graves and monuments, which they used for shelter, from the enemy's fire; — its left resting upon the Taney town road, and extending thence to the East, crossing the Baltimore Pike, and then bending backwards towards the South-east; on the right of the 11th came the 1st Corps, now, since the death of Gnl. Reynolds, commanded by Gnl. Newton,[24] formed in a line curving still more towards the South. — The troops of these two Corps were reformed on the morning of the 2nd, in order that each might be by itself, and to correct some

---

[24] John Newton, a Virginian, was a West Point graduate. During the Civil War, he held commands in both the east and the west. Remaining in the Regular Army, he rose to be Chief of Engineers. Warner, *Generals in Blue*, 344–45.

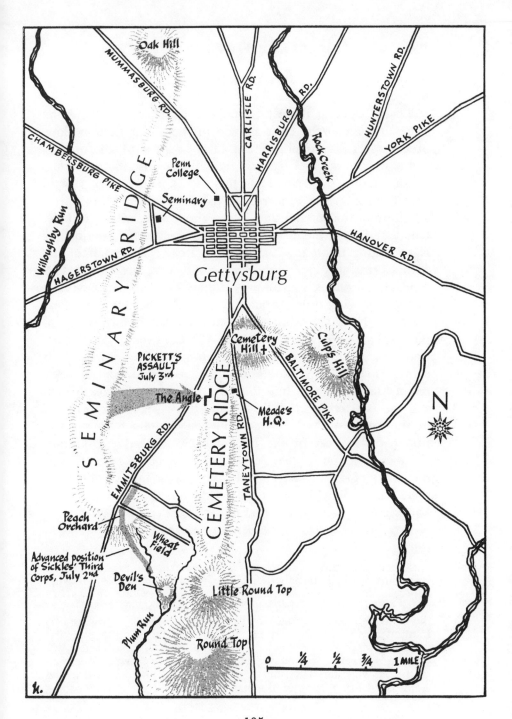

Oak Hill

MUMMASBURG RD.

CARLISLE RD.

HARRISBURG RD.

Rock Creek

HUNTERSTOWN RD.

YORK PIKE

CHAMBERSBURG PIKE

Penn College

Seminary

Willoughby Run

HAGERSTOWN RD.

HANOVER RD.

Gettysburg

S E M I N A R Y   R I D G E

PICKETT'S ASSAULT July 3rd

Cemetery Hill ✝

Culps Hill

BALTIMORE PIKE

The Angle

Meade's H.Q.

EMMITSBURG RD.

C E M E T E R Y   R I D G E

TANEYTOWN RD.

Peach Orchard

Wheat Field

Advanced position of Sickles' Third Corps, July 2nd

Devil's Den

Little Round Top

Plum Run

Round Top

N

0   ¼   ½   ¾   1 MILE

things not done well during the hasty formations here the day before.

To the right of the 1st Corps, and on an extension of the same line, along the crest and down the South Eastern slope of Culp's Hill, was posted the 12th Corps, Gnl. Slocum, its right, which was the extreme right of the line of the army, resting near a small stream called "Rock Run." No changes that I am aware of occurred in the formation of this Corps, on the morning of the 2nd. The 2nd Corps, after the brief halt that I have mentioned, moved up and took position, its right resting upon the Taney town Road, at the left of the 11th Corps, and extending the line thence, nearly a half a mile, almost due South, towards Round Top, with its Divisions in the following order, from right to left: the 3d, Gnl. Alex. Hays; — the 2nd, (Gibbon's) Gnl. [William] Harrow, (temporarily); — the 1st, Gnl. [John C.] Caldwell. The formation was, in line by brigade in column, the brigades being in colum [sic] by regiment, with forty paces interval between regimental lines; the 2nd and 3d Divisions having each one, and the 1st Division two Brigades — there were four Brigades in the 1st — similarly formed, in reserve, one hundred and fifty paces in rear of the line of their respective Divisions. That is, the line of the Corps, exclusive of its reserves, was the length of six regiments, deployed, and the intervals between them, some of which were left wide for the posting of the Batteries, and consisted of four common deployed lines, each of two ranks, of men; and a little more than one third was in reserve.[25]

---

[25] Thus Haskell describes each of the three divisions as having two brigades on its part of the front and either one or two brigades in reserve. Each brigade had one regiment on its section of the front and three behind it. However, a sketch map prepared by Lieutenant Colonel Nelson H. Davis of Meade's staff, evidently sometime after 11 A.M. on July 2, indicates that the situation was by then different. It shows only two brigades in reserve (one each in the 1st and 2nd Divisions). Thus it also shows eight brigades along the Corps' front or the length of *eight* regiments (not six,

The five Batteries, in all twenty-eight guns, were posted as follows: [Lt. George A.] Woodruff's, [1st U.S. Artillery] Regular, six twelve-pound Napoleons, brass, between the two Brigades in line of the 3d Division; [Capt. William A.] Arnold's "A" 1st R. I. six three inch Parrotts, rifled, and [Lt. Alonzo H.] Cushing's, ["A," 4th U.S. Artillery] Regular, four three inch Ordnance, rifled, between the 3d and 2nd Division, Capt. [John G.] Hazard's (commanded during the battle by Lieut. [T. Fred] Brown,) "B" 1st R. I. and Rhorty's [Rorty's] N.Y.[26] each six twelve-pound Napoleons, brass, between the 2nd and 1st Divisions.

I have been thus specific in in [sic] the description of the posting and formation of the 2nd Corps, because they were works that I assisted to perform; and also that the other Corps were similarly posted with reference to the strength of the lines, and the intermixing of Infantry and Artillery. From this, you may get a notion of the whole.

The 3d Corps, Gnl. Sickles, the remainder of it arriving upon the field this morning, was posted upon the left of the 2nd, extending the line still in the direction of Round Top, with its left resting near "Little Round Top." The left of the 3d Corps was the extreme left of the line of battle, until changes occurred which will be mentioned in the proper place. The 5th Corps, Gnl. Sykes,[27] coming on the Baltimore Pike about this time, was massed there near the line of battle, and held in reserve until some time in the afternoon, when it changed position as I shall describe.

I cannot give a detailed account of the Cavalry, for I saw but little of it. It was posted near the wings, and watched

as Haskell has it). There are also variations in the placement of the artillery. OR, Ser. 1, Vol. 27, Pt. 3, pp. 487, 1087.

[26] Capt. James McKay Rorty, Battery B, 1st N.Y. Artillery. This unit's initials appear as "N.G." in WHC.

[27] George Sykes replaced Meade as commander of the Fifth Corps. A West Point graduate, he led regular troops in the early months of the Civil War and then became a division commander in the Army of the Potomac. Warner, Generals in Blue, 492–93.

the roads and the movements of the enemy upon the flanks of the army, but further than this participated but little in the battle. Some of it was also used for guarding the trains which were far to the rear.[28] The Artillery Reserve, which consisted of a good many Batteries, though I cannot give the number, or the number of guns, was[29] posted between the Baltimore Pike and the Taney town Road, on very nearly the center of a direct line passing through the extremities of the wings. Thus it could be readily sent to any part of the line. The 6th Corps, Gnl. Sedgwick, did not arrive upon the field until some time afternoon; but it was now not very far away, and was coming up rapidly upon the Baltimore Pike. No fears were entertained that "Uncle John," as his men call Gnl. Sedgwick, would not be in the right place at the right time.

These dispositions were all made early, I think before eight o'clock, in the morning; — skirmishers were posted well out all around the line, and all put in readiness for battle. The enemy did not yet demonstrate himself. With a look at the ground now, I think you may understand the movements of the battle. From Round Top, by the line of battle, round to the extreme right, I suppose is about three miles. From this same eminence to the Cemetery extends a long ridge or hill — more resembling a great wave, than a hill however, — with its crest, which was the line of battle, quite direct, between the points mentioned. To the West of this, that is, towards the enemy, the ground falls away, by a very gradual descent, across the Emmitsburg Road, and then rises again forming another ridge, nearly parallel to the first, but inferior in altitude, and some thing over a thousand yards away. A belt of woods extends, partly along this second ridge, and partly

---

[28] There were sharp cavalry actions on July 3 which did not, however, significantly affect the battle's outcome. Coddington, *Gettysburg*, 520–25.

[29] In WHC the words from "though" through "guns" are omitted and "was" is rendered as "were."

farther to the West, at distances of from one thousand to thirteen hundred yards away from our line. Between these ridges, and along their slopes, that is, in front of the 2nd and 3d Corps, the ground is cultivated, and is covered with fields of wheat, now nearly ripe, with grass and pastures, with some peach orchards, with fields of waving corn, and some farm houses, and their out buildings along the Emmitsburg Road. There are very few places within the limits mentioned where troops or guns could move concealed. There are some oaks, of considerable growth, along the position[30] of the right of the 2nd Corps, — a group of small trees, sassafras and oak, in front of the right of the 2nd Division of this Corps, also; and considerable woods immediately in front of the left of the 3d Corps, and also to the West of, and near Round Top. At the Cemetery, where is Cemetery Ridge, to which the line of the 11th Corps conforms, is the highest point in our line, except Round Top. From this the ground falls quite abruptly to the town, the nearest point of which is some five hundred yards away from the line, and is cultivated, and checkered with stone fences. The same is the character of the ground occupied by, and in front of the left of the 1st Corps, which is also on a part of Cemetery Ridge. The right of this Corps, and the whole of the 12th, are along Culp's Hill, and in woods, and the ground is very rocky, and in places in front precipitous, — a most admirable position for defense from an attack in front, where, on account of the woods, no Artillery could be used with effect by the enemy. Then these last three mentioned Corps had, by taking rails, by appropriating stone fences, by felling trees, and digging the earth, during the night of the 1st of July, made for themselves excellent breast works, which were a very good thing indeed. The position of the 1st and 12th Corps was admirably strong, therefore. Within the line of battle is an irregular basin, somewhat

---

[30] WHC replaces the preceding four words with "woods immediately in front."

wooded and rocky in places, but presenting few obstacles to the moving of troops and guns, from place to place along the lines, and also affording the advantage that all such movements, by reason of the surrounding crests, were out of view of the enemy. On the whole this was an admirable position to fight a defensive battle, — good enough, I thought when I saw it first, and better I believe than could be found elsewhere in a circle of many miles. Evils, sometimes at least, are blessings in disguise; — for the repulse of our forces, and the death of Reynolds, on the 1st of July, with the opportune arrival of Hancock to arrest the tide of fugitives and fix it on these heights, gave us this position. — Perhaps the position gave us the victory. — On arriving upon the field, Gnl. Meade established his head quarters at a shabby little farm house, on the left of the Taney town Road, the house nearest the line, and a little more than five hundred yards in rear of what became the center of the position of the 2nd Corps, — a point where he could communicate readily and rapidly with all parts of the army. — The advantages of the position, briefly, were these: the flanks were quite well protected by the natural defences there, — Round Top up the left, and rocky, steep, untraversable ground upon the right. Our line was more elevated than that of the enemy, consequently our Artillery had a greater range and power than theirs. On account of the convexity of our line, every part of the line could be reinforced by troops having to move a shorter distance than if the line were straight, — further, for the same reason, the line of the enemy must be concave, and consequently longer, and with an equal force, thinner, and so weaker, than ours. Upon those parts of our line which were wooded, neither we nor the enemy could use Artillery; but they were so strong by nature aided by art, as to be readily defended by a small against a very large, body of Infantry. Where the line was open, it had the advantage of having open country in front; consequently the enemy here could not surprise us; we were on a crest, which besides the other advantages that I have mentioned, had this: the enemy must advance to the attack up an ascent, and must therefore move slower, and be, before coming upon us, longer under our fire, as well as more exhausted. These and some other things rendered our position admirable, — for a defensive battle.

So before a great battle was ranged the Army of the Potomac. The day wore on, the weather still sultry, and the sky overcast, with a mizzling effort at rain. When the audience has all assembled, time seems long until the curtain rises; so to day. "Will there be a battle to day?" — "Shall we attack the Rebel?" — "Will he attack us?" These and similar questions, later in the morning, were thought or asked a million times.

Meanwhile on our part all was put in the last state of readiness for battle. Surgeons were busy riding about selecting eligible places for Hospitals, and hunting streams, and springs, and wells. Ambulances and the Ambulance men were brought up near the lines, and stretchers gotten ready for use. — Who of us could tell but that he would be the first to need them? — The Provost Guards were busy driving up all stragglers, and causing them to join their regiments. Ammunition wagons were driven to suitable places, and pack mules bearing boxes of cartriges [sic]; and the commands were informed where they might be found. Officers were sent to see that the men had each his hundred rounds of ammunition. Generals and their Staffs were riding here and there among their commands to see that all was right. — A staff officer, or an orderly might be seen galloping furiously in the transmission of some order or message. — All, all was ready; — and yet the sound of no gun had disturbed the air or ear to-day.

And so the men stacked their arms — in long bristling rows they stood along the crests — and were at ease. Some men of the 2nd and 3d Corps pulled down the rail fences near and piled them up for breast-works in their front. Some loitered, —some went to sleep upon the ground, — some, a single man carrying twenty canteens slung over his shoulder, went for water, — some made them a fire and boiled a dipper of cof-

fee, — some with knees cocked up enjoyed the soldier's peculiar solace, a pipe of tobacco, — some were mirthful and chat-
ty, and some were serious and silent. Leaving them thus, — I
suppose of all arms and grades there were about a hundred
thousand of them somewhere about that field, — each to pass
the hour according to his duty or his humor, let us look to the
enemy.

Here let me state that according to the best information
that I could get, I think a fair estimate of the rebel force engaged in this battle would be a little upwards of a hundred
thousand men of all arms. Of course we can not now know,
but there are reasonable data for this estimate. At all events
there was no great disparity of numbers in the two opposing
armies. — We thought the enemy to be somewhat more numerous than we, and he probably was. But if ninety-five men
should fight with a hundred and five, the latter would not always be victors, — and slight numerical differences are of
much less consequence, in great bodies of men.[31]

Skillful generalship and good fighting are the jewels of war.
These concurring are difficult to overcome; and these, not
numbers, must determine this battle. During all the morning — and the night, too — the skirmishers of the enemy had
been confronting those of the 11th, 1st and 12th Corps. At
the time of the fight of the 1st, he was seen in heavy force North
of the town; —he was believed to be now in the same neighbor-

---

[31] Haskell's beliefs that the two armies each had over 100,000
men and that their sizes were not very different were shared by
several Union commanders. Meade thought that the Confederates
outnumbered him. Postwar estimates, based on conflicting and
incomplete returns, generally showed that Meade's force was much
the larger. The United States War Records Office computed to-
tals of 93,500 for the Union to 70,000 for the Confederates. But
Coddington's recent scholarly study of the battle gives strong ar-
guments for believing that the *effective* strengths of the opponents were, respectively, 85,500 and 75,000. All these figures in-
clude some effective soldiers whose units were present but were
never engaged. For a full discussion of the controversial question
of numbers, see Coddington, *Gettysburg*, 242–50.

hood in full force. But from the woody character of the country, and thereby the careful concealment of troops, which the Rebel is always sure to effect, during the early part of the morning almost nothing was actually seen by us of the invaders of the North. About nine o'clock in the morning, I should think, our glasses began to reveal them at the West and North-West of the town, a mile and a half away from our lines. They were moving towards our left, but the woods of Seminary Ridge so concealed them that we could not make out much of their movements. About this time some rifled guns in the Cemetery at the left of the 11th Corps, opened fire, — almost the first shots of any kind this morning, — and when it was found they were firing at a Rebel line of skirmishers merely, that were advancing upon the left of that, and the right of the 2nd Corps, the officer in charge of the guns was ordered to cease firing, and was rebuked for having fired at all. These skirmishers soon engaged those of the right of the 2nd Corps, who stood their ground and were reinforced to make the line entirely secure. The Rebel skirmish line kept extending further and further to their right, — toward our left, — they would dash up close upon ours, and sometimes drive them back a short distance, in turn to be repulsed themselves, — and so they continued to do, until their right was opposite the extreme left of the 3d Corps. By these means they had ascertained the position and extent of our line, — but their own masses were still out of view. From the time that the firing commenced, as I have mentioned, it was kept up, among the skirmishers until quite noon, often briskly; but with no definite results further than those mentioned, and with no considerable show of Infantry on the part of the enemy to support. There was a farm house and outbuildings in front of the 3d Division of the 2nd Corps, at which the skirmishers of the enemy had made a dash and dislodged ours posted there; and from there their sharp shooters began to annoy our line, of skirmishers and even the main line, with their long range rifles. I was up to the line, and a bullet from

one of the rascals hid there hissed by my cheek so close that
I felt the movement of the air distinctly. And so I was not
at all displeased, when I saw one of our regiments go down
and attack and capture the house and buildings and several
prisoners, after a spirited little fight, and by Gnl. Hays' order,
burn the buildings to the ground.[32] About noon the Signal
Corps, from the top of Little Round Top, with their powerful
glasses, and the Cavalry at our extreme left, began to report
the enemy in heavy force, making dispositions of battle, to
the West of Round Top, and opposite to the left of the 3d
Corps. Some few prisoners had been captured, some deserters
from the enemy had come in, — and from all sources by this
time we had much important and reliable information of the
enemy, — of his disposition and apparent purposes. The Rebel
Infantry consisted of three Army Corps, each consisting of
three Divisions, [James] Longstreet, [Richard S.] Ewell, — the
same whose leg Gibbon's shell knocked off at Gainesville on
the 28th of August last year, and A[mbrose] P. Hill, each in the
Rebel service having the rank of Lieut. General, were the commanders of these Corps. Longstreet's Division commanders
were [John B.] Hood, [Lafayette] McLaws, and [George E.]
Pickett; Ewell's were Rhodes [Robert E. Rodes], [Jubal A.]
Early, and [Edward] Johnson; and Hill's were [William D.]
Pender, [Henry] Heth, and [Richard H.] Anderson. Stewart
and Fitz Lee commanded Divisions of the Rebel Cavalry.[33]
The rank of these Division commands, I believe was that of
Major General. The Rebel had about as much Artillery as
we did;[34] but we never have thought much of this arm in the
hands of our adversaries. They have courage enough, but not

---

[32] Haskell refers to the buildings of the Bliss farm. While the
struggle for their possession began as related on July 2, General
Hays did not actually order the house and barn burned until the
following morning. *Ibid.*, 484–85.

[33] Major General James Ewell Brown Stuart commanded the
Confederate Cavalry Division. Brigadier General Fitzhugh Lee led
one of his brigades.

[34] In fact, while the Confederates had only 272 or 281 artillery

the skill, to handle it well. They generally fire far too high, and their ammunition is usually of a very inferior quality. And of late we have begun to despise the enemy's Cavalry too; — it used to have enterprise and dash, but in the late Cavalry contests ours has always been victor; and so now we think about all this *chivalry* is fit for is to steal a few of our mules occasionally, and their negro drivers. This army of the rebel Infantry, however, is good, — to deny this is useless, — I never had any desire to, — and if one should count up, it would possibly be found that they have gained more victories over us, than we have over them, — and they will now, doubtless, fight well, even desperately. And it is not horses or cannon that will determine the result of this confronting of the two armies, but the men with the muskets must do it — the Infantry must do the sharp work. So we watched all this posting of forces as closely as possible, for it was a matter of vital interest to us, and all information relating to it was hurried to the commander of the army. The Rebel line of battle was concave, bending around our own, with the extremities of the wings opposite to, or a little out side of, ours. Longstreet's Corps was upon their right; Hill's in the center; — these two Rebel Corps occupied the second or inferior ridge to the West of our position, as I have mentioned, with Hill's left bending towards, and resting near, the town, — and Ewell's was upon their left, his troops being in, and to the East of the town. This last Corps confronted our 12th, 1st, and the right of the 11th, Corps. When I have said that ours was a good *defensive* position, this is equivalent to saying that that of the enemy was not a good *offensive* one; for these are relative terms, and cannot be both predicated of the respective positions of the two armies at the same time. The reasons that theirs' was not a good offensive position, are the same already stated in favor of ours for defense. Excepting occasionally for a brief time

---

pieces, the Union artillerymen's varying counts of the Northern guns ranged from 362 to 374. Coddington, *Gettysburg*, 244

during some movement of troops, as when advancing to attack, their men and guns were kept constantly and carefully, by woods and inequalities of ground, out of our view.

Noon is past, — one o'clock is past, and save the skirmishing, that I have mentioned, and an occasional shot from our guns, at something or other of the nature of which the ones who fired it were ignorant, there was no fight yet. Our arms were still stacked, and the men were at ease. As I looked upon those interminable rows of muskets along the crests, and saw how cool and good spirited the men were who were lounging about on the ground among them, I could not, and did not, have any fears as to the result of the battle. The storm was near, and we all knew it well enough by this time, which was to rain death upon these crests and down these slopes, and yet the men who could not, and would not escape it, were as calm and cheerful generally, as if nothing unusual was about to happen! You see, these men were veterans, and had been in such places so often that they were accustomed to them. But I was well pleased with the tone of the men to-day, — I could almost see the foreshadowing of victory upon their faces, I thought. And I thought, too, as I had seen the mighty preparations go on to completion for this great conflict, — the marshaling of these two hundred thousand men and the guns, of the hosts that now but a narrow valley divided, that to have been in such a battle, and to survive on the side of the victors, would be glorious. Oh, the world is most unchristian yet!

Some what after one o'clock, P.M. — the skirmish firing had nearly ceased now, — a movement of the 3d Corps occurred which I shall describe. I cannot conjecture the reason of this movement. From the position of the 3d Corps, as I have mentioned, to the second ridge West, the distance is about a thousand yards; and there the Emmitsburg Road runs near the crest of the ridge. Genl. Sickles commenced to advance his whole Corps, from the general line, straight to the front, with a view to occupy this second ridge along, and near the road.

What his purpose could have been is past conjecture. It was
not ordered by Genl. Meade, as I heard him say, and he dis-
approved of it as soon as it was made known to him. Generals Hancock and Gibbon, as they saw the move in progress,
criticized its propriety sharply, as I know, and foretold quite
accurately what would be the result. I suppose the truth
probably is that Gnl. Sickles supposed he was doing for the
best; but he was neither born nor bred a soldier. But one
can scarcely tell what may have been the motives of such a
man, — a politician, and some other things, exclusive of the
Barton Key affair, — a man after show, and notoriety, and
newspaper fame, and the adulation of the mob! O, there is a
grave responsibility on those in whose hands are the lives of ten
thousand men; and on those who put stars upon men's shoulders, too! Bah! I kindle when I see some things that I have
to see. But this move of the 3d Corps was an important one:
— it developed the battle; — the results of the move to the
Corps itself we shall see. O, if this Corps had kept its strong
position upon the crest, and supported by the rest of the army,
had waited for the attack of the enemy![35]

It was magnificent to see those ten or twelve thousand
men, — they were good men — with their Batteries, and some
squadrons of Cavalry upon the left flank, all in battle order,
in several lines, with flags streaming, sweep steadily down the
slope, across the valley, and up the next ascent, towards their
destined position! From our position we could see it all. In
advance Sickles pushed forward his heavy line of skirmishers,
who drove back those of the enemy, across the Emmitsburg
Road, and thus cleared the way for the main body. The 3d
Corps now became the absorbing object of interest of all eyes.
The 2nd Corps took arms; and the 1st Division of this Corps,

---

[35] While many contemporaries (and most historians) shared Haskell's view of the Third Corps' advance, Sickles contended throughout his long life that he had secured a stronger position and had
prepared the way for the Union victory at Gettysburg. *Ibid.*, 346–
51.

was ordered to be in readiness to support the 3d Corps, should circumstances render support necessary. As the 3d Corps was the extreme left of our line, as it advanced, if the enemy was assembling to the West of Round Top with a view to turn our left, as we had heard, there would be nothing between the left flank of the Corps, and the enemy; and the enemy would be square upon its flank by the time it had attained the road. So when this advance line came near the Emmitsburg Road, and we saw the squadrons of Cavalry, mentioned, come dashing back from their position as flankers, and the smoke of some guns, and we heard the reports, away to Sickles' left, anxiety became an element in our interest in these movements. The enemy opened slowly at first, and from long range; but he was square upon Sickles' left flank. Gnl. Caldwell was ordered at once to put his Division, — the 1st, of the 2nd Corps, as mentioned — in motion, and to take post in the woods at the West[36] slope of Round Top, in such a manner as to resist the enemy should he attempt to come around Sickles' left and gain his rear. The Division moved as ordered, and disappeared from view in the woods, towards the point indicated at between two and three o'clock P.M. and the reserve brigade — the 1st, Col. [Francis E.] Heath, temporarily commanding — of the 2nd Division, was therefore moved up, and occupied the position vacated by the 3d Division.[37] About the same time the 5th Corps could be seen marching by the flank from its position on the Baltimore Pike, and in the openings of the woods heading for the same locality where the 1st Division of the 2nd Corps had gone. The 6th Corps had now come up, and was halted upon the Baltimore Pike. So the plot thickened. As the enemy opened upon Sickles with his Batteries, some five or six in all, I suppose, firing slowly, Sickles with as many replied, and with much more spirit. The

---

[36] "Left" in WHC.

[37] Haskell probably refers to the position vacated by the *1st* Division. In his reference to that unit in the previous sentence, he originally wrote "3d" but corrected it to "1st."

Artillery fire became quite animated, soon; but the enemy
was forced to withdraw his guns farther and farther away, and
ours advanced upon him. It was not long before the cannonade ceased altogether, the enemy having retired out of range,
and Sickles, having temporarily halted his command pending
this, moved forward again to the position he desired, or nearly
that. It was now about five o'clock, and we shall soon see what
Sickles gained by his move. First we hear more Artillery firing
upon Sickles left, — the enemy seems to be opening again, and
as we watched, the Rebel Batteries seem to be advancing, there.
The cannonade is soon opened again, and with great spirit
upon both sides. The enemy's Batteries press those of Sickles,
and pound the shot upon them, and this time they in turn
begin to retire to positions nearer the Infantry. The enemy
seems to be fearfully in earnest, this time. And what is more
ominous than the thunder or the shot of his advancing guns,
this time, in the intervals between his Batteries, far to Sickles'
left, appear the long lines, and the colums [sic] of the Rebel
Infantry, now unmistakably moving out to the attack. The
position of the 3d Corps becomes at once one of great peril,
and it is probable that its commander by this time began to
realize his true situation. All was astir now on our crest, —
Generals and their Staffs were galloping hither and thither —
the men were all in their places, and you might have heard
the rattle of ten thousand ramrods, as they drove home and
"thugged" upon the little globes and cones of lead. As the
enemy was advancing upon Sickles' flank, he commenced a
change, or at least a partial one, of front, by swinging back
his left and throwing forward his right, in order that his lines
might be parallel to those of his adversary, his Batteries mean
time doing what they could to check the enemy's advance; but
this movement was not completely executed before new Rebel
Batteries opened upon Sickles' right flank, — his former front,
— and in the same quarter appeared the Rebel Infantry also.
Now came the dreadful battle picture, of which we for a time
could be but spectators. Upon the front and right f[l]ank of

Sickles came sweeping the Infantry of Longstreet and Hill.
Hitherto there had been skirmishing and Artillery practice —
now the battle begins; for amid the heavier smokes, and larger
tongues of flame of the Batteries, now began to appear the
countless flashes, and the long fiery sheets of the muskets, and
the rattle of the vollies [*sic*] mingled with the thunder of the
guns. We see the long gray lines come sweeping down upon
Sickles' front, and mix with the battle smoke; now the same
colors emerge from the bushes and orchards upon his right,
and envelope his flank in the confusion of the conflict.

O, the din, and the roar, and those thirty thousand Rebel
wolf cries! What a Hell is there down that valley!

These ten or twelve thousand men of the 3d Corps fight
well, but it soon becomes apparent that they must be swept
from the field, or perish there where they are doing so well,
so thick and overwhelming a storm of Rebel fire involves them.
It was fearful to see, but these men, such as ever escape, must
come from that conflict as best they can. To move down and
support them there with other troops is out of the question, for
this would be, to do as Sickles did, to relinquish a good position, and advance to a bad one. There is no other alternative, — the 3d Corps must fight itself out of its position of
destruction! What was it ever put there for?

In the mean time some other dispositions must be made,
to meet the enemy, in the event that Sickles is overpowered.
With this Corps out of the way, the enemy would be in a position to advance upon the line of the 2nd Corps, not in a
line parallel with its front, but they would come obliquely
from the left. To meet this contingency the left of the 2nd
Division of the 2nd Corps is thrown back slightly, and two
Regiments, the 15th Mass. Col. [George H.] Ward, and the
82nd N.Y., Lieut. Col. [James] Huston,[38] are advanced down
to the Emmitsburg Road, to a favorable position nearer us
than the fight has yet come, and some new Batteries from the

---

[38] "Horton" in WHC.

Artillery reserve are posted upon the crest near the left of the 2nd Corps. This was all Gnl. Gibbon could do, — other dispositions were made, or were now being made upon the field, which I shall mention presently. The enemy is still giving Sickles fierce battle, — or rather the 3d Corps, for Sickles has been borne from the field minus one of his legs, and Gnl. [David Bell] Birney now commands, — and we of the 2nd Corps, a thousand yards away, with our guns and men are, and must be, still idle spectators of the fight.

The Rebel, as anticipated, tries to gain the left of the 3d Corps, and for this purpose is now moving into the woods at the West of Round Top. We knew what he would find there. No sooner had the enemy gotten a considerable force into the woods mentioned, in the attempted execution of his purpose, than the roar of the conflict was heard there also. The 5th Corps and the 1st Division of the 2nd were there at the right time, and promptly engaged him; — and there too the battle soon became general and obstinate. Now the roar of battle has become twice the volume, that it was before, and its range extends over more than twice the space. The 3d Corps has been pressed back considerably, and the wounded are streaming to the rear by hundreds, but still the battle there goes on, with no considerable abatement on our part. The field of actual conflict extends now from a point to the front of the left of the 2nd Corps, away down to the front of Round Top, and the fight rages with the greatest fury. The fire of Artillery and Infantry and the yells of the Rebels fill the air with a mixture of hidious [sic] sounds. When the 1st Division of the 2nd Corps first engaged the enemy, for a time it was pressed back somewhat, but under the able and judicious management of Gnl. Caldwell, and the support of the 5th Corps, it speedily ceased to retrograde, and stood its ground; and then there followed a time, after the 5th Corps became well engaged, when from appearances we hoped the troops already engaged would be able to check entirely, or repulse the further assault of the enemy. But fresh bodies of the Rebels con-

tinued to advance out of the woods to the front of the position of the 3d Corps, and to swell the numbers of the assailants of this already hard pressed command. — The men there
begin to show signs of exhaustion, — their ammunition must
be nearly expended, — they have now been fighting more than
an hour, and against greatly superior numbers. From the
sound of the firing at the extreme left, and the place where
the smoke rises above the tree tops there, we know that the
5th Corps is still steady, and holding its own there; and as
we see the 6th Corps now marching and near at hand to that
point, we have no fears for the left, — we have more apparent
reason to fear for ourselves.

The 3d Corps is being overpowered, — here and there its
lines begin to break, — the men begin to pour back to the
rear in confusion, — the enemy are close upon them, and
among them, — organization is lost, to a great degree, — guns
and caissons are abandoned and in the hands of the enemy, —
the 3d Corps, after a heroic, but unfortunate fight, is being
litterally [sic] swept from the field. That Corps gone what is
there between the 2nd Corps, and these yelling masses of the
enemy? Do you not think that by this time we began to feel
a personal interest in this fight? We did indeed. We had
been mere observers of all this, — the time was at hand when
we must be actors in this drama.

Up to this hour Gnl. Gibbon had been in command of the
2nd Corps, since yesterday, but Gnl. Hancock relieved of his
duties elsewhere, now assumed command. Five or six hundred
yards away the 3d Corps was making its last opposition; and
the enemy was hotly pressing his advantage there, and throwing in fresh troops whose line extended still more along our
front, when Generals Hancock and Gibbon rode along the
lines of their troops; and at once cheer after cheer — not Rebel,
mongrel cries, but genuine cheers, — rang out all along the
line, above the roar of battle, for "Hancock", and "Gibbon,"
and "our Generals." These were good. — Had you heard their
voices, you would have known these men would fight. Just

at this time we saw another thing that made us glad: — we looked to our rear, and there, and all up the hillside, which was the rear of the 3d Corps before it went forward, were rapidly advancing large bodies of men from the extreme right of our line of battle, coming to the support of the part now so hotly pressed. There was the whole 12th Corps, with the exception of about one Brigade, that is, the larger portions of the Divisions of Gnls. Williams[39] and Geary;[40] the 3d Division of the 1st Corps, Gnl. Doubleday, and some other Brigades from the same Corps — and some of them were moving at the double quick, — they formed lines of battle at the foot of the hill by[41] the Taney town Road, and when the broken fragments of the 3d Corps were swarming by them towards the rear, without halting or wavering they came sweeping up, and with glorious old cheers, under fire, took their places on the crest in line of battle to the left of the 2nd Corps. Now Sickles' blunder is repaired. — Now Rebel Chief hurl forward your howling lines and columns! Yell out your loudest, and your last, for many of your best will never yell, or wave the spurious flag again!

The battle still rages all along the left, where the 5th Corps is; and the West slope of Round Top is the scene of the conflict; and nearer us there was but short abatement, as the last of the 3d Corps retired from the field; for the enemy is flushed with his success; he has been throwing forward Brigade after Brigade, and Division after Division, since the battle began, and his advancing line now extends almost as far to our right

---

[39] Alpheus S. Williams had temporarily replaced Slocum as commander of the entire Twelfth Corps when the latter was given command of Meade's right wing on the morning of July 2. A lawyer and newspaper publisher from Michigan, Williams had served in the Mexican War and in the Army of the Potomac since 1861. After Gettysburg, he held divisional and corps commands in the western theater. Warner, *Generals in Blue*, 559–60.

[40] John W. Geary's 2nd Division in fact got lost and failed to reach this portion of the field. Coddington, *Gettysburg*, 433–35.

[41] WHC omits the preceding three words.

as the right of the 2nd Division of the 2nd Corps. The whole
slope in our front is full of them; — and in various formations,
in line, in column, and in masses which are neither, with yells,
and thick vollies [sic], they are rushing towards our crest. The
3d Corps is out of the way. — Now we are in for it. The Battery men are ready by their loaded guns. All along the crest
is ready. Now Arnold and Brown. — Now Cushing, and Woodruff, and Rhorty [Rorty]! — you three shall survive to-day!
— They drew the cords that moved the friction primers, and
gun after gun, along all the Batteries, in rapid succession,
leaped where it stood and bellowed its canister upon the enemy. The enemy still advance. The Infantry open fire, —
first the two advance regiments the 15th Mass. and the 82
N.Y. — then here and there throughout the length of the long
line, at the points where the enemy comes nearest, — and
soon the whole crest, Artillery and Infantry, is one continued
sheet of fire. From Round Top to near the Cemetery stretches
an uninterrupted field of conflict. There is a great army upon
each side, now hotly engaged.

To see the fight, while it went on in the valley below us,
was terrible: — what must it be now when we are in it, and
it is all around us, in all its fury?

All senses for the time are dead but the one of sight. The
roar of the discharges, and the yells of the enemy all pass
unheeded; but the impassioned soul is all eyes, and sees all
things, that the smoke does not hide. How madly the battery
men are driving home the double charges of canister in those
broad mouthed Napoleons, whose fire seems almost to reach
the enemy. — How rapidly these long blue-coated lines of Infantry, deliver their file fire down the slope.

But there is no faltering, — the men stand nobly to their
work. Men are dropping dead or wounded on all sides, by
scores and by hundreds; and the poor mutilated creatures,
some with an arm dangling, some with a leg broken by a bullet,
are limping and crawling towards the rear. They make no
sound of complaint or pain, but are as silent as if dumb, and

mute. A sublime heroism seems to pervade all, and the intuition, that to lose that crest, and all is lost. How our officers in the work of cheering on and directing the men, are falling. We have heard that Gnl. [Samuel K.] Zook, and Col. [Edward E.] Cross, in the 1st Division of our Corps are mortally wounded, — they both commanded Brigades, — now near us Col. Ward of the 15th Mass. — he lost a leg at Ball's Bluff, — and Lieut. Col. Huston of the 82nd N.Y. are mortally struck while trying to hold their commands, which are being forced back. Col. [Paul J.] Revere 20th Mass. grandson of old Paul Revere, of the Revolution is killed, — Lieut. Col. Max Thoman, commanding 59th N.Y. is mortally wounded, and a host of others that I cannot name. — These were of Gibbon's Division. Lieut. Brown is wounded among his guns, — his position is a hundred yards in advance of the main line, — the enemy is upon his Battery, and he escapes, but leaves three of his six guns in the hands of the enemy.

The fire all along our crest is terrific, and it is a wonder how any thing human could have stood before it, and yet the madness of the enemy drove them on, clear up to the muzzle of the guns, — clear up to the lines of our Infantry, — but the lines stood right in their places. Gnl. Hancock with his Aides rode up to Gibbon's Division, under the smoke. — Gnl. Gibbon, with myself, was near, — and there was a flag dimly visible, coming towards us from the direction of the enemy. "Here, what are these men falling back for?" said Hancock. The flag was no more than fifty yards away, but it was the head of a Rebel column, which at once opened fire with a volley. Lieut. [W.D.W.] Miller, Gnl. Hancock's Aide fell twice struck, but the General was unharmed, and he told the 1st Minn. which was near, to drive these people away. That splendid Regiment, the less than three hundred that are left out of fifteen hundred that it has had, swings around upon the enemy, gives them a volley in their faces, and advances upon them with the bayonet. The Rebels fled in confusion; but Col Colville [William Colvill, Jr.], Lieut. Col. [Charles P.] Adams, and Major [Mark W.] Downie, are all badly, dangerously wounded, and many of the other officers and men will never fight again. More than two-thirds fell.[42]

Such fighting as this cannot last long, — it is now near sundown, — and the battle has gone on wonderfully long already. But if you will stop to notice it, a change has occurred. — The Rebel cry has ceased, and the men of the Union begin to shout there, under the smoke, and their lines to advance. See, the Rebels are breaking! They are in confusion in all our front! — The wave has rolled upon the rock, and the rock has smashed it. Let us shout too!

First upon their extreme left the Rebels broke, where they had almost pierced our lines; thence the repulse extended rapidly to their right: they hung longest about Round Top, where the 5th Corps punished them; but in a space of time incredibly short, after they first gave signs of weakness, the whole force of the Rebel assault, along the whole line, in spite of waving red flags, and yells, and the entreaties of officers, and the pride of the chivalry, fled like chaff before the whirlwind, back down the slope, over the valley, across the Emmitsburg Road, shattered, without organization, in utter confusion, fugitive into the woods, and victory was with the arms of the Republic. The great Rebel assault, the greatest ever made upon this continent, has been made and signally repulsed, and upon this part of the field the fight of to-day is now soon over. Pursuit was made as rapidly and as far as practicable; but owing to the proximity of night, and the long distance which would have to be gone over before any of the enemy, where they would be likely to halt, could be overtaken, further success was not attainable to-day. When the Rebel rout first commenced, a large number of prisoners, some thousands at least, were captured; — almost all their dead, and such of their wounded as could

---

[42] Haskell's report of the proportion of casualties among the 1st Minnesota was accurate, despite the later myth that the regiment had suffered a uniquely high casualty rate of 82 percent. Letter of Robert W. Meinhard, *Civil War Times Illustrated*, 27(January 1989): 6, 42.

not themselves get to the rear were within our lines; several
of their flags were gathered up, and a good many thousand
muskets, — some nine or ten guns and some caissons lost by
the 3d Corps, and the three of Brown's Battery — these last
were in Rebel hands but a few minutes, — were all safe now
with us, the enemy having had no time to take them off.

Not less, I estimate, than twenty thousand men were killed
or wounded in this fight. Our own losses must have been nearly half this number; — about four thousand in the 3d Corps;
— fully two thousand in the 2nd; — and I think two thousand in the 5th; — and I think the losses of the 1st, 12th, and the
little more than a Brigade of the 6th, — all of that Corps which
were actually engaged, — would reach nearly two thousand
more. Of course it will never be possible to know the numbers
upon either side who fell in this particular part of the general
battle, but from the position of the enemy, and his numbers,
and the appearance of the field, his loss must have been as
heavy as, I think much heavier than, our own; and my estimates are probably short of the actual loss.[43]

The fight done, the sudden revulsions of sense and feeling
follow, which more or less characterize all similar occasions.
How strange the stillness seems! The whole air roared with
the conflict but a moment since, — now all is silent, not a
gun-shot sound is heard — and the silence comes distinctly,
almost painfully to the senses. — And the sun purples the
clouds in the West, and the sultry evening steals on as if there
had been no battle, and the furious shout and the cannon's
roar had never shook the earth. And how look those fields —
we may see them before dark — the ripening grain, the luxuriant corn, the orchards, the grassy meadows, and in their
midst the rural cottage of brick or wood? They were beautiful
this morning. They are desolate now, — trampled by the count-

---

[43] On the other hand, the most recent historian of the battle
estimates that casualties (including prisoners) in all of the second
day's fighting totalled about 16,500, of whom 10,000 were Fed-
erals. Coddington, *Gettysburg*, 442, 768.

less feet of the combattants [*sic*], — plowed and scarred by the shot and shell, the orchards splintered, the fences prostrate, the harvests trodden in the mud. And more dreadful than the sight of all this, thickly strewn over all their length and breadth, are the habiliments of the soldier, — the knapsacks, cast aside in the stress of the fight, or after the fatal lead had struck; — haversacks, yawning with the rations, the owner will never call for; canteens of cedar of the Rebel men of Jackson and of cloth-covered tin of the men of the Union; — blankets and trowsers, and coats, and caps; and some are blue and some are gray; — muskets, and ramrods, and bayonets, and swords, and scabbards, and belts, some bent and cut by the shot, or shell; — broken wheels, exploded caissons, and limber-boxes, and dismantled guns; — and all these are sprinkled with blood; — horses, some dead, a mangled heap of carnage, some alive, with a leg shot clear off, or other frightful wound, appealing to you with almost more than brute gaze as you pass; — and last, but not least numerous, many thousands of men, — and there was no rebellion here now, — the men of South Carolina were quiet by the side of those of Massachusetts, — some composed with upturned faces, sleeping the last sleep, some mutilated and frightful, some wretched, fallen, bathed in blood, survivors still and unwilling witnesses of the rage of Gettysburg.

And yet with all this before them, as darkness came on, and the dispositions were made and the outposts thrown out, for the night, the Army of the Potomac was quite mad with joy. No more light-hearted guests ever graced a banquet, than were these men as they boiled their coffee, and munched their soldiers' supper, to-night. Is it strange?

Otherwise, they would not have been soldiers. And such sights, as all these will continue to be seen, as long as war lasts in the world; and when war is done, then is the end, and the days of the milennium [*sic*] at hand.

The Ambulances commenced their work as soon as the battle opened; — the twinkling lanterns through the night, and

the sun of to-morrow saw them still with the same work unfinished.

I wish that I could write, that with the coming on of darkness, ended the fight of to-day, — but such was not the case.
The armies have fought enough to-day, and ought to sleep
to-night, one would think; — but not so thought the Rebel.
Let us see what he gained by his opinion. When the troops,
including those of the 12th Corps, had been withdrawn from
the extreme right of our line, in the afternoon, to support the
left, as I have mentioned, thereby of course weakening that
part of the line so left, the Rebel Ewell, either becoming
aware of the fact, or because he thought he could carry our
right at all events, late in the afternoon commenced an assault upon that part of our line. His battle had been going
there simultaneously with the fight on the left, but not with
any great degree of obstinacy on his part. He had advanced
his men through the woods, and in front of the formidable
position lately held by the 12th Corps cautiously, and to his
surprise, I have no doubt, found our strong defenses upon the
extreme right entirely abandoned. These he at once took possession of, and simultaneously made an attack upon our right
flank, which was now near the summit of Culp's hill, and
upon the front of that part of the line. That small portion
of the 12th Corps, which had been left there, and some of the
11th Corps, sent to their assistance did what they could to
check the Rebels; but the 11th Corps men were getting shot at
there and they did not like to stay; matters began to have a
bad look in that part of the field; — a portion of the 1st Division of the 1st Corps, was sent there for support; the 6th Wis.
among others, and this improved matters; — But still as we
had but a small number of men there, all told, the enemy with
their great numbers, were having too much prospect of success; and it seems that, probably emboldened by this, Ewell
had resolved upon a night attack, upon that wing of our army,
and was making his dispositions accordingly. The enemy had
not at sundown, actually carried any part of our rifle pits

there, save the ones abandoned; but he was getting troops assembled upon our flank; and all together, with our weakness there at that time, matters did not look as we would like to have them. Such was then the posture of affairs, when the fight upon our left, that I have mentioned, was done. Under such circumstances it is not strange that the 12th Corps, as soon as its work was done upon the left, was quickly ordered back to the right, to its old position. There it arrived in good time; not soon enough, of course, to avoid the mortification of finding the enemy in the possession of a part of the works the men had labored so hard to construct, but in ample time before dark, to put the men well in the pits we already held, and to take up a strong defensible position, at right angles to, and in rear of, the main line, in order to resist those flanking dispositions of the enemy. The army was secure again. The men in the works would be steady against all attacks in front, as long as they knew that their flank was safe. Until between ten and eleven o'clock at night, the woods upon the right, resounded with the discharges of musketry. Shortly after or about dark the enemy made a dash upon the right of the 11th Corps. They crept up the windings of a valley, not in a very heavy force, but from the peculiar mode in which this Corps does outpost duty, quite unperceived in the dark until they were close upon the main line. — It is said, I do not know it to be true, that they spiked two guns of one of the 11th Corps Batteries; — and that the Battery men had to drive them off with their sabres and rammers; — and that there was some fearful Dutch swearing on the occasion, *"donner wetter"* among other similar impious oaths, having been freely used. The enemy here were finally repulsed by the assistance of Col. [Samuel S.] Carroll's[44] Brigade of the 3d Division of the 2nd Corps, and the 106th Pa. from the 2nd Division of the same Corps, was, by Gnl. Howard[']s request sent there to do outpost duty. It seems to have been a matter of utter madness

---

[44] "Correll" in WHC.

and folly upon the part of the enemy to have continued their night attack, as they did upon the right. Our men were securely covered by ample works; and even in most places a log was placed a few inches above the top of the main breastwork, as a protection to the heads of the men as they thrust out their pieces beneath it to fire. Yet in the darkness the enemy would rush up, clambering over rocks, and among trees, even to the front of the works; but only to leave their riddled bodies there upon the ground, or to be swiftly repulsed headlong into the woods again. In the darkness the enemy would climb trees close to the works, and endeavor to shoot our men by the light of the flashes; — when discovered a thousand bullets would whistle after them in the dark, and some would hit, — and then the Rebel would make up his mind to come down.

Our loss was light, almost nothing in this fight, — the next morning the enemy's dead were thick all along this part of the line. Near eleven o'clock, the enemy wearied with his disastrous work, desisted; and thereafter until morning not a shot was heard in all the armies.

So much for the battle, — there is another thing that I wish to mention, of the matters of the 2nd of July.

After evening came on, and from reports received, all was known to be going satisfactorily upon the right, Gnl. Meade summoned his Corps Commanders to his Head Quarters for consultation. A consultation is held upon matters of vast moment to the country; and that poor little farm house is honored with more distinguished guests than it ever had before, or than it will ever have again, probably.

Do you expect to see a degree of ceremony, and severe military aspect characterize this meeting, in accordance with strict military rules, and commensurate with the moment of the matters of their deliberation? Name it: "Major General Meade, Commander of the Army of the Potomac, with his Corps Generals, holding a council of war, upon the field of Getysburg," and it would sound pretty well, — and that was

what it was; and you might make a picture of it and hang it
up by the side of "Napoleon and his Marshals," and "Washington and his Generals," may be, at some future time. But for
the artist to draw his picture from, I will tell how this council appeared. Meade, Sedgwick, Slocum, Howard, Hancock,
Sykes, Newton, Pleasonton[45] — commander of the Cavalry —
and Gibbon were the Generals present. — Hancock, now that
Sickles is wounded has charge of the 3d Corps, and Gibbon
again has the 2nd.[46] Meade is a tall, spare man, with full
beard, which with his hair, originally brown, is quite thickly
sprinkled with gray, — has a Romanish face, very large nose,
and a white large forehead, prominent and wide over the eyes,
which are full and large, and quick in their movements, and
he wears spectacles. His *fibres* are all of the long and sinewy
kind. His habitual personal appearance is quite careless, and
it would be rather difficult to make him look well dressed.
Sedgwick is quite a heavy man, — short, thick-set, and muscular, with florid complexion, dark, calm, straight looking
eyes, with full, heavyish features, which with his eyes, have
plenty of animation when he is aroused, — he has a magnificent profile, — well cut, with the nose and forehead forming
almost a straight line, curly short chestnut hair and full beard,
cut short, with a little gray in it. He dresses carelessly, but
can look magnificently when he is well dressed. Like Meade,
he looks, and is, honest and modest. — You might see at once,

---

[45] Alfred Pleasonton, a West Point graduate and Mexican War
veteran. Serving in the Army of the Potomac, he took command
of its Cavalry Corps in June, 1863. In 1864, because Grant wished
to replace him with Sheridan, he was banished to the west. Warner,
Generals in Blue, 373–74.

[46] Hancock actually had charge over both the Second and Third
Corps on the Union left, while Slocum commanded the right.
Generals David B. Birney and Alpheus S. Williams, who were in
immediate command, respectively, of the Third and Twelfth
Corps, were also present. Other generals who crowded into the
little room were Daniel Butterfield, Meade's Chief of Staff, and
Gouverneur K. Warren, the Army's Chief Engineer. Coddington,
Gettysburg, 402, 449, 749, 757.

why his men, because they love him, call him "Uncle John,"
not to his face of course, but among themselves. Slocum is
small, rather spare, with black straight hair, and beard, which
latter is unshaven and thin, large full, quick black eyes, white
skin, sharp nose, wide cheek bones, and hollow cheeks and
small chin. His movements are quick and angular, — and he
dresses with a sufficiet [sic] degree of elegance. Howard is medium in size, has nothing marked about him, is the youngest
of them all, I think, — has lost an arm in the war, — has
straight brown hair and beard, — shaves his short upper lip,
over which his nose slants down, dim blue eyes, and on the
whole appears a very pleasant, affable, well dressed little gentleman. Hancock is the tallest, and most shapely, and in many
respects is the best looking officer of them all. His hair is
very light brown, straight and moist, and always looks, well,
— his beard is of the same color, of which he wears the moustache and a tuft upon the chin; complexion ruddy, features
neither large nor small, but well cut, with full jaw and chin,
compressed mouth, straight nose, full deep blue eyes, and a
very mobile, emotional countenance. He always dresses remarkably well, and his manner is dignified, gentlemanly and
commanding. I think if he were in citizens clothes, and should
give commands in the army to those who did not know him,
he would be likely to be obeyed at once, and without any
question as to his right to command. Sykes is a small, rather
thin man, well dressed and gentlemanly, brown hair and beard
which he wears full, with a red, pinched, rough looking skin,
feeble blue eyes, large[47] nose, with the general air of one who
is weary, and a little ill natured. Newton is a well-sized, shapely, muscular, well dressed man, with brown hair, with a very
ruddy, clean-shaved, full face, blue eyes, blunt, round features.
walks very erect, curbs in his chin, and has somewhat of that
smart sort of swagger, that people are apt to suppose characterizes soldiers. Pleasonton is quite a nice little dandy, with

---

[47] "Long" in WHC.

brown hair and beard, — a straw hat with a little jocky [sic] rim, which he cocks upon one side of his head, with an unsteady eye, that looks slily [sic] at you, and then dodges.

Gibbon, the youngest of them all save Howard, is about the same size as Slocum, Howard, Sykes and Pleasonton, and there are none of these who will weigh one hundred and fifty pounds. He is compactly made, neither spare nor corpulent, with ruddy complexion, chestnut brown hair, with a clean-shaved face, except his moustache, which is decidedly reddish in color, medium-sized, well-shaped head, sharp, moderately-jutting brows, deep-blue, calm eyes, sharp, slightly-aquiline nose, compressed mouth, full jaws and chin, with an air of calm firmness in his manner.

He always looks well dressed. I suppose Howard is about thirty-five, and Meade about forty-five, years of age; — the rest are between these ages, but not many are under forty. As they come to the council now there is the appearance of fatigue about them, which is not customary, but is only due to the hard labors of the past few days. They all wear clothes of dark blue, — some have top boots, and some not, and except the two-starred strap upon the shoulders of all save Gibbon, who has but one star, there was scarcely a piece of regulation uniform about them all. There were their swords, of various pattern, but no sashes, — the Army hat, but with the crown pinched into all sorts of shapes, and the rim slouched down, and shorn of all its ornaments but the gilt band, — except Sykes who wore a blue cap, — and Pleasonton with his straw hat, with broad black band. Then the mean little room where they met, — its only furniture consisted of a large wide bed in one corner; a small pine table in the center, upon which was a wooden pail of water, with a tin cup for drinking, and a candle, stuck to the table by putting the end in tallow melted down from the wick; and five or six straight-backed rush-bottom chairs. The Generals came in, — some sat, some kept walking or standing, two lounged upon the bed, — some were constantly smoking cigars. And thus disposed, they deliberated, — whether

the army should fall back from its present position, to one
in rear which it was said was stronger; — should attack the
enemy on the morrow, wherever he could be found; — or
should stand there upon the horse-shoe crest, still on the defensive, and await the further movements of the enemy.

The latter proposition was unanimously agreed to. — Their
heads were sound. The Army of the Potomac would just halt
right there, and allow the Rebel to come up and smash his
head against it, to any reasonable extent he desired, — as he
had to-day. After some two hours the council dissolved, and
the officers went their several ways.

Night, sultry and starless, droned on; and it was almost midnight that I found myself peering my way from the line of
the 2nd Corps, back down to the General's Head Quarters,
which were an Ambulance in the rear, in a little peach orchard. All was silent now, but the sound of the Ambulances,
as they were bringing off the wounded; and you could hear
them rattle here and there about the field and see their lanterns. I am weary and sleepy almost to such an extent as not
to be able to sit my horse. And my horse can hardly move,
— the spur will not start him, — what can be the reason, — I
know that he has been touched by two or three bullets to-day,
but not to wound or lame him to speak of. — Then in riding
by a horse that is hitched, in the dark I got kicked, — had I
not a very thick boot, the blow would have been likely to
have broken my ankle, — it did break my temper as it was,
— and as if it would cure matters I foolishly spurred my horse
again. — No use, — he would not but walk. — I dismounted
— I could not lead him along at all, — so out of temper, I rode
at the slowest possible walk to the Head Quarters, which I
reached at last. Generals Hancock and Gibbon, were asleep
in the Ambulance. With a light I found what was the matter
with "Billy." A bullet had entered his chest just in front of
my left leg as I was mounted, and the blood was running down
all his side and leg, and the air from his lungs came out of
the bullet hole. I begged his pardon mentally for my cruelty

in spurring him, and should have done so in words if he could have understood me. Kind treatment as is due to the wounded he could understand, and he had it. Poor Billy, — He and I were first under fire together, and I rode him at the 2nd Bull Run, and the 1st and 2nd Fredericksburg, and at Antietam after brave "Joe" was killed; but I shall never mount him again — Billy's battles are over.

"George,[48] make my bed here upon the ground, by the side of this Ambulance. — Pull off my sabre and my boots, — that will do!" Was ever princly [sic] couch, or softest down so soft as those rough blankets, there upon the unroofed sod? At midnight they received me for four hours delicious, dreamless oblivion of weariness and of battle. So to me ended the 2nd of July.

At four o'clock on the morning of the 3d I was awakened by Gnl. Gibbon's pulling me by the foot, and saying: "Come, don't you hear that?" I sprang up to my feet. — Where was I? — A moment and my dead senses, and memory were alive again, and the sound of brisk firing of musketry to the front and right of the 2nd Corps, and over at the extreme right of our line, where we heard it last, in the night, brought all back to my memory. We surely were on the field of battle; and there were palpable evidences to my senses,[49] that to-day was to be another of blood.

Oh, for a moment the thought of it was sickening to every sense and feeling! But the motion of my horse as I galloped over the crest a few minutes later, and the serene splendor of the morning now breaking through rifted clouds, and spreading over all the landscape, soon reassured me. Come day of battle, up Rebel hosts, and thunder with your arms; — we are all ready to do and to die for the Republic!

I found a sharp skirmish going on in front of the right of

[48] Possibly George Hamlin, Haskell's servant in 1861 and 1862. Haskell's file in U.S., War Dept., Adjutant General's Office, Compiled Service Records for 6th Wisconsin, National Archives.
[49] WHC shows this as "reason."

the 2nd Corps, between our outposts and those of the enemy; but save this, — and none of the enemy but his outposts were in sight, — all was quiet in all that part of the field. On the extreme right of the line the sound of musketry was quite heavy; and this I learned was brought on by the attack of the 2nd Division, 12th Corps, Gnl. [John W.] Geary, upon the enemy in order to drive him out of our works which he had sneaked into yesterday, as I have mentioned. The attack was made at the earliest moment in the morning when it was light enough to discern objects to fire at.

The enemy could not use the works, but was confronting Geary in woods, and had the cover of many rocks and trees; so the fight was an irregular one, now breaking out and swelling to a vigorous fight, now subsiding to a few scattering shots; and so it continued by turns until the morning was well advanced, when the enemy was finally wholly repulsed, and driven from the pits, and the right of our line was again reestablished in the place it first occupied. The heaviest losses the 12th Corps sustained in all the battle, occurred during this attack; — and they were here quite severe. I heard Gnl. Meade express dissatisfaction at Gnl. Geary for making this attack, as a thing not ordered, and not necessary; as the works of ours were of no intrinsic importance, and had not been captured from us, by a fight; and Geary's position was just as good as they, where he was during the night. And I heard Gnl. Meade say that he sent an order to have this fight stopped; but I believe the order was not communicated to Geary until after the repulse of the enemy.[50] Later in the forenoon the enemy, again tried to carry our right by storm. — We heard that old Rebel Ewell had sworn an oath that he would break our right. — He had Stonewall Jackson's Corps, and possibly

---

[50] Geary's superiors, Generals Slocum and Williams, had planned the attack; but Ewell's Confederate assault, mentioned below, began before the Union drive could get well under way. Meade did criticize Geary for supposedly permitting excessive firing. Coddington, *Gettysburg*, 465–75.

imagined himself another Stonewall, — but he certainly *hank-ered* after the right of our line, — and so up through the woods, and over the rocks, and up the steeps he sent his storming par-ties, — our men could see them now in the day time. —

But all the Rebel's efforts were fruitless, save in one thing — slaughter to his own men. These assaults were made with great spirit and determination; but as the enemy would come up, our men lying behind their secure defenses would just singe them with the blaze of their muskets, and riddle them, as a hail-storm, the tender blades of corn. The Rebel oath was not kept, any more than his former one to support the constitution of the United States. The Rebel loss was very heavy indeed here, — ours but trifling. I regret that I cannot give more of the details of this fighting upon the right, — it was so determined upon the part of the enemy, both last night, and this morning, — so successful to us. About all that I actu-ally saw of it during its progress, was the smoke, — and I heard the discharges, — my information is derived from officers who were personally in it. Some of our heavier Artillery assisted our Infantry in this by firing, with the pieces elevated far from the rear, over the heads of our men, — at a distance from the enemy of two miles I suppose. Of course they could have done no great damage. It was nearly eleven o'clock, that the battle in this part of the field subsided, not to be again renewed. All the morning we felt no apprehension for this part of the line; — for we knew its strength, and that our troops engaged, the 12th Corps, and the 1st Division, Wadsworth's, of the 1st, could be trusted.

For the sake of telling one thing at a time, I have antici-pated events somewhat, in writing of this fight upon the right. I shall now go back to the starting point, four o'clock this morning, and, as other events occurred during the day, second to none in the battle in importance, which I think I saw as much of as any man living, I will tell you something of them, and what I saw, and how the time moved on. The outpost skirmish that I have mentioned, soon subsided. I suppose it

was the natural escape of the wrath which the men had during
the night hoarded up against each other, and which, as soon
as they could see in the morning, they could no longer con-
tain, but must let it off through their musket barrels, at their
adversaries. At the commencement of the war such firing
would have awaked the whole army, and roused it to its feet
and to arms; — not so now. The men upon the crest lay
snoring in their blankets, even though some of the enemy's
bullets dropped among them, as if bullets were harmless as
the drops of dew around them. As the sun arose to-day the
clouds became broken, and we had once more glimpses of sky,
and fits of sunshine, — a rarity, to cheer us. From the crest,
save to the right of the 2nd Corps, no enemy, not even his
outposts, could be discovered, along all the position where he
so thronged upon the 3d Corps yesterday. All was silent
there, — the wounded horses were limping about the field;
the ravages of the conflict were still fearfully visible, — the
scattered arms and the ground thickly dotted with the dead, —
but no hostile foe. The men were roused early, in order that
their morning meal might be out of the way in time for whatever should occur. Then ensued the hum of an army, not in
ranks, chatting in low tones, and running about and jostling
among each other, rolling and packing their blankets and tents.
They looked like an army of rag-gatherers, while shaking these
very useful articles of the soldier's outfit, — for you must
know that rain and mud in conjunction have not had the effect to make them very clean; and the wear and tear of service have not left them entirely whole. But one could not
have told by the appearance of the men, that they were in battle yesterday, and were likely to be again to-day. They packed
their knapsacks, boiled their coffee, and munched their hard
bread, just as usual, — just like old soldiers, who know what
campaigning is; and their talk is far more concerning their
present employment, — some joke or drollery, — than concerning what they saw or did yesterday.

As early as practicable the lines all along the left are revised and reformed, — this having been rendered necessary by yesterday's battle, and also by what is anticipated to day.

It is the opinion of many of our Generals that the Rebel will not give us battle to-day, — that he had enough yesterday, — that he will be heading towards the Potomac at the earliest practicable moment, if he has not already done so; — but the better, and controling [*sic*] judgment is, that he will make another grand effort to pierce or turn our lines, — that he will either mass and attack the left again, as yesterday, — or direct his operations against the left of our center, the position of the 2nd Corps, and try to sever our line. I infer that Genl. Meade was of the opinion that the attack to-day would be upon the left, — this from the dispositions he ordered, — I know that Gnl. Hancock anticipated the attack upon the center.[51]

The dispositions to-day upon the left are as follows: The 2nd and 3d Divisions of the 2nd Corps are in the positions of yesterday; then on the left come Doubleday's — the 3d — Division and Col. [George J.] Stannard's Brigade of the 1st Corps; — then Caldwell's[52] — the 1st — Division of the 2nd Corps; then the 3d Corps, temporarily under the command of Hancock, since Sickle's [*sic*] wound; — the 3d Corps is upon the same ground in part, and on the identical line where it first formed yesterday morning, and where, had it stayed, instead of moving out to the front, we should have many more men to-day, and should not have been upon the brink of disaster yesterday, — on the left of the 3d is the 5th Corps, — with a short front, and deep line; — then comes the 6th Corps, all but one brigade, which is sent over to the 12th.

The 6th, a splendid corps, almost intact in the fight of yesterday, is the extreme left of our line, which terminates to the South of Round Top, and runs along its Western base, in the

[51] There is some evidence that Meade, too, expected the attack to be upon his center. *Ibid.,* 483–84.
[52] "Colwell" in WHC.

woods, and thence to the Cemetery. This corps is burning to pay off the old scores made on the 4th of May there back of Fredericksburg. Note well the position of the 2nd and 3d Divisions of the 2nd Corps, — it will become important.

There are nearly six thousand men and officers in these two Divisions here upon the field, — the losses were quite heavy yesterday, — some regiments are detached to other parts of the field, — so all told there are less than six thousand men now in the two Divisions, who occupy a line of about a thousand yards.[53] The most of the way along this line upon the crest was a stone fence, constructed of small rough stones, a good deal of the way badly pulled down; — but the men had improved it and patched it with rails from the neighboring fences, and with earth, so as to render it in many places a very passable breast work against musketry, and flying fragments of shells.

These works are so low, as to compel the men to kneel or lye [sic] down, generally to obtain cover. Near the right of the 2nd Division, and just by the little group of trees that I have mentioned there, this stone fence made a right angle, and extended thence to the front, about twenty or thirty yards, where with another less than a right angle it followed along the crest again. (Thus ⬛ ⬛ .)[54] The lines were conformed to these breast-works and to the nature of the ground upon the crest, so as to occupy the most favorable places, — to be covered, and still be able to deliver effective fire upon the enemy should he come there. In some places a second line was so posted as to be able to deliver its fire over the heads of the first line behind the works; but such formation was not practicable all of the way. But all the force of these two Divisions was in line, in position, without reserves, and in such a manner that every man of them could have fired his piece at the same instant. The Division flags, that of the 2nd

---

[53] The actual length of the line was 2000 feet. Coddington, *Gettysburg*, 476.

[54] WHC omits the parentheses and the matter between them.

Division, being a white trefoil upon a square blue field, and of the 3d Division a blue trefoil upon a white rectangular field, — waved behind the Divisions at the points where the Generals of Division were supposed to be; the Brigade flags, similar to these but with a triangular field, were behind the Brigades; and the national flags of the Regiments were in the lines of their Regiments. To the left of the 2nd Division, and advanced something over a hundred yards, were posted a part of Stannard's Brigade, two regiments or more, behind a small bush-crowned crest that ran in a direction oblique to the general line. These were well covered by the crest, and wholly concealed by the bushes, so that an advancing enemy would be close upon them before they could be seen. Other troops of Doubleday's Division were strongly posted in rear of these in the general line.

I could not help wishing all the morning that this line of the two Divisions of the 2nd Corps were stronger, — it was, so far as numbers constitute strength, the weakest part of our whole line of battle. What if, I thought, the enemy should make an assault here to-day, with two or three heavy lines, — a great overwhelming mass, would he not sweep through that thin six thousand?

But I was not Gnl. Meade, who alone had power to send other troops there; and he was satisfied, with that part of the line as it was. He was early on horseback this morning, and rode along the whole line, looking to it himself, and with glass in hand sweeping the woods and fields in the direction of the enemy, to see if ought [sic] of him could be discovered. His manner was ca[l]m and serious, but earnest. There was no arrogance of hope, or timidity of fear discernible in his face; but you would have supposed he would do his duty, conscientiously all well, and would be willing to abide the result. You would have seen this in his face. He was well pleased with the left of the line to-day, it was so strong, with good troops; — he had no apprehension for the right where the fight, now was going on, on account of the admirable position of our forces there; — he was not of the opinion that the enemy would attack the center, our artillery had such sweep there, and this was not the favorite point of attack with the Rebel; besides, should he attack the center, the General though[t] he could reinforce it in good season. I heard Gnl. Meade speak of these matters to Hancock and some others, at about nine o'clock in the morning, while they were up by the line, near the 2nd Corps.

No further changes of importance, except those mentioned, were made in the disposition of the troops this morning, except to replace some of the Batteries that were disabled yesterday, by others from the Artillery Reserve, and to brace up the lines well with guns wherever there were eligible places, from the same source. The line is all in good order again, and we are ready for general battle.

Save the operations upon the right, the enemy, so far as we could see, was very quiet all the morning. Accasionally [sic] the outposts would fire a little, and then cease. Movements would be discovered which would indicate the attempt on the part of the enemy to post a Battery; — our Parrotts would send a few shells to the spot, then silence would follow.

At one of these times a painful accident happened to us, this morning; 1st Lieut. Henry Ropes, 20 Mass. in Gnl. Gibbon's Division, a most estimable gentleman, and officer, intelligent, educated, refined, one of the noble souls that came to the country's defense, while lying at his post with his regiment, in front of one of the Batteries, which fired over the Infantry, was instantly killed by a badly made shell, which, or some portion of it, fell but a few yards in front of the muzzle of the gun. The same accident killed or wounded several others. The loss of Ropes would have pained us at any time, and in any manner; — in this manner his death was doubly painful.

Between ten and eleven o'clock over in a peach orchard in front of the position of Sickles yesterday, some little show of the enemy's Infantry was discovered, — a few shells scattered the gray-backs, — they again appeared, and it becoming apparent that they were only posting a skirmish line, no further molestation was offered them. A little after this some of the enemy's flags could be discerned over near the same quarter, above the top, and behind a small crest of a ridge, — there seemed to be two or three of them, — possibly they were guidons, — and they moved too fast to be carried on foot. Possibly, we thought, the enemy is posting some Batteries there. — We knew in about two hours from this time better about the matter. Eleven o'clock came, — the noise of battle has ceased upon the right, — not a sound of a gun or musket can be heard on all the field, — the sky is bright with only the white fleecy clouds floating over from the West, — the July sun streams down its fire upon the bright iron of the muskets in stacks upon the crest, and the dazzling brass of the Napoleons — the army lolls, and longs for the shade, of which some get a hands [*sic*] breadth, from a shelter tent stuck upon a ramrod, — the silence and sultriness of a July noon are supreme. Now it so happened that just about this time of day a very original and interesting thought occurred to Gnl. Gibbon and several of his Staff: that it would be a very good thing, and a very good time, to have something to eat. When I announce to you that I had not tasted a mouthful of food since yesterday noon, and that all I had had to drink since that time but the most miserable muddy warm water, was a little drink of whiskey that Major [James C.] Biddle, Gnl. Meade's Aide-de-Camp, gave me last evening, and a cup of strong coffee that I gulped down as I was first mounting this morning; and further, that save the four or five hours in the night, there was scarcely a moment, since that time but what I was in the saddle, you may have some notion of the reason of my assent to this extraordinary proposition. Nor will I mention the doubts I had as to the feasibility of the execution of this very novel proposal, except to say that I knew this morning, that our larder was low; — not to put too fine a point upon it, that we had nothing but some potatoes and sugar, and coffee in the world. And I may as well say here, that of such, in scant proportions, would have been our repast, had it not been for the riding of miles by two persons, one an officer, to procure supplies, — and they only succeeded in getting some few chickens, some butter, and one huge loaf of bread, which last was bought of a soldier, because he had grown faint in carrying it, and was afterwards rescued with much difficulty, and after a long race from a four-footed hog, which had got hold of and had actually eaten a part of, it. "There is a divinity," &c.[55]

Suffice it, this very ingenious and unheard of contemplated proceeding, first announced by the General, was accepted and at once undertaken by his Staff.[56] Of the absolute quality of what we had to eat, I could not pretend to judge, — but I think an unprejudiced person would have said of the bread, that it was good, — so of the potatoes, before they were boiled; of the chickens, he would have questioned their age, but they were large and in good *running* orders, the toast was good, and the butter, — there were those who when coffee was given them, called for tea, and *vice versa,* and were so ungracious as to suggest that the water that was used in both, might have come from near a barn. Of course it did not. We all came down to the little peach orchard where we had stayed last night, and wonderful to see and tell, ever mindful of our needs, had it all ready, had our faithful John. There was an enormous pan of stewed chickens, and the potatoes, and toast, all hot, and the bread and the butter, and tea, and coffee.

There was satisfaction derived from just naming them all over. We called John an angel, and he snickered and said, he *"knowed"* we'd come. Gnl. Hancock is of course invited to partake, and without delay we commence operations. — Stools are not very numerous, — two in all — and these the

---

[55] *There's a divinity that shapes our ends,*
Rough-hew them how we will.
WILLIAM SHAKESPEARE, *Hamlet,* Act V, Scene II.
[56] For a different account of this luncheon, see Gibbon, *Personal Recollections,* 146.

two generals have by common consent. — Our table was the
top of a mess-chest, — by this the Generals sat, — the rest of
us sat upon the ground, cross-legged like the picture of a smoking Turk, and held our plates upon our laps. How delicious
was the stewed chicken. — I had a cucumber pickle in my
saddle bags, — the last of a lunch left there two or three days
ago, — which George brought, and I had half of it. We were
just well at it, when Genl. Meade rode down to us from the
line, accompanied by one of his Staff, and by Gnl. Gibbons
[*sic*] invitation they dismounted and joined us. For the General commanding the Army of the Potomac, George, by an
effort worthy of the person and the occasion, finds an empty
cracker box for a seat. — The Staff officer must sit upon the
ground with the rest of us. — Soon Generals Newton and
Pleasonton, each with an Aide, arrive. By an almost super-
human effort a roll of blankets is found, which, upon a pirtch,[57]
is long enough to seat these Generals both, and room is made
for them. — The Aides sit with us. And fortunate to relate,
there was enough cooked for us all, and from Gnl. Meade to
the youngest 2nd Lieutenant we all had a most hearty, and
well relished dinner. Of the "past" we were "secure."[58] The
Generals ate, and after lighted cigars, and under the flickering
shade of a very small tree, discoursed of the incidents of yesterday's battle, and of the probabilities of to-day. Gnl. Newton humorously spoke of Gnl. Gibbon as "this young North-
Carolinian," and how he was becoming arrogant and above
his position because he commanded a Corps. Gnl. Gibbon
retorted by saying that Gnl. Newton had not been long enough
in such a command, only since yesterday, to enable him to
judge of such things. Gnl. Meade still thought that the enemy would attack his left again to day, towards evening; but
he was ready for them, — Gnl. Hancock, that the attack would

---

[57] While this word is not "pinch," as printed in WHC, it is
too illegible to be certain of the above reading.
[58] "The past, at least, is secure." DANIEL WEBSTER, Second Reply
to Hayne, January 26, 1830.

be upon the position of the 2nd Corps. It was mentioned that Gnl. Hancock would again resume[59] command of the 2nd Corps, from that time, so that Gnl. Gibbon would again return to the 2nd Division.

Gnl. Meade spoke of the Provost Guards, that they were good men, and that it would be better to-day to have them in the ranks,[60] than to stop straggls [sic] and skulkers, as these latter would be good for but little even in the ranks; and so he gave the order that all the Provost Guards should at once temporarily rejoin their Regiments. Then Gnl. Gibbon called up Capt. [Wilson B.] Farrel[l], 1st Minn. who commanded the Provost Guard of his division, and directed him, for that day, to join the regiment. "Very well, sir," said the Captain, as he touched his hat, and turned away. He was a quiet excellent gentleman, and through [sic] soldier. I knew him well, and esteemed him. I never saw him again. He was killed in two or three hours from that time, and over half of his splendid company, were either killed or wounded.

And so the time passed on, each General now and then dispatching some order or message by an officer or orderly, until about half past twelve, when all the Generals, one by one, first Gnl. Meade, rode off their several ways. And Genl. Gibbon and his Staff, alone remained.

We dozed in the heat, and lolled upon the ground, with half open eyes. Our horses were hitched to the trees, munching some oats. A great lull rests upon all the field. Time was heavy; — and for want of something better to do, I yawned and looked at my watch; — it was five minutes before one o'clock. I returned my watch to its pocket, and thought possibly that I might go to sleep, and stretched myself upon the ground accordingly. *"Ex uno disce omnes."*[61] My atitude

---

[59] "Assume" in WHC.

[60] Both here and later in the sentence, WHC prints this word as "works."

[61] "From one you may learn all."

[*sic*] and purpose were those of the General and the rest of the staff.

What sound was that? — There was no mistaking it! — The distinct sharp sound of one of the enemy's guns, square over to the front, caused us to open our eyes and turn them in that direction, when we saw directly above the crest the smoke of the bursting shell, and heard its noise. — In an instant, before a word was spoken, as if that was the signal gun for general work, loud, startling, booming, the report of gun after gun, in rapid succession, smote our ears, and their shells plunged down and exploded all around us. — We sprang to our feet. — In briefest time the whole Rebel line to the West, was pouring out its thunder and its iron upon our devoted crest. The wildest confusion for a few moments obtained among us. The shells came bursting all about. — The servants ran terror-stricken for dear life and disappeared. — The horses, hitched to the trees or held by the slack hands of orderlies, neighed out in fright, and broke away and plunged riderless through the fields. The General at the first, had snatched his sword, and started on foot for the front. I called for my horse; no body responded. I found him tied to a tree near by, eating oats, with an air of the greatest composure, which under the circumstances, even then struck me as exceedingly ridiculous. — He alone of all beasts or men near, was cool. I am not sure but that I learned a lesson then from a horse. Anxious alone for his oats, while I put on the bridle and adjusted the halter, he delayed me by keeping his head down; so I had time to see one of the horses of our mess-wagon struck and torn by a shell; — the pair plunge, — the driver has lost the rein, — horses, driver, and wagon go into a heap by a tree. — Two mules close at hand, packed with boxes of ammunition, are knocked all to pieces by a shell. — Gnl. Gibbon's groom has just mounted his horse, and is starting to take the General's to him, when the flying iron meets him and tears open his breast, — he drops dead, and the horses gallop away. No more than a minute since the first shot was fired, and I am mounted and riding after the General. The mighty din that now rises to heaven and shakes the earth, is not all of it the voice of the rebellion; for our guns, the guardian lions of the crest, quick to awake when danger comes, have opened their fiery jaws, and begun to roar, — the great hoarse roar of battle. I overtake the General half way up to the line, — before we reach the crest his horse is brought by an orderly, — leaving our horses just behind a sharp declivity of the ridge, on foot we go up among the Batteries. How the long streams of fire spout from the guns, — how the rifled shells hiss, — how the smoke deepens and rolls! But where is the Infantry? Has it vanished in smoke? Is this a nightmare, or a juggler's devilish trick? — All too real. The men of the Infantry have seized their arms, and behind their works, behind every rock, in every ditch, wherever there is any shelter, they hug the ground, silent, quiet, unterrified, little harmed. The enemy's guns now in action, are in position at their front of the woods along the second ridge, that I have before mentioned, and towards their right, behind a small crest in the open field, where we saw the flags this morning. Their line is some two miles long, concave on the side towards us, and their range is from one thousand to eighteen hundred yards. A hundred and twenty-five Rebel guns, we estimate, are now active, firing twenty-four pound, twenty, twelve and ten pound projectiles, solid shot and shells, spherical, conical, spiral. The enemy's fire is chiefly concentrated upon the position of the 2nd Corps. From the Cemetery to Round Top, with over a hundred guns, and to all parts of the enemy's line, our Batteries reply, of twenty and ten pound Parrotts, ten pound rifled Ordnances and twelve pound Napoleons, using projectiles as various in shape and name as those of the enemy.[62] Capt. Hazard, commanding the Artillery Brigade of the 2nd Corps, was vigilant among the Batteries of his command, and they were all doing well.

---

[62] The total number of guns involved on both sides of this great cannonade was 170 to 179 for the Confederates against about 118 along the shorter Union line. Coddington, *Gettysburg*, 486, 497.

All was going on satisfactorily. We had nothing to do, therefore, but to be observers of the grand spectacle of battle. Capt.
[Francis] Wessels, Judge Advocate of the Division, now joined
us, and we sat down just behind the crest, close to the left
of Cushing's Battery, to bide our time, to see, to be ready to
act, when the time should come, which might be at any moment. Who can describe such a conflict as is raging around
us! To say that it was like a summer storm, with the crash
of thunder, the glare of lightning, the shrieking of the wind,
and the clatter of hail-stones, would be weak. The thunder
and lightning of these two hundred and fifty guns, and their
shells, whose smoke darkens the sky, are incessant, all per-
vading, in the air above our heads, on the ground at our feet,
remote, near, deafening, ear-piercing, astounding; and these
hail-stones, are massy iron charged with exploding fire. And
there is little of human interest in a storm; — it is an absorbing element of this. You may see flame and smoke, and hurrying men, and human passion, at a great conflagration; but
they are all earthly, and nothing more. These guns are great
infuriate demons, not of the earth, whose mouths blaze with
smoky tongues of living fire, and whose murky breath, sulphur-
laden, rolls around them and along the ground, the smoke
of Hades. These grimy men, rushing, shouting, their souls
in phrenzy, plying the dusky globes, and the igniting spark, are
in their league, and but their willing ministers. We thought,
that at the second Bull Run, at the Antietam, and at Fredericksburg on the 11th of December, we had heard heavy
cannonading; — they were but holy day salutes compared with
this. Besides the great ceaseless roar of the guns, which was
but the background of the others, a million various minor
sounds engaged the ear. The projectiles shriek long and sharp,
— they hiss, — they scream, — they growl, — they sputter, —
all sounds of life and rage; and each has its different note, and
all are discordant. Was ever such a chaos[63] of sound before.

---

[63] "Chorus" in WHC.

We note the effect of the enemy's fire among the Batteries, and along the crest. We see the solid shot strike axle, or pole, or wheel, and the tough iron and heart of oak snap and fly like straws. The great oaks there by Woodruff's guns heave down their massy branches with a crash, as if the lightning had smote them. The shells swoop down among the Battery horses, standing there apart, — a half a dozen horses start, — they tumble, — their legs stiffen, — their vitals and blood smear the ground. And these shot and shells have no respect for men either. We see the poor fellows hobbling back from the crest, or unable to do so, pale and weak lying on the ground, with the mangled stump of an arm or leg, dripping their life blood away, or with a cheek torn open, or a shoulder smashed. And many, alas! hear not the roar as they stretch upon the ground, with upturned faces, and open eyes, though a shell should burst at their very ears. Their ears, and their bodies this instant are only mud. We saw them but a moment since there among the flame, with brawny arms and muscles of iron, wielding the rammer and pushing home the cannon's plethoric load.

Strange freaks these round shot play! — We saw a man coming up from the rear with his full knapsack on, and some canteens of water held by the straps, in his hands. He was walking slowly and with apparent unconcern, though the iron hailed around him. A shot struck the knapsack, and it and its contents flew thirty yards in every direction, — the knapsack disappeared like an egg, thrown spitefully against a rock. The soldier stopped, and turned about in puzzled surprise, — put up one hand to his back to assure himself that the knapsack was not there, and then walked slowly on again unharmed, with not even his coat torn. — Near us was a man crouching behind a small disintegrated stone, which was about the size of a common water-bucket. He was bent up, with his face to the ground, in the attitude of a pagan worshipper, before his idol. It looked so absurd to see him thus, that I went and said to him: "Do not lie there like a toad. — Why not go to your regiment and be a man!" He turned up his face with a stupid, terrified look upon me, and then without a word turned his nose again to the ground. An orderly that was with me at the time, told me a few moments later, that a shot struck the stone, smashing it in a thousand fragments, but did not touch the man, though his head was not six inches from the stone.

All the projectiles that came near us were not so harmless. Not ten yards away from us, a shell burst among some small bushes, where sat three or four orderlies holding horses; — two of the men and one horse were killed. Only a few yards off a shell exploded over an open limber box in Cushing's Battery; and almost at the same instant, another shell, over a neighboring box. In both the boxes the ammunition blew up with an explosion that shook the ground, throwing fire, and splinters, and shells far into the air and all around, and destroying several men. We watched the shells bursting in the air, as they came hissing in all directions. Their flash was a bright gleam of lightning radiating from a point, giving place in the thousandth part of a second, to a small, white, puffy cloud, like a fleece of the lightest, whitest wool. These clouds were very numerous. We could not often see the shell before it burst; but some times, as we faced towards the enemy, and looked above our heads, the approach would be heralded by a prolonged hiss, which always seemed to me to be a line of something tangible, terminating in a black globe, distinct to the eye, as the sound had been to the ear. The shell would seem to stop; and hang suspended in the air an instant, and then vanish in fire and smoke and noise. We saw the missels [sic] tear and plow the ground. All in rear of the crest for a thousand yards, as well as among the Batteries, was the field of their blind fury. Ambulances, passing down the Taney town Road, with wounded men, were struck. — The Hospitals near this road were riddled. — The house which was Gnl. Meade's Head Quarters was shot through several times; and a great many horses of officers and orderlies were lying dead around it. Riderless horses, galloping madly through the fields, were brought up, or down, rather, by these invisible horse-tamers, and they would not run any more. Mules with ammunition, pigs wallowing about, cows in the pastures, whatever was animate or inanimate, in all this broad range, were no exception to their blind havoc. The percussion shells would strike, and thunder, and scatter the earth and their whistling fragments; the Whitworth bolts would pound, and ricochet, and howl[64] far away sputtering, with the sound of a mass of hot iron plunged in water; and the great solid shot would smite the unresisting ground with a sounding "thud," as the strong boxer crashes his iron fist into the jaws of his unguarded adversary. Such were some of the sights and sounds of this great iron battle of missels [sic]. Our Artillery men upon the crest, budged not an inch, nor intermitted, but, though caisson and limber were smashed, and guns dismantled, and men and horses, killed, there amidst smoke and sweat, they gave back without grudge or loss of time in the sending, in kind whatever the enemy sent, globe, and cone, and bolt, hollow or solid, — an iron greeting to the rebellion, — the compliments of the wrathful Republic. An hour has droned its flight, since first the war began, — there is no sign of weariness or abatement on either side. So long it seemed, that the din and crashing around began to appear the normal condition of nature there, and fighting, man's element. The General proposed to go among the men, and over to the front of the Batteries, so at about two o'clock he and I started. We went along the lines of the Infantry; as they lay there flat upon the earth, a little to the front of the Batteries. — They were suffering little, and were quiet, and cool. How glad we were that the enemy were no better gunners, and that they cut the shell fuses too long. To the question asked the men: "What do you think of this?" — the replies would be: "O, this is bully," — "We are getting to like it," — "O, we don't mind this." And so they lay under

---

[64] "Bowl" in WHC.

the heaviest cannonade that ever shook the continent, and among them a thousand times more jokes, than heads, were cracked.

We went down in front of the line some two hundred yards, and as the smoke had a tendency to settle upon a higher plain than where we were, we could see near the ground distinctly all over the field, as well back to the crest where were our own guns, as to the opposite ridge where were those of the enemy. No Infantry was in sight save the skirmishers, and they stood silent, and motionless, — a row of gray posts through the field on one side, confronted by another of blue. Under the grateful shade of some elm trees, where we could see much of the field, we made seats of the ground, and sat down. Here all the more repulsive features of the fight were unseeen by reason of the smoke. Man had arranged the scenes, and for a time had taken part in the great drama; but at last as the plot thickened, conscious of his littleness, and inadequacy to the mighty part, he had stepped aside and given place to more powerful actors. So it seemed; for we could see no men about the Batteries. On either crest we could see the great flaky streams of fire, and they seemed numberless, of the opposing guns, and their white banks of swift convolving smoke; but the sound of the discharges was drowned in the universal ocean of sound. Over all the valley, the smoke, a sulphury arch, stretched its lurid span; and through it always, shrieking on their unseen courses, thickly flew a myriad iron deaths.

With our grim horizon on all sides round toothed thick with Battery flame, under that dissonant canopy of warring shells, we sat, and saw,[65] and heard in silence. What other expression had we that was not mean, for such an awful universe of battle?

A shell struck our breast work of rails up in sight of us, and a moment afterwards we saw the men bearing some of their wounded companions away from the same spot; and dir-

---

[65] WHC omits the two words preceding.

ectly two men from there came down toward where we were, and sought to get shelter in an excavation near by where many dead horses, killed in yesterday's fight, had been thrown. General Gibbon said to these men, more in a tone of kindly expostulation, than of command: "My men, do not leave your ranks to try to get shelter here. All these matters are in the hands of God, and nothing that you can do will make you safer in one place than in another." — The men went quietly back, to the line, at once. The General then said to me: "I am not a member of any church, but I have always had a strong religious feeling; and so in all these battles I have always believed that I was in the hands of God; and that I should be unharmed or not, according to his will. For this reason, I think it is, I am always ready to go where duty calls, no matter how great the danger." Half past two o'clock, an hour and a half since the commencement, and still the cannonade did not in the least abate; but soon thereafter some signs of weariness, and a little slackening of fire began to be apparent upon both sides. First we saw Brown's Battery retire from the line, too feeble for further battle. Its position was a little to the front of the line. Its commander was wounded, and many of its men were so, or worse, — some of its guns had been disabled, — many of its horses killed — its ammunition was nearly expended. Other Batteries in similar case, had been withdrawn before, to be replaced by fresh ones, and some were withdrawn afterwards. Soon after the Battery named had gone, the General and I started to return, passing towards the left of the Division, and crossing the ground where the guns had stood. The stricken horses were numerous, and the dead and wounded men lay about, and as we passed these latter, their low piteous call for water would invariably come to us, if they had yet any voice left. I found canteens of water near, — no difficult matter where a battle has been — and held them to livid lips, and even in the faintness of death, the eagerness to drink told of their terrible torture of thirst. But we must pass on. Our Infantry was still unshaken, and in all the cannonade suffered very little. — The Batteries had been handled much more severely. I am unable to give any figures. A great number of horses had been killed, — in some Batteries more than half of all. Guns had been dismounted, — a great many caissons, limbers, and carriages had been destroyed, — and usually from ten to twenty-five men to each Battery had been struck, at least along our part of the crest. All together the fire of the enemy had injured us much, both in the modes that I have stated, and also by exhausting our ammunition, and fouling our guns, so as to render our Batteries unfit for further immediate use. The scenes that met our eyes on all hands among the Batteries were fearful. All things must end, and the great cannonade was no exception to the general law of earth. In the number of guns active at one time, and in the duration and rapidity of their fire, this Artillery engagement, up to this time must stand alone and pre-eminent in this war. — It has not been often, or many times, surpassed, in the battles of the world. Two hundred and fifty guns, at least, rapidly fired, for two mortal hours! Cypher out the number of tons of gunpowder and iron that made those two hours hideous!

Of the injury of our fire upon the enemy, except the facts that ours was the superior position, if not better served and constructed Artillery, and that the enemy's Artillery, hereafter during the battle, was almost silent, we know little.[66] Of course during the fight we often saw the enemy's caissons explode, and the trees sent,[67] by our shot, crashing about his ears, but we can from these alone infer but little of general results. At three o'clock almost precisely the last shot hummed, and bounded, and fell, and the cannonade was over. The purpose of General Lee in all this fire of his guns, — we know it now, we did not at the time, so well — was to disable our Artillery and break up our Infantry, upon the position of the

[66] The Confederates had almost exhausted their batteries' ammunition and had little in reserve. Coddington, *Gettysburg*, 499.
[67] "Rent" in WHC.

2nd Corps, so as to render them less an impediment to the
sweep of his own Brigades and Divisions over our crest, and
through our lines. He probably supposed our Infantry was
massed behind the crest, and the Batteries; and hence his fire
was so high, and his fuses to the shells were cut so long, too
long. The Rebel General failed in some of his plans in this
behalf, as many Generals have failed before, and will again.
The Artillery fight over, men began to breathe more freely,
and to ask: — "What next I wonder?" The Battery men were
among their guns, some leaning to rest, and wipe the sweat
from their sooty faces, — some were handling ammunition
boxes, and replenishing those that were empty. Some Batteries
from the Artillery Reserve were moving up to take the places
of the disabled ones: — the smoke was clearing from the crests.
— There was a pause between acts, with the curtain down, soon
to rise upon the great final act, and catastrophe of Gettysburg.
We had passed by the left of the 2nd Division, coming from
the 1st, — when we crossed the crest, the enemy was not in
sight, and all was still, — we walked slowly along in rear of
the troops, by the ridge cut off now from a view of the enemy,
or his position, and were returning to the spot where we had
left our horses. Gnl. Gibbon had just said that he inclined
to the belief that the enemy was falling back, and that the
cannonade was only one of his noisy modes of covering the
movement. I said that I thought that fifteen minutes would
show that, by all his bowling, the Rebel did not mean retreat.
We were near our horses when we noticed Brig. Gnl. [Henry
J.] Hunt, Chief of Artillery of the Army, near Woodruff[']s
Battery, swiftly moving about on horseback, and apparently
in a rapid manner giving some orders about the guns. Thought
we, what could this mean! In a moment afterwards we met
Capt. Wessels, and the orderlies who had our horses, — they
were on foot leading the horses. — Capt. Wessels was pale,
and he said, excited: "General, they say the enemy's Infantry is
advancing." We sprang into our saddles — a score of bounds

brought us upon the all-seeing crest. To say that none[68] grew
pale and held their breath at what we and they there saw, would
not be true. Might not six thousand men be brave and without shade of fear, and yet, before a hostile eighteen thousand,[69]
armed, and not five minutes' march away, turn ashy white?
None on that crest now need be told that *the enemy is advancing*. Every eye could see his legions, an overwhelming,
resistless tide of an ocean of armed men, sweeping upon us!
Regiment after Regiment, and Brigade after Brigade, move
from the woods, and rapidly take their places in the lines
forming the assault. Pickett's proud Division, with some additional troops, hold their right; Pettigrew's, (Heth's) their
left.[70] The first line at short interval, is followed by a second,
and that a third succeeds; and columns between support the
lines. More than half a mile their front extends; — more than
a thousand yards the dull gray masses deploy, man touching
man, rank pressing rank, and line supporting line. Their red
flags wave; their horsemen gallop up and down; the arms of
eighteen thousand men, barrel and bayonet, gleam in the sun,
a sloping forrest [*sic*] of flashing steel. Right on they move,
as with one soul, in perfect order, without impediment of
ditch, or wall, or stream, over ridge and slope, through orchard, and meadow, and cornfield, magnificent, grim, irresist-
ible. All was orderly and still upon our crest, — no noise,
and no confusion. The men had little need of commands, for
the survivors of a dozen battles knew well enough what this
array in front portended; and already in their places, they
would be prepared to act when the right time should come.

---

[68] WHC reads "men."
[69] A careful scholarly calculation puts the strength of the Confederate assaulting force at 13,500 officers and men. Coddington,
Gettysburg, 462, 777. Another well-reasoned reckoning puts it at
11,900. George R. Stewart, *Pickett's Charge: A Microhistory of the
Final Attack at Gettysburg, July 3, 1863* (Boston, 1959), 172–73.
[70] James J. Pettigrew led the division of the wounded Henry
Heth in the assault. WHC here substitutes "Worth" for the latter's name.

The click of the locks as each man raised the hammer, to feel with his finger that the cap was on the nipple; the sharp jar as a musket touched a stone upon the wall when thrust, in aiming, over it; and the clinking[71] of the iron axles, as the guns were rolled up by hand a little further to the front, were quite all the sounds that could be heard. Cap-boxes were slid around to the front of the body; — cartridge-boxes opened; — officers opened their pistol holsters. Such preparation, little more, was needed. The trefoil flags, colors of the Brigades and Divisions, moved to their places in rear; but along the lines in front, the grand old ensign that first waved in battle at Saratoga, in 1777, and which these people coming would rob of half its stars, stood up, and the west-wind kissed it as the sergeants sloped its lance towards the enemy. — I believe that not one above whom it then waved, but blessed his God that he was loyal to it, and whose heart did not swell with pride towards it, as the emblem of the Republic, before that treason's flaunting rag in front. — Gnl. Gibbon rode down the lines, cool and calm, and in an unimpassioned voice he said to the men: "Do not hurry, men, and fire too fast; — let them come up close before you fire, and then aim low, and steadily." The coolness of their General was reflected in the faces of his men. Five minutes had elapsed since first the enemy had emerged from the woods, — no great space of time, surely, if measured by the usual standards by which men estimate duration, — but it was long enough for us to note and weigh some of the elements of mighty moment, that surrounded us: — the disparity of numbers between the assailants and the assailed; — that few as were our numbers, we could not be supported or reinforced until support would not be needed, or would be too late; — that upon the ability of the two trefoil Divisions to hold the crest, and repel the assault, depended not only their own safety or destruction, but also the honor of the Army of the Potomac, and defeat or victory at Gettysburg. — Should

---

[71] "Clicking" in WHC.

these advancing men pierce our line, and become the entering wedge, driven home, that would sever our army asunder, what hope would there be afterwards, and where the blood-earned fruits of yesterday? — It was long enough for the Rebel storm to drift across more than half the space that had at first separated it from us. None, or all, of these considerations either depressed or elevated us — they might have done the former, had we been timid, the latter, had we been confident and vain, — but, we were there waiting, and ready to do our duty; — that done, results could not dishonor us.

Our skirmishers open a spattering fire along the front, and, fighting, retire upon the main line, — the first drops, the heralds of the storm, sounding on our windows. Then the thunders of our guns, first Arnold's then Cushing's, and Woodruff's and the rest, shake and reverberate again through the air, and their sounding shells smite the enemy. — The General said I had better go and tell General Meade of this advance; — to gallop to Gnl. Meade's Head Quarters, — to learn there that he had changed them to another part of the field, — to dispatch to him, by the Signal Corps, in Gnl. Gibbon's name the message: "The enemy is advancing his Infantry in force upon my front," —and to be again upon the crest, were but the work of a minute. — All our available guns are now active, and from the fire of shells, as the range grows shorter and shorter, they change to shrapnel, and from shrapnel to canister; but in spite of shells, and shrapnel, and canister, without wavering or halt, the hardy lines of the enemy continue to move on. The Rebel guns make no reply to ours; and no charging shout rings out to-day, as is the Rebel wont; but the courage of these silent men amid our shot, seems not to need the stimulus of other noise. The enemy's right flank sweeps near Stanard's [sic] bushy crest, and his concealed Vermonters rake it with a well delivered fire of musketry; — the gray lines do not halt or reply, but withdrawing a little from that extreme, they still move on. And so across all that broad open ground they have come, nearer and nearer, nearly half the

way with our guns bellowing in their faces, until now a hundred yards, no more, divide our ready left, from their advancing
right. The eager men there are impatient to begin. — Let them.
— First Harrow's breast-works flame, — then Hall's, — then
Webb's.[72] As if our bullets were the fire-coals that touched
off their muskets, the enemy in front halts, and his countless
level barrels blaze back upon us. — The 2nd Division is struggling in battle; — the rattling storm soon spreads to the right,
and the blue trefoils are vieing [sic] with the white. All along
each hostile front, a thousand yards, with narrowest space between, the vollies [sic] blaze and roll; as thick the sound as
when a summer hailstorm pelts the city roofs; as thick the fire
as when the incessant lightning fringes a summer cloud. —
When the Rebel Infantry had opened fire, our Batteries soon
became silent; and this without their fault, for they were foul
by long previous use, they were the targets of the concentrated
Rebel bullets, and some of them had expended all their canister. But they were not silent before Rhorty [sic] was killed,
Woodruff had fallen mortally wounded, and Cushing, firing
almost his last canister, had dropped dead among his guns, shot
through the head by a bullet. The conflict is left to the Infantry alone. Unable to find my General when I had returned
to the crest after transmitting his message to Genl. Meade, and
while riding in the search, having witnessed the development
of the fight, from the first fire upon the left, by the main lines,
until all of the two Divisions were furiously engaged, I gave
up hunting as useless, — I was convinced Gnl. Gibbon could not
be on the field, — I left him mounted, — I could easily have
found him now had he so remained, — but now, save myself
there was not a mounted officer near the engaged lines, — and
was riding towards the right of the 2nd Division with pur-

---

[72] Commanders of the components of the line of battle of the
2nd Division, Second Corps, named from left to right: General
William Harrow, 1st Brigade; Colonel Norman J. Hall, 3rd Brigade; General Alexander S. Webb, 2nd (or "Philadelphia") Brigade.

pose to stop there, as the most eligible position to watch the
further progress of the battle, there to be ready to take part,
according to my own notions, whenever and wherever occasion
was presented. The conflict was tremendous, but I had seen
no wavering in all our line. Wondering how long the Rebel
ranks, deep though they were, could stand our sheltered vollies [sic], I had come near my destination, when — Great Heav-
en! — were my senses mad! — the larger portion of Webb's
Brigade, — my God, it was true — there by the group of trees,
and the angles of the wall, was breaking from the cover of
their works, and without orders or reason, with no hand lifted
to check them, was falling back a fear-stricken flock of confusion! The fate of Gettysburg hung upon a spider's single
thread! — A great magnificent passion came on me at the instant, not one that overpowers and confounds, but one that
blanches the face, and sublimes every sense and faculty. My
sword that had always hung idle by my side, the sign of rank
only, in every battle, I drew bright and gleaming, the symbol
of command. Was not that a fit occasion, and these fugitives
the men on whom, to try the temper of the Solingen steel? All
rules and proprieties were forgotten all considerations of person, and danger, and safety, despised; for as I met the tide
of these rabbits, the damned red flags of the rebellion began
to thicken and flaunt along the wall they had just deserted,
and one was already waving over one of the guns of the dead
Cushing. I ordered these men to *"halt,"* and *"face about,"* and
"fire," and they heard my voice, and gathered my meaning,
and obeyed my commands. On some unpatriotic backs, of
those not quick of comprehension, the flat of my sabre fell,
not lightly; and at its touch their love of country returned;
and with a look at me as if I were the destroying angel, as I
might have become theirs, they again faced the enemy.[73] Genl.
Webb soon came to my assistance. He was on foot, but he was

---

[73] While Haskell may exaggerate the extent of the panic, sizable
parts of Webb's small brigade did fall back before the final thrust
of the Confederate charge. Coddington, *Gettysburg*, 516–17.

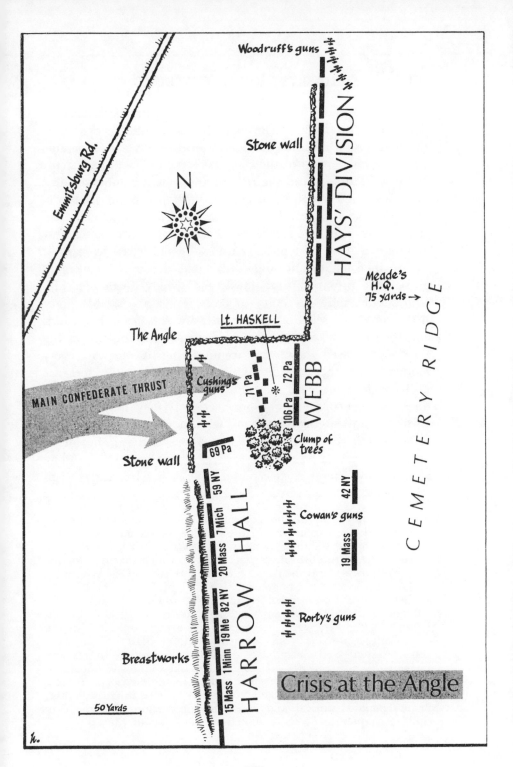

Woodruff's guns

Stone wall

HAYS' DIVISION

Emmitsburg Rd.

N

Meade's
H.Q.
75 yards →

The Angle

Lt. HASKELL

CEMETERY RIDGE

Cushing's
guns

71 Pa

72 Pa

106 Pa

WEBB

MAIN CONFEDERATE THRUST

Clump of
trees

Stone wall

69 Pa

59 NY

7 Mich

20 Mass

42 NY

Cowan's guns

19 Mass

HARROW HALL

82 NY

19 Me

1 Minn

Rorty's guns

15 Mass

Breastworks

Crisis at the Angle

50 Yards

h.

active, and did all that one could do to repair the breach, or
to avert its calamity.[74] The men that had fallen back, facing
the enemy soon regained confidence in themselves, and became
steady. This portion of the wall was lost to us, and the enemy
had gained the cover of the reverse side, where he now stormed
with fire; but Webb's men, with their bodies in part protected by the abruptness of the crest, now sent back in the enemy's faces as fierce a storm. Some scores of venturesome Rebels, that in their first push at the wall, had dared to cross at
the further angle, and those that had desecrated Cushing's
guns, were promptly shot down, and speedy death met him
who should raise his body to cross it again. At this point
little could be seen of the enemy, by reason of his cover,
and the smoke, except the flash of his muskets, and his waving
flags. Those red flags were accumulating at the wall every
moment, and they maddened us as the same color does the
bull. Webb's men are falling fast, and he is among them to
direct and encourage; but however well they may now do,
with that walled enemy in front, with more than a dozen flags
to Webb's three, it soon becomes apparet [sic] that in not many
minutes they will be overpowered, or that there will be none
alive for the enemy to overpower. Webb has but three Regi-

---

[74] Webb was a graduate of West Point and previously a staff
officer in the Army of the Potomac. He had been promoted to
general and given command of the brigade only a few days before
the battle of Gettysburg. Warner, *Generals in Blue*, 544–45. He
played a major role in rallying his brigade, which that day totaled
only 953 officers and men and suffered 494 casualties. Wounded,
he later received the Congressional Medal of Honor for his role
at Gettysburg. Coddington, *Gettysburg*, 516–18, 528, 806. Webb
did not mention Haskell in his report. *OR.*, Ser. 1, Vol. 27, Pt.
1, pp. 428–29. Afterward, however, when he was president of the
City College of New York, he read without disagreement Haskell's essay on Gettysburg. He told Haskell's brother that Frank
Haskell ". . .was one we all respected & liked and any document
bearing his name will carry great weight in the 2d Corps." Alexander S. Webb to H.M. Haskell, November 3, 1881, in Haskell Mss.,
Pennsylvania Historical and Museum Commission. See the concluding chapter for Webb's subsequent opinion of the essay.

ments, all small, the 69th, 71st, and 72nd Penn. — the 106th
Penn. except two companies, is not here to day, — and he must
have speedy assistance, or this crest will be lost. Oh, where
is Gibbon, — where is Hancock, — some General — any body,
with the power and the will to support that wasting, melting
line? — No general came, and no succor! I thought of Hays
upon the right; but from the smoke and war along his front, it
was evident that he had enough upon his hands, if he staid
the in rolling tide of the Rebels there. — Doubleday upon the
left, was too far off, and too slow, and on another occasion I
had begged him to send his idle Regiments to support another
line, battling with thrice its numbers, and this *"Old Sumpter
[sic] Hero"* had declined.[75] As a last resort I resolved to see if
[Norman J.] Hall and Harrow could not send some of their
commands to reinforce Webb. I galloped to the left in the
execution of my purpose, and as I attained the rear of Hall's
line, from the nature of the ground there, and the position of
the enemy, it was easy to discover the reason and the manner
of this gathering of Rebel flags in front of Webb. The enemy, emboldened by his success in gaining our line by the
group of trees and the angle of the wall, was concentrating all
his right against, and was further pressing, that point. There
was the stress of his assault, — there would he drive his fiery
wedge to split our line. In front of Harrow's and Hall's Brigades he had been able to advance no nearer than where he
first halted to deliver fire: and these commands had not yielded an inch. To effect the concentration before Webb, the
enemy would march the regiment on his extreme right of
each of his lines, by the left flank, to the rear of the troops,
still halted and facing to the front, and so continuing to draw
in his right, when they were all massed in the position desired, he would again face them to the front, and advance to

---

[75] Abner Doubleday, against whom Haskell here again displays
animus, was a veteran of the Sumter bombardment. Nicknamed
"Forty-eight Hours," he had a reputation for being slow and lack-
ing initiative. Warner, *Generals in Blue,* 129–30.

the storming. This was the way he made the wall before Webb's line blaze red with his battle flags; and such was the purpose there of his thick-crowding battalions.[76] — Not a moment must be lost. Col. Hall I found just in rear of his line, sword in hand, cool, vigilant, noting all that passed, and directing the battle of his Brigade. The fire was constantly diminishing now in his front, in the manner by the movement of the enemy, that I have mentioned: — drifting to the right. "How is it going?," — Col. Hall asked me as I rode up. — "Well, but Webb is hotly pressed, and must have support, or he will be over-powered. — Can you assist him?" — "Yes." — "You cannot be too quick." — "I will move my Brigade at once." — "Good." — He gave the order, and in briefest time I saw five friendly colors hurrying to the aid of the imperilled three; and each color represented true, battle-tried men, that had not turned back from Rebel fire that day nor yesterday, though their ranks were sadly thinned.[77] To Webb's Brigade, pressed back, as it had been from the wall, the distance was not great, from Hall[']s right. — The Regiments marched by the right flank. Col. Hall superintended the movement in person. Col. [Arthur F.] Devereux cooly commanded the 19th Mass. — his Major, [Edmund] Rice, had already been wounded and carried off. — Lieut. Col. [George N.] Macy of the 20th Mass. had just had his left hand shot off, and so Capt. [Henry L.] Abbott gallantly led over this fine Regiment; — the 42nd N.Y. followed their excellent Colonel, [James E.] Mallon; — Lieut. Col.

---

[76] While the "group of trees" was the Confederates' objective, it is probable that the concentration of their troops on Webb's front resulted from the convergence of attacking units rather than from the elaborate maneuvering here described. Coddington, *Gettysburg*, 502–519.

[77] In his report, Colonel Hall, the commander of the 3rd Brigade, Gibbon's Division, claimed that he himself had seen part of Webb's line give way and had brought up reinforcements. Thus, while not mentioning Haskell's request for aid, he did speak in "highest terms" of Haskell's "magnificent conduct . . . in bringing forward regiments and in nerving the troops to their work by word and fearless example." *OR*, Ser. 1, Vol. 27, Pt. 1, p. 440.

[Amos E.] Steele, [Jr.,] 7th Mich. had just been killed, and this Regiment, and the handful of the 59th N.Y. followed their colors. The movement, as it did, attracting the enemy's fire, and executed in haste, as it must be, was difficult; but in reasonable time, and in order that is serviceable, if not regular, Hall's men are fighting gallantly side by side with Webb's, before the all important point. I did not stop to see all this movement of Hall's; but from him I went at once further to the left, to the 1st Brigade. — Gnl. Harrow I did not see,[78] but his fighting men would answer my purpose as well. The 19th Me., the 15th Mass., the 82nd N.Y.,[79] and the shattered old thunderbolt, the 1st Minn. — poor Farrell was dying there upon the ground, where he had fallen, — all men that I could find, I took over to the right at the *double quick*. As we were moving to, and near, the other Brigades of the Division, from my position on horseback, I could see that the enemy's right, under Hall's fire was beginning to stagger and to break. "See," I said to the men, "see the *'chivalry,'* See the gray-backs run!" The men saw, and as they swept to their places by the side of Hall's and opened fire, they roared; and this in a manner that said more plainly than words, — for the deaf could have seen it in their faces, and the blind could have heard it in their voices, — *the crest is safe.*

The whole Division concentrated, and changes of position, and new phases, as well on our part, as on that of the enemy, having as indicated occurred, for the purpose of showing the exact present posture of affairs, some further description is necessary. Before the 2nd Division the enemy is massed, the main bulk of his force covered by the ground that slopes to his rear, with his front at the stone wall. Between his front and us extends the very apex of the crest. All there are left of the White Trefoil Division, — yesterday morning there were

---

[78] Harrow, however, evidently saw Haskell, for in his report he stated that the latter "greatly distinguished himself by his constant exertion in the most exposed places." *Ibid.,* p. 421.
[79] WHC has "32nd N.Y."

three thousand eight hundred; — this morning there were less than three thousand; — at this moment there are somewhat over two thousand; — twelve Regiments in three Brigades, are below, or behind the crest, in such a position that by the exposure of the head and upper part of the body, above the crest, they can deliver their fire in the enemy's faces along the top of the wall. By reason of the disorganization incidental, in Webb's Brigade, to his men's having broken and fallen back, as mentioned, in the two other Brigades, to their rapid and difficult change of position under fire, and in all the Division, in part, to severe and continuous battle, formation of Companies, and Regiments in regular ranks is lost; but commands, Companies, Regiments, and Brigades, are blended and intermixed, — an irregular, extended mass, — men enough, if in order, to form a line of four or five ranks along the whole front of the Division. The twelve flags of the Regiments wave defiantly at intervals along the front; at the stone wall, at unequal distances from ours, of forty, fifty, or sixty yards, stream nearly double this number of the battle flags of the enemy. These changes accomplished on either side, and the concentration complete, although no cessation or abatement in the general din of conflict since the commencement had at any time been appreciable, now it was as if a new battle, deadlier, stormier than before had sprung from the body of the old, — a young Phenix of Combat, whose eyes stream lightning, shaking his arrowy wings over the yet glowing ashes of his progenitor. The jostling swaying lines on either side boil, and roar, and dash their flamy spray, two hostile billows of a fiery ocean. Thick flashes stream from the wall; — thick vollies [*sic*] answer from the crest. No threats or expostulation now; — only example and encouragement. All depths of passion are stirred, and all combattive [*sic*][80] fire, down to their deep foundations. Individuality is drowned in a sea of clamor; and timid men, breathing the breath of the multitude, are brave. The frequent

---

[80] WHC has "combatives."

dead and wounded lie where they stagger and fall; — there is no humanity for them now, and none can be spared to care for them. The men do not cheer, or shout, — they growl; and over that uneasy sea, heard with the roar of musketry, sweeps the muttered thunder of a storm of growls. Webb, Hall, Devereux, Mallon, Abbott, among the men where all are heros [sic], are doing deeds of note. Now the loyal wave rolls up as if it would overleap its barrier, the crest, — pistols flash with the muskets. — "Forward to the wall,"[81] is answered by the Rebel counter-command, "Steady, men," — and the wave swings back. — Again it surges, and again it sinks. These men of Pennsylvania, on the soil of their own homesteads, the first and only to flee the wall, must be the first to storm it. "Major —— *lead* your men over the crest, — they will follow." "By the tactics I understand my place is in rear of the men." "Your pardon, sir; I see *your* place is in rear of the men. I thought you were fit to lead." — "Capt Suplee[82] come on with your men." ["]Let me first stop this fire in the rear, or we shall be hit by our own men." "Never mind the fire in the rear; let us take care of this in front first." — "Sergeant forward with your color. Let the Rebels see it close to their eyes once more before they die." The Color Sergeant of the 72 Pa. grasping the stump of the severed lance in both his hands, waved the flag above his head, and rushed towards the wall. — "Will you see your color storm the wall alone!" One man only starts to follow. Almost half way to the wall, down go color bearer

---

[81] WHC begins this sentence with "My," thus attributing the command to Haskell and, by implication, perhaps the following quotations as well. While this word appears in the original manuscript, it is inserted above a caret mark in what appear to be different handwriting and ink. Thus, like other changes, it is probably the work of Harvey Haskell, the original editor.

[82] While WHC erroneously renders this as "Sapler," Haskell almost certainly refers to Captain Andrew C. Suplee of the 72nd Pennsylvania, whom the regimental and brigade commanders mentioned favorably in their reports. *OR*, Ser. 1, Vol. 27, pt. 1, pp. 427, 433.

and color to the ground, — the gallant Sergeant is dead. —
The line springs, — the crest of the solid ground, with a great
roar, heaves forward its maddened load, men, arms, smoke,
fire, a fighting mass; — it rolls to the wall; — flash meets flash;
— the wall is crossed; — a moment ensues of thrusts, yells,
blows, shots, and undistinguishable conflict, followed by a
shout, universal, that makes the welkin ring again; and — the
last and bloodiest fight of the great battle of Gettysburg is
ended and won.

Many things cannot be described by pen or pencil, — such
a fight is one. Some hints and incidents may be given but
a description, a picture, never. From what is told, the ima-
gination may for itself construct the scene; otherwise he who
never saw, can have no adequate idea of what such a battle
is.

When the vortex of battle passion had subsided, hopes,
fears, rage, joy, of which the maddest and the noisiest was
the last, and we were calm enough to look about us, we saw,
that as with us, the fight with the 3d Division was ended; and
that in that Division was a repetition of the scenes immediately about us. — In that moment the judgment almost refused to credit the senses. Are these abject wretches about us,
whom our men are now disarming and driving together in
flocks, the jaunty men of Pickett's Division, whose sturdy lines
and flashing arms, but a few moments, since, came sweeping
up the slope to destroy us? Are these red cloths that our men
toss about in derision, the "fiery Southern crosses," thrice ar-
dent, the battle-flags of the rebellion, that waved defiance
at the wall? We know, but so sudden has been the transition,
we yet can scarce believe.

Just as the fight was over, and the first outburst of victory
had a little subsided, when all in front of the crest was noise,
and confusion, — prisoners being collected, small parties in
pursuit of them far down into the field, flags waving, officers
giving quick, sharp commands to their men, — I stood apart
for a few moments, upon the crest, by that group of trees which

ought to be historic forever, a spectator of the thrilling scene around. Some few musket shots were still heard in the 3d Division; and the enemy's guns, almost silent since the advance of his Infantry, until the moment of his defeat, were dropping a few sullen shells among friend and foe upon the crest, — rebellion fosters such humanity. Near me, saddest sight, of the many of such a field, and not in keeping with all this noise, were mingled, alone the thick dead of Maine, and Minnesota, and Michigan, and Massachusetts, and the Empire and the Keystone states, who, not yet cold, with the blood still oozing from their death wounds, had given their lives to the country upon the stormy field, — so mingled upon that crest let their honored graves be. — Look with me, about us. — These dead have been avenged already. Where the long lines of the enemy's thousands so proudly advanced, see how thick the silent men of gray are scattered. — It is not an hour since those legions were sweeping along so grandly, — now sixteen hundred of that fiery mass, are strewn among the trampled grass, dead as the clods they load; more than seven thousand, probably eight thousand, are wounded, some there with the dead, in our hands, some fugitive far towards the woods, — among them Generals Pettigrew, [Richard B.] Garnett, [James L.] Kemper, and Armstead [sic], the last three mortally,[83] and the last one in our hands, — "Tell Gnl. Hancock," he said to Lieut. [W.G.] Mitchell, Hancock's Aide-de-Camp, to whom he handed his watch, "that I know I did my country a great wrong when I took up arms against her, for which I am sorry, but for which I cannot live to atone,"[84] — four thou-

---

[83] While Kemper's wound was not in fact fatal, he also was captured.

[84] Lewis A. Armistead, a North Carolinian and Virginian, had attended West Point and served in the Mexican War. A Confederate from the beginning of the Civil War, he had led his brigade to what would later be called "High Tide" or the "High Water Mark of the Confederacy." A few moments before he allegedly made the quoted statement to Mitchell, he had inspired his men by charging across the stone wall with his hat on his upraised sword.

sand, not wounded, are prisoners of war, — more in number
of the captured, than the captors. — Our men are still "gathering them in." Some hold up their hands, or a handkerchief,
in sign of submission; some have hugged the ground to escape
our bullets, and so are taken; few made resistance after the
first moment of our crossing the wall; some yield submissively
with good grace; some with grim, dogged aspect, showing that
but for the other alternative, they could not submit to this.
— Colonels, and all less grades of officers, in the usual proportions, are among them, and all are being stripped of their
arms. Such of them as escaped wounds and capture, are flee-
ing routed and panic-stricken, and disappearing in the woods.
Small arms, more thousands than we can count, are in our
hands, scattered over the field. And those defiant battle-flags,
some inscribed with; "1st Manassas," the numerous battles of
the Peninsula, "2nd Manassas," "South Mountain," "Sharpsburg," (our Antietam,) "Fredericksburg," "Chancellorsville,"
and many more names, our men have, and are showing about,
over thirty of them.[85]

Such was really the closing scene of the grand drama of
Gettysburg. After repeated assaults upon the right and the left,
where, and in all of which repulse had been his only success,
this persistent and presuming enemy forms his chosen troops,
the flower of his army, for a grand assault upon our center.
The manner and result of such assault have been told, — a loss
to the enemy of from twelve thousand to fourteen thousand,
killed, wounded, and prisoners, and of over thirty battle flags.
This was accomplished by not over six thousand men, with a
loss on our part of not over two thousand five hundred, killed
and wounded.[86]

Ezra J. Warner, *Generals in Gray: Lives of the Confederate Commanders* (Baton Rouge, 1959), 11–12; Coddington, *Gettysburg*, 517.
  [85] Hancock reported that the Second Corps had captured thirty-
three colors but that six had been "secreted as individual trophies."
OR, Ser. 1, Vol. 27, Pt. 1, p. 377.
  [86] Confederate casualties probably totaled about 7500 out of some
11,900 engaged. Union losses approximated 1500 out of 5750. For

Would to Heaven Gnls. Hancock and Gibbon could have stood there where I did, and have looked upon that field! It would have done two men, to whom the country owes much, good to have been with their men in that moment of victory, — to have seen the results of those dispositions which they had made, and of that splendid fighting which men schooled by their discipline, had executed. But they are both severely wounded, and have been carried from the field. One person did come then that I was glad to see there; and that was no less than Major General Meade, whom the Army of the Potomac was fortunate enough to have at that time to command it. See how a great General looked upon the field, and what he said and did, at the moment, and when he learned, of his great victory. To appreciate the incident I give, it should be borne in mind, that one coming up from the rear of the line, as did Gnl. Meade, could have seen very little of our own men, who had now crossed the crest, and although he could have heard the noise, he could not have told its occasion, or by whom made, until he had actually attained the crest. One who did not know results, so coming, would have been quite as likely to have supposed that our line there had been carried and captured by the enemy, so many gray Rebels were on the crest, as to have discovered the real truth. — Such mistake was really made by one of our own officers, as I shall relate. —

Gnl. Meade rode up, accompanied alone by his son,[87] who is his Aide-de-Camp, — an escort, if select, not large for a commander of such an army. The principal horseman was no bedizened hero of some holy day review, but he was a plain man, dressed in a serviceable summer suit of dark blue cloth, without badge or ornament, save the shoulder-straps of his grade, and a light, straight sword of a General, a General Staff, officer. He wore heavy, high top-boots and buff gauntlets;

a good discussion of the speculations and calculations behind these figures, see Stewart, *Pickett's Charge*, 172–73, 263–66, 295–97.
[87] Captain George Meade.

and his soft black felt hat was slouched down over his eyes.
His face was very white, not pale, and the lines were marked,
and earnest, and full of care. As he arrived near me, coming
up the hill, he asked in a sharp, eager voice: "How is it going
here?" "I believe, General, the enemy's attack is repulsed:"
I answered. Still approaching, and a new light began to come
in his face, of gratified surprise, with a touch of incredulity,
of which his voice was also the medium, he further asked:
"*What? is the assault entirely repulsed?*"[88] — his voice quicker
and more eager than before. "It is, Sir:" I replied. By this
time he was on the crest; and when his eye had for an instant
swept over the field, taking in just a glance of the whole, —
the masses of prisoners, — the numerous captured flags, which
the men were derisively flaunting about, — the fugitives of the
routed enemy, disappearing with the speed of terror in the
woods, — partly at what I had told him, partly at what he saw,
he said impressively, and his face was lighted: "*Thank God.*"
And then his right hand moved as if it would have caught
off his hat and waved it; but this gesture he suppressed, and
instead he waved his hand, and said "Hur-rah." The son,
with more youth in his blood, and less rank upon his shoulders,
snatched off his cap, and roared out his three "hurrahs," right
heartily. The general then surveyed the field, some minutes,
in silence. He at length asked who was in command. — He had
heard that Hancock and Gibbon were wounded, — and I told
him that Gnl. Caldwell was the senior officer of the Corps,
and Gnl. Harrow, of the Division. He asked where they were,
but before I had time to answer that I did not know, he resumed: "No matter; I will give my orders to you and you
will see them executed." He then gave direction that the troops
should be re-formed as soon as practicable, and kept in their
places, as the enemy might be mad enough to attack again;

---

[88] Meade had already learned from another officer that the Confederates had begun to turn back. Coddington, *Gettysburg*, 531.
WHC replaces "entirely" with "already."

he also gave directions concerning the posting of some reinforcements which he said would soon be there, adding: *"If
the enemy does attack, charge him in the flank, and sweep him
from the field, do you understand."* The General then, a
gratified man, galloped in the direction of his head quarters.

Then the work of the field went on. First, the prisoners
were collected and sent to the rear. "There go the men" the
Rebels were heard to say, by some of our Surgeons who were
in Gettysburg, at the time Pickett's Division marched out to
take position; "There go the men that will go through your
d——d Yankee lines, for you." A good many of them did
"go through our lines, for us," but in a very different way
from the one they intended, — not impetuous victors, sweeping
away our thin line with ball and bayonet; but crest-fallen cap-
tives, without arms, guarded by the true bayonets of the Union, with the cheers of their conquerors ringing in their ears.
There was a grim truth after all in this Rebel remark. Collected, the prisoners began their dreary march, a miserable,
melancholy stream of dirty gray to pour over the crest to our
rear. Many of the officers were well dressed, fine, proud gentlemen, such men as it would be a pleasure to meet, when the
war is over. I had no desire to exult over them, and pity and
sympathy were the general feelings of us all upon the occasion.
The cheering of our men, and the unceremonious handling of
the captured flags were probably not gratifying to the prisoners, but not intended for taunt or insult to the men, they could
take no exception to such practices. When the prisoners were
turned to the rear, and were crossing the crest, Lieut. Col.
[C. H.] Morgan, Gnl. Hancock's Chief of Staff, was conducting
a Battery from the Artillery Reserve, towards the 2nd Corps.
As he saw the men in gray coming over the hill, he said to the
officer in command of the Battery: "See up there, the enemy
has carried the crest. — See them come pouring over. — The
Old Second Corps is gone; and you had better get your Battery away from here as quickly as possible, or it will be captured." The Officer was actually giving the order to his men

to move back, when closer observation discovered that the gray backs that were coming had no arms, and then the truth flashed upon the minds of the observers. The same mistake was made by others.

In view of results of that day, — the successes of the arms of the country, would not the people of the whole country, standing then upon the crest with Gnl. Meade, have said, with him: "Thank God"?

I have no knowledge, and little notion, of how long a time elapsed from the moment the fire of the Infantry commenced, until the enemy was entirely repulsed, in this his grand assault. I judge, from the amount of fighting, and the changes of position that occurred, that probably the fight was of nearly an hour[']s duration — but I cannot tell, and I have seen none who knew. — The time seemed but a very few minutes, when the battle was over.

When the prisoners were cleared away, and order was again established upon our crest, where the conflict had impaired it, until between five and six o'clock, I remained upon the field, directing some troops to their positions, in conformity to the orders of Gnl. Meade. The enemy appeared no more in front of the 2nd Corps; but while I was engaged as I have mentioned, farther to our left some considerable force of the enemy moved out, and made show of attack. Our Artillery now in good order again, in due time opened fire, and the shells scattered the *Butternuts,* as clubs do the gray snow-birds of winter, before they came within range of our Infantry. This, save unimportant outpost firing, was the last of the battle.

Of the pursuit of the enemy, and the movements of the army subsequent to the battle, until the crossing of the Potomac by Lee, and the closing of the campaign, it is not my purpose to write. Suffice it, that on the night of the 3d of July the enemy withdrew his left, Ewell's Corps, from our front, and on the morning of the 4th we again occupied the village of Gettysburg; and on that national day victory was proclaimed to the country; — that floods of rain on that day prevented army movements of any considerable magnitude; the day being passed by our Army, in position upon the field, in burying our dead, and some of those of the enemy, and in making the movements already indicated; — that on the 5th, the pursuit of the enemy was commenced, — his dead were buried by us, — and the Corps of our Army, upon various roads, moved from the battle field.

With a statement of some of the results of the battle, as to losses, and captures, and of what I saw in riding over the field, when the army[89] was gone, my account is done.

Our own losses in "killed, wounded, and missing," I estimate at *Twenty-three thousand.*[90] Of the "missing" the larger proportion were prisoners, lost on the 1st of July. Our loss in prisoners, not wounded, probably was *four thousand.* The losses were distributed among the different Army Corps about as follows; — In the 2nd Corps, which sustained the heaviest loss of any Corps, a little over *Four thousand, five hundred,* of whom the "missing" were a mere nominal number; — in the 1st Corps, a little over *Four thousand,* of whom a good many were "missing;" — in the 3d Corps, *Four thousand,* of whom some were missing; — in the 11th Corps, nearly *Four thousand,* of whom the most were "missing"; — and the rest of the loss, to make the aggregate mentioned, was shared by the 5th, 6th, and 12th Corps, and the Cavalry. Among these the "missing" were few; and the losses of the 6th Corps and of the Cavalry, were light. I do not think the official reports will show my estimate of our losses to be far from correct, for I have taken great pains to question Staff Officers upon the subject, and have learned approximate numbers from them. We

---

[89] WHC reads "enemy" instead.
[90] Haskell's estimate of total Union losses was virtually identical with the figure of 23,049 reached by the best postwar authority, Thomas L. Livermore, in *Numbers and Losses in the Civil War in America, 1861–65* (Boston, 1900), 102.

lost no gun or flag, that I have heard of, in all the battle. — Some small arms, I suppose were lost on the 1st of July.

The enemy's loss in killed, wounded and prisoners, I estimate, at *Forty thousand*,[91] and from the following *data*, and for the following reasons: So far as I can learn we took *Ten thousand* prisoners, who were not wounded, — many more than these were captured, but several thousands of them were wounded. I have so far as practicable, ascertained the number of dead the enemy left upon the field, approximately, by getting the reports of different burying parties; — I think his dead upon the field were *Five thousand,* almost all of whom, save those killed on the 1st of July, were buried by us, — the enemy not having them in their possession. In looking at a great number of tables of killed and wounded in battles, I have found that the proportion of the killed to the wounded is as *one,* to *five,* or more than five, rarely less than five. So with the killed at the number stated, *Twenty-five thousand,* would probably be wounded. Hence the aggregate that I have mentioned.[92] I think *fourteen thousand* of the enemy, wounded, and unwounded, fell into our hands. Great numbers of his small arms, two or three guns, and forty or more — was there ever such bannered harvest? — of his regimental battle-flags, were captured by us. Some day possibly we may learn the enemy's loss, but I doubt if he will ever tell truly how many flags he did not take home with him. I have great confidence, however, in my estimates, for they have been carefully made, and after much inquiry, and with no desire or motive to overestimate the enemy's loss.

The magnitude of the Armies engaged, the number of the

---

[91] The standard estimate of Confederates losses is only 28,063. *Ibid.,* 103. Yet a modern scholar believes that the official tabulations of Southern losses are too low — both because of errors and because the Confederate "wounded" only included men declared unfit for duty by a physician. Coddington, *Gettysburg,* 808.

[92] WHC omits all the words beginning with "would" in the previous sentence through "have" in this sentence.

casualties, the object sought by the Rebel, the result, will all contribute to give Gettysburg a place among the great historic battles of the world. That General Meade's concentration was rapid, — over thirty miles a day were marched by several of the Corps, — that his position was skillfully selected, and his dispositions good, — that he fought the battle hard and well, — that his victory was brilliant and complete, I think all should admit. I cannot but regard it, as highly fortunate to us, and commendable in General Meade, that the enemy was allowed the initiative, the offensive, in the main battle; — that it was much better to allow the Rebel, for his own destruction, to come up and smash his lines and colums [sic], upon the defensive solidity of our position, than it would have been to hunt him, for the same purpose, in the woods, or to unearth him from his rifle pits. In this manner our losses were lighter, and his heavier, than if the case had been reversed. And whatever the books may say of troops' fighting the better who make the attack, I am satisfied that in this war, Americans, the Rebels, as well as ourselves, are best on the defensive. The proposition is deduceable [sic] from the battles of the war, I think, and my observation confirms it.

But men there are, who think that nothing was gained or done well in this battle, because some other General did not have the command, or because any portion of the army of the enemy was permitted to escape capture or destruction. — As if one army of a hundred thousand men could encounter another of the same numbers, of as good troops, and annihilate it! — Military men do not claim or expect this; — but the McClellan destroyers do; the doughty knights of purchasable newspaper quills; the formidable warriors from the brothels of politics; men of much warlike experience against — honesty and honor; of profound attainments in — ignorance; who have the maxims of Napoleon, whose spirit they as little understand as they do most things, to quote, to prove all things; but who, unfortunately, have much influence in the country, and with the government, and so over the army. It is very pleasant for

these people, no doubt, at safe distances from guns, in the en-
joyment of a lucrative office, or of a fraudulently obtained
government contract, surrounded by the luxuries of their own
firesides, where mud, and flooding storms, and utter weariness
never penetrate, to discourse of battles, and how campaigns
should be conducted, and armies of the enemy, destroyed; But
it should be enough, perhaps, to say, that men, here or elsewhere, who have knowledge enough of military affairs, to en-
title them to express an opinion on such matters, and accurate
information enough to realize the nature and the means of
this desired destruction of Lee's army, before it crossed the
Potomac into Virginia, will be most likely to vindicate the
Pennsylvania campaign of General Meade, and to see that he
accomplished all that could have been reasonably expected of
any General, of any army. Complaint has been, and is, made
specially against Meade, that he did not attack Lee near Williamsport, before he had time to withdraw across the river.
These were the facts concerning this matter:

The 13th of July was the earliest day when such an attack,
if practicable at all, could have been made. The time before
this, since the battle, had been spent in moving the army from
the vicinity of the field, finding something of the enemy, and
concentrating before him. On that day the army was concentrated, and in order of battle, near the turnpike that leads
from Sharpsburg, to Hagerstown, Md. the right resting at or
near the latter place, the left near Jones's Cross-roads, some
six miles in the direction of Sharpsburg, and in the following
order from left to right; the 12th Corps, the 2nd, the 5th, the
6th, the 1st, the 11th, — the 3d being in reserve behind the
2nd. The mean distance to the Potomac was some six miles, and
the enemy was between Meade and the river. The Potomac,
swelled by the recent rain, was boiling and swift, and deep,
a magnificent place to have drowned all this Rebel crew. I
have not the least doubt but that Gnl. Meade would have liked
to drown them all, if he could, but they were unwilling to be
drowned, and would fight first. To drive them into the river,

then, they must first be routed. Gnl. Meade, I believe, favored
an attack upon the enemy at that time, and he summoned his
Corps commanders to a council upon the subject. The 1st
Corps was represented by Wadsworth; the 2nd, by William
Hays;[93] the 3d, by French, the 5th, by Sykes; the 6th, by Sedgwick; the 11th, by Howard; the 12th, by Slocum; and the
Cavalry, by Pleasonton. Of the eight Generals, three, Wadsworth, Howard, and Pleasonton, were in favor of immediate
attack; and five, Hays, French, Sykes, Sedgwick, and Slocum,
were not in favor of attack until better information was obtained of the position and situation of the enemy. Of the
pros, Wadsworth only temporarily represented the 1st Corps,
in the brief absence of Newton, who, had a battle occurred,
would have commanded; Pleasonton, with his horses, would
have been a spectator only; and Howard, with the *"Brilliant
11th Corps,"* would have been trusted no where, but a safe
distance from the enemy, — not by Gnl. Howard's fault, however, for he is a good and brave man. Such was the position
of those who felt sanguinarily inclined. Of the *cons* were all
of the fighting Generals of the fighting Corps, save the 1st.
This then was the feeling of these Generals; — all, who would
have had no responsibility or part, in all probability, *hankered*
for a fight; those who would have had both part and responsibility, did not. The attack was not made. At daylight on the
morning of the 14th, strong reconnaissances from the 12th,
2nd and 5th Corps, were the means of discovering, that between the enemy, except a thousand or fifteen hundred of his
rear guard,[94] who fell into our hands, and the Army of the
Potomac, rolled the rapid unbridged river. — The Rebel,
Genl. Pettigrew was here killed. The enemy had constructed
bridges, had crossed, during all the preceding night, but so

---

[93] Hays received the command of the Corps after the wounding
of Hancock.
[94] Haskell here repeats the exaggerated Union report of this
action. The captured Confederates probably totaled 719. Coddington, *Gettysburg,* 570–71.

close were our Cavalry and Infantry upon him in the morning
that the bridges were destroyed, before his rear guard had all
crossed.

Among the considerations influencing these Generals against
the propriety of attack at that time, were probably the following: The army was wearied and worn down by four weeks of
constant forced marching or battle, in the midst of heat, mud,
and drenching showers, burdened with arms, accoutrements,
blankets, sixty to a hundred cartridges, and five to eight days'
rations. What such weariness means, few save soldiers know.
Since the battle the army had been constantly diminished by
sickness or prostration, and by more straggling than I ever saw
before. Poor fellows, they could not help it. The men were
near the point when further efficient physical exertion was
quite impossible. Even the sound of the skirmishing which
was almost constant, and the excitement of impending battle,
had no effect to arouse for an hour the exhibition of their
wonted former vigor. The enemy's loss in battle, it is true,
had been far heavier than ours; but his army was less weary
than ours, for in a given time since the first of the campaign,
it had marched far less, and with lighter loads. — These Rebels
are accustomed to hunger and nakedness, customs to which our
men do not take readily — And the enemy had straggled less,
for the men were going away from battle, and towards home;
and for them to straggle, was to go into captivity, whose end
they could not conjecture. The enemy was some where in position, in a ridgy, wooded country, abounding, in strong defensive positions, his main bodies concealed, protected by rifle-
pits and epaulements,[95] acting strictly on the defensive. His
dispositions, his positions even, with any considerable degree of
accuracy, were unknown; nor could they be known, except by
reconnaissances in such force, and carried to such extent, as

---

[95] A type of earthwork. The Confederates had indeed prepared
unusually strong field fortifications for their men and guns. Coddington, *Gettysburg*, 565–66.

would have constituted them attacks, liable to bring on at any moment a general engagement, and at places where we were least prepared, and least likely to be successful. To have had a battle there, then, Gnl. Meade would have had to attack a cunning enemy in the dark, where surprises, undiscovered rifle-pits and batteries, and unseen bodies of men might have met his forces, at every point. With his not greatly superior numbers, under such circumstances, had Gnl. Meade attacked, would he have been victorious? The vote of those Generals at the council shows their opinion, — my own is that he would have been repulsed with heavy loss, with little damage to the enemy. — Such a result might have satisfied the bloody politicians better than the end of the campaign as it was; but I think the country did not need that sacrifice of the Army of the Potomac at that time, — that enough odor of sacrifice came up to its nostrils from the 1st Fredericksburg field, to stop their snuffing for some time. — I felt the probability of defeat strongly at the time, when we all supposed that a conflict would certainly ensue; for always before a battle, — at least it so appears[96] to me, — some dim presentiment of results, some unaccountable foreshadowing, pervades the army. — I never knew the result to prove it untrue — which rests with the weight of a conviction. Whether such shadows are cause, or consequence, I shall not pretend to determine; but when, as they often are, they are general, I think they should not be wholly disregarded by the commander. I believe the Army of the Potomac is always willing, often eager, to fight the enemy, whenever, as it thinks, there is a fair chance for victory; — that it always will fight, let come victory or defeat, whenever it is ordered so to do. Of course the army, both officers, and men, had very great disappointment, and very great sorrow, that the Rebels *escaped* — so it was called, — across the river; — the disappointment was genuine, at least to the extent that disappointment is like surprise; but the sorrow, to

---

[96] WHC has "happens."

judge by looks, tones, and actions, rather than by words, was not of that deep, sable character, for which there is no balm.

Would it be an imputation upon the courage or patriotism of this army, if it was not rampant for fight at this particular time, and under the existing circumstances? Had the enemy stayed upon the left bank of the Potomac twelve hours longer, there would have been a great battle there near Williamsport, on the 14th of July.

After such digression, if such it is, I return to Gettysburg.

As good generalship is claimed for General Meade in this battle, so was the conduct of his subordinate commanders. I know, and have heard, of no bad conduct or blundering, on the part of any officer, save that of Sickles, on the 2nd of July; and that was so gross, and came so near being the cause of irreparable disaster, that I cannot discuss it with moderation. — I hope this man may never return to the Army of the Potomac, or elsewhere to a position, where his incapacity, or something worse, may be fruitless destruction to thousands again. — The conduct of the officers and men was good. — The 11th Corps behaved badly, but I have yet to learn the occasion, when, in the opinion of any save their own officers, and themselves, the men of this Corps have behaved well, on the march, or before the enemy, either under Siegel, or any other commander. — With this exception, and some minor cases, of very little consequence in the general result, our troops, whenever and wherever the enemy came, stood against their[97] storms of impassable fire. Such was the Infantry, — such the Artillery, — the Cavalry did less, but it did all that was required.

The enemy, too, showed a determination and valor worthy of a better cause; — their conduct in this battle even makes me proud of them as Americans. — They would have been victorious over any but the best of soldiers. Lee and his Generals presumed too much upon some past successes, and did not estimate how much they were due, on their part to position,

---

[97] In WHC, "them."

as at Fredericksburg, or on our part to bad generalship, as at
the 2nd Bull Run and Chancellorsville.

The fight of the 1st of July we do not, of course, claim as
a victory; — but even that probably would have resulted dif-
ferently, had Reynolds not been struck. — The success of the
enemy in the battle ended with the 1st of July. The Rebels
were joyous and jubilant, — so said our men in their hands,
and the citizens of Gettysburg, — at their achievements on that
day. Fredericksburg and Chancellorsville were remembered
by them. — They saw victory already won, or only to be
snatched from the streaming coat-tails of the 11th Corps, or
the *"raw Pennsylvania militia"* as they thought they were, when
they saw them run; and already the spires of Baltimore, and
the dome of the national capitol, were forecast upon their glad
vision, — only two or three days' march away through the
beautiful vallies [*sic*] of Pennsylvania and *"my"* Maryland.
Was there ever any thing so fine before! How splendid it
would be to enjoy the poultry and the fruit, the meats, the
cakes, the beds, the clothing, the *whiskey*, without price, in
this rich land of the Yankee! It would indeed! But on the
2nd of July something of a change came over the spirit of
these dreams. They were surprised at results, and talked less,
and thought more, as they prepared supper, that night. — After the fight of the 3d, they talked only of the means of their
own safety from destruction. Picketts' [*sic*] splendid Division
had been almost annihilated, they said; and they talked not of
how many were lost, but of who had escaped. They talked of
those "Yanks", that had *clubs* on their flags and caps, — the
trefoils of the 2nd Corps, that are like *clubs* in cards.

The battle of Gettysburg is distinguished in this war, not
only as by far the greatest and severest conflict that has occurred, but for some other things that I may mention. The
fight of the 2nd of July, on the left, which was almost a sepa-
rate and complete battle, is, so far as I know, alone in the following particulars; the numbers of men actually engaged at
one time, and the enormous losses that occurred, in killed and

wounded, in the space of about two hours. If the truth could
be obtained, it would probably show a much larger number of
casualties, in this, than my estimate in a former part of these
sheets. Few battles of the war, that have had so many casualties altogether, as those of the two hours on the 2nd of July.
The 3d of July is distinguished. Then occurred the "great
cannonade" — so we call it, — and so it would be called in
any war, and in almost any battle. And besides this, the main
operations, that followed, have few parallels in history, none
in this war, of the magnitude and magnificence of the assault,
single, and simultaneous, the disparity of the numbers engaged, and the brilliancy, completeness, and overwhelming
character of the result, in favor of the side, numerically the
weakest. I think I have not, in giving the results of this encounter, overestimated the numbers or the losses of the enemy.
We learned on all hands, by prisoners, and by their newspapers,
that over two Divisions moved up to the assault, — Pickett's
and Pettigrew's — that this was the first engagement of Pickett's in the battle, and the first of Pettigrew's, save a light
participation on the 1st of July. — The Rebel Divisions usually
number nine or ten thousand, or did at that time, as we understood. — Then I have seen something of troops, and think I
can estimate their number somewhat. — The number of the
Rebels killed here, I have estimated in this way: — the 2nd
and 3d Divisions of the 2nd Corps buried the Rebel dead in
their own front, and where they fought upon their own grounds,
— by count they buried over *one thousand eight hundred*. I
think no more than about *two hundred* of these were killed on
the 2nd of July, in front of the 2nd Division, and the rest
must have fallen upon the 3d. My estimates that depend upon
this contingency, may be erroneous, but to no great extent.
The rest of the particulars of this assault, our own losses, and
our captures, I know are approximately accurate. Yet the
whole sounds like romance, a grand stage piece of blood.

Of all the Corps d'Armeé, for hard fighting, severe losses,
and brilliant results, the palm should be, as by the army it is,

awarded to the *"Old Second."* It did more fighting than any other Corps, inflicted severer loss upon the enemy, in killed and wounded, and sustained a heavier like loss; and captured more flags than all the rest of the army, and almost as many prisoners as the rest of the army. The loss of the 2nd Corps in killed and wounded in this battle, — there is no other test of hard fighting, — was almost as great as that of all Gnl. Grant's forces, in the battles that preceded, and in, the siege of Vicksburg. Three eights [*sic*] of the whole Corps were killed and wounded. Why does the Western Army suppose that the Army of the Potomac does not fight? Was ever a more absurd supposition! The Army of the Potomac is grand! Give it good leadership — let it alone, — and it will not fail to accomplish all that reasonable men desire.

Of Gibbon's white trefoil Division, if I am not cautious, I shall speak too enthusiastically. This Division has been accustomed to distinguished leadership. Sumner, Sedgwick, and Howard have honored, and been honored by, its command. It was repulsed under Sedgwick at Antietam, and under Howard at Fredericksburg; it was victorious under Gibbon, at the 2nd Fredericksburg, and at Gettysburg. At Gettysburg its loss in killed and wounded was over *one thousand seven hundred,* near one half of all engaged; it captured *seventeen* battle-flags, and *two thousand three hundred prisoners.* Its bullets hailed on Pickett's Division, and killed or mortally wounded four Rebel Generals, [William] *Barksdale,* on the 2nd of July, with the three on the 3d, *Armstead* [*sic*], *Garnett,* and *Kemper.* In losses, in killed and wounded, and in captures from the enemy of prisoners and flags, it stands pre-eminent among all the Divisions at Gettysburg.[98]

---

[98] While Haskell's corps and division had borne the brunt of the fighting on Gettysburg's third day, the First and the Third Corps had been similarly involved on the previous two days and had suffered comparable losses in killed and wounded. The reported casualties of Gibbon's division during the battle itself were 1546 killed or wounded and 101 missing, for a total of 1647. *OR,* Ser. 1, Vol. 27, Pt. 1, pp. 173–87. In referring to "the second

Under such Generals as Hancock and Gibbon brilliant results may be expected. Will the country remember them?

It is understood in the Army that the President thanked the slayer of Barton Key, for *saving the day* at Gettysburg.[99] Does the country know any better than the President, that Meade, Hancock, and Gibbon, were entitled to some little share of such credit?

At about six o'clock on the afternoon of the 3d of July, my duties done upon the field, I quitted it to go to the General. My brave horse, *Dick,* — poor creature his good conduct in the battle that afternoon had been complimented by a Brigadier, — was a sight to see. He was litterally [*sic*] covered with blood. Struck repeatedly, his right thigh had been ripped open in a ghastly manner by a piece of shell, and three bullets were lodged deep in his body; and from his wounds the blood oozed and ran down his sides and legs, and with the sweat formed a bloody foam. Dick's was no mean part in that battle. Good conduct in men under such circumstances as he was placed, might result from a sense of duty; — his was the result of his bravery. — Most horses would have been unmanageable, with the flash and roar of arms about, and the shooting; Dick was utterly cool, and would have obeyed the rein had it been a straw. To Dick belongs the honor of first mounting that stormy crest before the enemy, not forty yards away, whose bullets smote him; and of being the only horse there during the heat of the battle. Even the enemy noticed Dick, and one of their reports of the battle mentions the *"solitary horseman,"* who rallied our wavering line. He enabled me to do twelve times as much as I could have done on foot. It would not be dignified for an officer on foot to run; — it is entirely so,

---

Fredericksburg," Haskell means the Union assault on the heights during the Chancellorsville campaign.

[99] Lincoln had visited Sickles, who was convalescing at Washington. The general had given the President an account of Gettysburg designed to magnify his role in the battle. Swanberg, *Sickles,* 221–24.

mounted, to gallop. I do not approve of officers dismounting in battle, which is the time of all when they most need to be mounted, for thereby they have so much greater facilities for being everywhere present. Most officers, however, in close action, dismount. Dick deserves well of his country, and one day should have a horse-monument. If there be, *"ut sapientibus placet,"*[100] an equine elysium, I will send to Charon the brass coin, the fee for Dick's passage over, and on the other side of the Styx, in those shadowy clover-fields he may nibble the blossoms forever.

I had been struck upon the thigh by a bullet, which I think must have glanced, and partially spent its force, upon my saddle. It had pierced the thick cloth of my trowsers, and two thicknesses of underclothing, but had not broken the skin; leaving me with an enormous bruise, that for a time benumbed the entire leg. At the time of receiving it, I heard the thump, and noticed it and the hole in the cloth, into which I thrust my finger; and I experienced a feeling of relief I am sure, when I found that my leg was not pierced.[101] I think, when I dismounted from my horse after that fight, that I was no very comly [*sic*] specimen of humanity. Drenched with sweat, the white of battle, by the reaction, now turned to burning red, I felt like a boiled man; and had it not been for the exhilaration at results, I should have been miserable. This kept me up, however, and having found a man to transfer the saddle from poor Dick, who was now disposed to lie down by loss of blood and exhaustion, to another horse, I hobbled on among the hospitals in search of General Gibbon.

The skulkers were about, and they were as loud as any in their rejoicings at the victory; and I took a malicious pleasure, as I went along and met them, in taunting the *sneaks* with their cowardice, and telling them, — it was not true, — that

---

[100] "As it is pleasing to wise men."
[101] Gibbon reported Haskell as having been "wounded slightly." Haskell, Compiled Service Records, 6th Wisconsin, in U.S., War Dept., A.G.O., National Archives.

Gnl. Meade had just given the order to the Provost Guards
to arrest and shoot all men they could find away from their
regiments who could not prove a good account of themselves.
To find the General was no easy matter. I inquired for both
Gnls. Hancock and Gibbon — I knew well enough that they
would be together, — and for the hospitals of the 2nd Corps.
My search was attended with many incidents that were pro-
vokingly humorous. The stupidity of most men is amazing.
I would ask of a man I met: "Do you know, sir, where the 2nd
Corps hospitals are?" — "The 12th Corps Hospital is there!."
— Then I would ask sharply: "Did you understand me to ask
for the 12th Corps hospital?" — "No!" — "Then why tell me
what I do not ask, or care to know." Then stupidity would
stare, or mutter about the ingratitude of some people for kindness. Did I ask for the Generals I was looking for, they would
announce the interesting fact, in reply, that they had seen
some other Generals. Some were sure, that Gnl. Hancock, or
Gibbon, was dead. They had seen his dead body. — This was
a falsehood, and they knew it. — Then it was Gnl. Longstreet.
— This was also, as they knew, a falsehood.

Oh, sorrowful was the sight to see so many wounded! The
whole neighborhood in rear of the field became one vast hospital, of miles in extent. Some could walk to the hospitals,
such as could not, were taken upon stretchers from the places
where they fell, to selected points, and thence the ambulances
bore them, a miserable load, to their destination. Many were
brought to the buildings along the Taney town road, and too
badly wounded to be carried further, died and were buried
there, Union and Rebel soldiers together. At every house,
and barn, and shed the wounded were; by many a cooling
brook, or many a shady slope, or grassy glade the red flags
beckoned them to their tented asylums; and there they gathered,
in numbers a great army, a mutilated, bruised mass of humanity. Men with gray hair and furrowed cheeks, and soft lipped,
beardless boys were there; for those bullets have made no distinction between age and youth. Every conceivable wound

that iron and lead can make, blunt or sharp, bullet, ball, and shell, piercing, bruising, tearing, was there; — sometimes so light that a bandage and cold water would restore the soldier to the ranks again; — sometimes so severe that the poor victim in his hopeless pain, remediless save by the only panacea for all mortal suffering, invoked that. The men are generally cheerful, and even those with frightful wounds, often are talking with animated faces of nothing but the battle and the victory; but some are downcast, their faces distorted with pain. Some have undergone the Surgeon's work; some, like men at a ticket office, await impatiently their turn, — to have an arm or a leg cut off. Some walk about with an arm in a sling; some sit idly upon the ground; some at full length lie upon a little straw, or a blanket, with their brawny, now blood-stained, limbs bare, and you may see where the minie bullet has struck, or the shell has torn. From a small round hole upon many a manly brest [sic], the red blood trickles; but the palid [sic] cheek, the hard drawn breth [sic], and dim closed eyes, tell how near the source of life it has gone. The Surgeons with coats off, and sleeves rooled [sic] up, and the hospital attendants with green bands upon their caps, are about their work; and their faces and clothes are spattered with blood; and though they look weary and tired, their work goes systematically and steadily on, — how much and how long they have worked, the piles of legs, arms, feet, hands, fingers, about, partially tell. Such sounds are heard, sometimes, — you would not have heard them upon the field, — as convince that bodies, bones, sinews and muscles are not made of insensible stone. Near by appears a row of small fresh mounds placed side by side, — they were not there day before yesterday, — they will become more numerous every day.

Such things I saw as I rode along. At last I found the Generals. — Gnl. Gibbon was sitting in a chair that had been *borrowed* some where, with his wounded shoulder bare, and an attendant was bathing it with cold water. — Gnl. Hancock was near by in an ambulance. — They were at the tents of the 2nd Corps hospitals, which were on Rock Run. As I approached Gnl. Gibbon, when he saw me he began to "hurrah," and wave his right hand, — he had heard the result. — I said: "O, General, long and *well* may you wave," — and he shook me warmly by the hand. Gnl. Gibbon was struck by a bullet in the left shoulder, which had passed from the front, through the flesh, and out behind, fracturing the shoulder blade, and inflicting a severe, but not dangerous wound. He thinks he was the mark of a sharp shooter of the enemy, hid in the bushes, near where he and I had sat so long during the cannonade; and he was wounded and taken off the field before the fire of the main lines of Infantry had commenced; he being, at the time he was hit, near the left of his Division. Gnl. Hancock was struck a little later, near the same part of the field, by a bullet piercing, and almost going through his thigh, without touching the bone however. His wound was severe also. He was carried back out of range, but before he would be carried off the field, he lay upon the ground in sight of the crest, where he could see something of the fight, until he knew what would be the result.

And then at Gnl. Gibbon[']s request, I had to tell him, and a large voluntary crowd of the wounded who pressed around, now, for the wounds they showed, not rebuked for closing up to the Generals, the story of the fight. I was nothing loth; and I must say, though I used sometimes before the war, to make speeches, that I never had so enthusiastic an audience before. Cries of "good," "glorious," frequently interrupted me, the storming of the wall was applauded by enthusiastic tears, and the waving of battered, bloody hands.[102] By the custom of the

---

[102] Gibbon thus received his first detailed account of the repulse of Pickett's charge from Haskell. Even years later, Gibbon praised his aide's gallantry and use of authority "as a staff officer of his absent general" to bring up reinforcements. Quoting liberally from Haskell's essay on the battle, Gibbon recalled, ". . . I have always thought that to him more than to any one man, are we indebted for the repulse of Lee's assault." Gibbon, *Personal Recollections*, 153.

service the General had the right to have me along with him, while away with his wound; but duty and inclination attracted me still to the field, and I obtained the General's consent to stay. Accompanying Gnl. Gibbon to Westminster, the nearest point to which railroad trains then ran, and seeing him transferred from an ambulance to the cars for Baltimore, on the 4th, the next day I returned to the field, to his Division, since his wounding in the command of Gnl. Harrow.

On the 6th of July, while my bullet bruise was yet too inflamed and sensitive for me to be good for much in the way of duty, — the Division was then halted for the day some four miles from the field on the Baltimore turnpike, — I could not repress the desire or omit the opportunity to see again where the battle had been. With the right stirrup-strap shortened in a manner to favor the bruised leg, I could ride my horse at a walk, without serious discomfort.[103] It seemed very strange, upon approaching the horse-shoe crest again, not to see it covered with the thousands of troops, and the horses and guns, but they were all gone, — the armies, to my seeming, had vanished, — and on that lovely summer morning the stillness and silence of death pervaded the localities where so recently the shouts and the cannon had thundered. The recent rains had washed out many an unsightly spot, and smoothed many a harrowed trace of the conflict; but one still needed no guide save the eyes, to follow the track of that storm which the storms of heaven were powerless soon to entirely efface. The spade and shovel, so far as a little earth for the human bodies would render their task done, had completed their work, — a great labor, that, — but one still might see under some concealing bush, or sheltering rock, what once had been a man; and the thousands of stricken horses, still lay scattered as they had died. The scattered small arms and the accoutre-

---

[103] Haskell made this ride over the field in the company of Charles Fairchild, who had come to help care for his wounded brother, Colonel Lucius Fairchild of the 2nd Wisconsin. Charles [Fairchild] to mother, July 6, 1863, in the Fairchild Papers, SHSW.

ments had been collected and carried away, almost all that
were of any value; but great numbers of bent and splintered
muskets, rent knapsacks and haversacks, bruised canteens, shreds
of caps, coats, trowsers, of blue or gray cloth, worthless belts
and cartridge-boxes, torn blankets, ammunition boxes, broken
wheels, smashed limbers, shattered gun carriages, parts of har-
ness, — of all that men or horses wear or use in battle, were
scattered broad-cast over miles of the field. From these one
could tell where the fight had been hottest. The rifle pits
and epaulements, and the trampled grass, told where the lines
had stood, and the batteries, — the former being thicker where
the enemy had been, than those of our own construction. No
soldier was to be seen; but numbers of civilians and boys, and
some girls even, were curiously loitering about the field, and
their faces showed not sadness or horror, but only staring wonder or smirking curiosity. They looked for mementoes of the
battle to keep, they said; but their furtive attempts to conceal
an uninjured musket, or an untorn blanket, — they had been
told that all property left here, belonged to the government,
— showed that the love of gain was an ingredient at least of
their motive for coming here. Of course there was not the
slightest objection to their taking any thing they could find,
now; but their manner of doing it was the objectionable thing.
— I could now understand why soldiers had been asked a dollar
of a small strip of old linnen [sic] to bind their own wound,
and not be compelled to go off to the hospitals. Never elsewhere upon any field have I seen such abundant evidences of
a terrific fire of cannon and musketry, as upon this. Along
the enemy's position, where our shells and shot had struck
during the cannonade of the third, the trees had cast their
trunks and branches as if they had been icicles shaken by a
blast. And graves of the Rebels' making, and dead horses, and
scattered accoutrements, showed that other things besides trees
had been struck by our projectiles. I must say, that, having
seen the work of their guns upon the same occasion, I was
gratified to see these things. Along the slope of Culp[']s Hill,

in front of the position of the 12th, and the 1st Division of
the 1st, Corps, the trees were almost litterally [sic] peeled, from
the ground up some fifteen or twenty feet, so thick upon them
were the scars the bullets had made. Upon a single tree, in
several instances,[104] not over at [sic] foot and a half in dia-
meter, I actually counted as many as two hundred and fifty
bullet marks. The ground was covered by the little twigs that
had been cut off by the hailstorm of lead. Such were the evidences of the storm under which Ewell's bold Rebels, assaulted
our breast-works on the night of the 2nd, and the morning
of the 3d, of July. And those works looked formidable, zig-
zaging [sic] along those rocky crests even now, when not a musket was behind them. What madness on the part of the enemy
to have attacked them! All along through these bullet stormed
woods were interspersed little patches of fresh earth, raised
a foot or so above the surrounding ground, — some were very
near the front of the works, — and near by upon a tree, whose
bark had been smoothed by an axe, written in red chalk would
be the words, not in fine handwriting: *"75 Rebils berid
hear,"*[105] "☞ *54* Rebs *there"* — and so on. Such was the burial, and such was the epitaph, of many of these famous men,
once lead [sic] by the mighty Stonewall Jackson. Oh, this
damned rebellion will make brutes of us all, if it is not soon
quelled! Our own men were buried in graves not trenches;
and upon a piece of board, or stave of a barrel, or bit of
cracker-box, placed at the head, were neatly cut or pencilled
the name and regiment of the one buried in each. — This
practice was general; but of course there must be some excep-
tions, for some times the cannon's load had not left enough
of a man to recognize or name. The reasons here for the more
careful interment of our own dead, than such as was given to
the dead of the enemy, are obvious, and I think satisfactory:
Our own dead were usually buried not long after they fell,

---

[104] WHC omits "in several instances."
[105] WHC corrects the spelling here.

and without any general order to that effect. It was a work
that the men's hearts were in, as soon as the fight was over,
and opportunity offered, to hunt out their dead companions,
to make them a grave in some convenient spot, and decently
composed, with their blankets wrapt about them, to cover them
tenderly with earth, and mark their resting place. Such buri-
als were not without as scalding tears as ever fell upon the
face of coffinned [sic] mortality. The dead of the enemy could
not be buried until after the close of the whole battle. The
army was about to move, — some of it was already upon the
march, before such burial commenced. Tools save those carried by the pioneers, were many miles away with the trains,
and the burying parties were required to make all haste in
their work, in order to be ready to move with their regiments.
To make long shallow trenches; to collect the Rebel dead,
often hundreds in one place; and to cover them hastily with a
little earth, without name, number, or mark, save the shallow
mound above them, — their names of course they did not
know, — was the best that could be done. I should have been
glad to have seen more formal burial even of these men of the
rebellion, both because hostilities should cease with death, and
of the respect I have for them as my brave, though deluded,
countrymen. — I found fault with such burial at the time,
though I knew that the best was done that could be under the
circumstances; but it may perhaps soften somewhat the rising
feelings upon this subject of any who may be disposed to share
mine, to remember that under similar circumstances, — had the
issue of the battle been reversed, — our own dead would have
had no burial at all, at the hands of the enemy; but stripped
of their clothing, their naked bodies would have been left to
rot, and their bones to whiten, upon the top of the ground
where they fell. Plenty of such examples of Rebel magnani-
mity are not wanting; and one occurred on this field too. Our
dead that fell into the hands of the enemy upon the 1st of
July, had been plundered of all their clothing, but they were

left unburied, until our own men buried them after the Rebels had retreated, at the end of the battle.

All was bustle and noise in the little town of Gettysburg, as I entered it on my tour of the field. From the afternoon of the 1st, to the morning of the 4th, of July, the enemy was in possession. Very many of the inhabitants had, upon the first approach of the enemy, or upon the retirement of our troops, fled their homes and the town, not to return until after the battle. Now the town was a hospital, where gray and blue mingled in about equal proportions. The public buildings, the court-house, the churches, and many private dwellings were full of wounded. There had been in some of the streets a good deal of fighting; and bullets had thickly spattered the fences and walls; and shells had riddled the houses from side to side. And the Rebels had done their work of pilage [sic] there too. In spite of the smooth-sounding general order of the Rebel commander, enjoining a sacred regard for private property, — the order was really good, and would sound marvelously well abroad, or in history, — all stores of drugs and medicines, of clothing, tin ware and all groceries, had been rifled, and emptied, without pay, or offer of recompense. Libraries public and private had been entered, and the books scattered about the yards, or destroyed. Great numbers of private dwellings had been entered and occupied without ceremony, and whatever was liked, had been appropriated, or wantonly destroyed. Furniture had been smashed, and beds ripped open; and apparently unlicensed pillage had reigned. Citizens and women who had remained had been kindly relieved of their money, their jewelry, and their watches, — all this by the high-toned chivalry, the army of the magnanimous Lee![106] Put these things by the side of the acts of the "vandal

---

[106] Undoubtedly there was looting at Gettysburg. See, for example, Mary Elizabeth Massey, *Bonnet Brigades* (New York, 1966), 222. During their entire invasion, the Confederates often did not observe the letter or spirit of Lee's order. Nevertheless, even an

Yankees," in Virginia, and then let mad Rebeldom prate of
honor! But the people, the women and children, that had fled,
were returning, or had returned, to their homes, — such homes,
— and amid the general havoc, were restoring as they could order to the desecrated firesides. And the faces of them all plainly told, that, with all they had lost, and bad as was the condition of all things they found, they were better pleased with
such homes, than with wandering houseless in the fields, with
the Rebels there. All had treasures of incidents, of the battle,
and of the occupation of the enemy, — wonderful sights, escapes, witnessed encounters, wounds, the marvelous passage of
shells or bullets, — which upon the asking, or even without,
they were willing to share with the stranger. I heard of no
more than one or two cases, of any personal injury received by
any of the inhabitants. One woman was said to have been
killed, while at her wash tub, sometime during the battle; but
probably by a stray bullet, coming a very long distance, from
our own men.[107] For the next hundred years Gettysburg will
be rich in legends and traditions of the battle. I rode through
the Cemetery on "Cemetery Hill." How those quiet sleepers
must have been astounded in their graves when the twenty-
pound Parrott guns, thundered above them, and the solid
shot crushed their grave stones! The flowers, roses and creep-
ing vines, that pious hands had planted to bloom and shed
their odors over the ashes of dear[108] ones gone, were trampled
upon the ground, and black with the cannon's soot. A dead
horse lay by the marble shaft, and over it the marble finger
pointed to the sky. The marble lamb that had slept its white
sleep on the grave of a child, now lies blackened upon a broken

---

historian who is inclined to make the worst of their conduct indicates that it was hardly "unlicensed pillage." Coddington, *Gettysburg,* 153–79.

[107] Haskell probably refers to young Jennie Wade, who was shot
while baking bread in her home and became the "feminine martyr"
of the battle. Massey, *Bonnet Brigades,* 223.

[108] WHC reads "dead."

gun-carriage. Such are the incongruities and jumblings of battle.

I looked away to *the group of trees,* — the Rebel gunners know what ones I mean, and so do the survivors of Pickett's Division, — and a strange facination [*sic*] led me thither. How thick are the marks of battle as I approach, — the graves of the men of the 3d Division of the 2nd Corps, — the splintered oaks, — the scattered horses, — seventy-one dead horses were on a spot some fifty yards square, near the position of Woodruff's Battery, and where he fell.

I stood solitary upon the crest by *"the trees"* where less than three days ago I had stood before; but now how changed is all the eye beholds. Do these thick mounds cover the fiery hearts, that in the battle rage, swept the crest and stormed the wall? I read their names — them alas, I do not know, — but I see the regiments marked on their frail monuments, — "20th Mass. Vols." — "69 P.V." — "1st Minn. Vols." — and the rest, — they are all represented, and as they fought, commingled here. So I am not alone, — these my brethren of the fight are with me. — Sleep, noble brave! The foe shall not desecrate your sleep. — Yonder thick trenches will hold them. — As long as patriotism is a virtue, and treason a crime, your deeds have made this crest, your resting place, hallowed ground!

But I have seen and said enough of this battle. The unfortunate wounding of my General so early in the action of the 3d of July, leaving important duties which in the unreasoning excitement of the moment, I in part assumed, enabled me to do for the successful issue something, which under other circumstances would not have fallen to my rank or place. Deploring the occasion for taking away from the Division in that moment of its need its soldierly, appropriate head, so cool, so clear, I am yet glad, as that was to be, that his example and his tuition have not been entirely in vain to me, and that my impulses then prompted me to do somewhat as he might have done, had he been on the field. The encomiums of officers, so numerous, and some of so high rank, generously accorded me for my conduct upon that occasion, — I am not without vanity, — were gratifying. My position as a Staff Officer gave me an opportunity to see much, — perhaps as much as any one person, — of that conflict. My observations were not so particular, as if I had been attached to a smaller command; not so general, as may have been those of a Staff Officer of the General commanding the army; but of such as they were — my heart was there, and I could do no less than to write something of them — in the intervals between marches, and during the subsequent repose of the army, at the close of the campaign. I have put somewhat upon these pages. I make no apology for the egotism, if such there is, of this account; — it is not designed to be a history, but simply *my account,* of the battle. It should not be assumed, if I have told of some occurrences, that there were not other important ones. I would not have it supposed that I have attempted to do full justice to the good conduct of the fallen, or the survivors, of the 1st and 12th Corps. — Others must tell of them: — I did not see their work. A full account of *the battle as it was,* will never, can never, be made. Who could sketch the changes, the constant shifting, of the bloody panorama! It is not possible. The official reports may give results, as to losses, with statements of attacks, and repulses; they may also note the means by which results were attained, which is a statement of the number and kind of the forces employed; but the connection between means and results, the mode, the battle proper, these reports touch lightly. Two prominent reasons at least exist which go far to account for the general inadequacy of these official reports; — or to account for their giving no true idea of what they assume to describe: — the literary infirmity of the reporters; and their not seeing themselves and their commands, as others would have seen them. And factions, and parties, and politics, the curses of this Republic, are already putting in their unreasonable demands for the foremost honors of this field. "Gnl. Hooker won Gettysburg." How? Not with the army in person, or by infinitessimal [*sic*] influence; — leaving it almost four days before the battle, when both armies were scattered, and fifty miles apart? Was ever claim so absurd? Hooker, and he alone, won the result at Chancellorsville. "Gnl. Howard won Gettysburg." — "Sickles saved the day." Just Heaven save the poor Army of the Potomac from its friends! It has more to dread, and less to hope from them, than from the red bannered hosts of the rebellion. The states prefer, each her, claim for the sole brunt and winning of the fight. "Pennsylvania won it." — "New York won it." — Did not Old Greece, or some tribe from about the sources of the Nile win it? For modern Greeks, — from Cork — and African Hannibals were there. Those intermingled graves along the crest, bearing the names of every loyal state save one or two, should admonish these geese to cease their cackle. One of the armies of the country won the battle; and that army supposes that General Meade led it upon that occasion. If it be not one of the lessons that this war teaches, that we have a country, paramount, and supreme over faction, and party, and state, then was the blood of fifty thousand citizens shed on this field in vain. For the reasons mentioned, of this battle greater than Waterloo a history, just, comprehensive, complete, will never be written. By-and-by, out of the chaos of trash and falsehood, that newspapers hold, out of the disjointed mass of reports, out of the traditions and tales that come down from the field, some eye that never saw the battle, will select, and some pen will write what will be named *the history*. With that the world will be, and if we are alive we must be, content.

Already as I rode down from the hights [*sic*], Nature's mysterious loom was at work, joining and weaving on her ceaseless web the shells had broken there! Another Spring shall green these trampled slopes, and flowers, planted by unseen hands, shall bloom upon these graves; another Autumn and the yellow harvest shall ripen there, — all not in less, but higher, perfection for this poured out blood. In another decade of years, in another century, or age, we hope that the Union, by the same means, may repose in a securer peace, and bloom in a higher civilization. Then what matter it, if lame Tradition glean on this field and hand down her garbled sheaf; — if deft Story with furtive fingers plait her ballad wreaths, deeds of her heros [sic] here; — or if stately History fill as she list her arbitrary tablet, the sounding record of this fight: — Tradition, Story, History, all, will not efface the true grand Epic of Gettysburg.

Haskell[109]

*   *   *   *   *

Sandy Hook, Md. near
Harper's Ferry, July 17, 1863.

I have a moment to write, as we came here yesterday, and are not likely to move to-day. The whole Army is assembled near here, ready to cross into Virginia at any hour. When I wrote you last a battle was iminent [sic], but it *"did not come off"*, — the other party having commenced to leave that night; — and they were all across by the next morning except 1500 of their rear guard, which we captured on the morning of the 14th.

We shall probably cross into Va. to-morrow, and then — God only knows the rest. — The purpose is, — to destroy the Rebel Army. The details of this destruction are not arranged. Look to the Politicians at Washington for all such matters. They can *fix it*. Shoemakers, Quacks, and the like know these things — Generals in the field do not.

I am getting along well, and feel all right. — I must say that I was rather glad that the Rebs got into Va. without a battle, for we were so tired that it seemed very hard to again fight so soon after Gettysburgh [sic]. But now long marches, and fatigues innumerable are again before us.

I suppose I ought to feel glad at all our recent successes,

---

[109] WHC adds Haskell's first name and middle initial and the direction "To H. M. Haskell" — components of a letter that are not in the original manuscript.

and I do, that we have had all over the country, but I do wish
they would give the Army of the Potomac some assistance
from the idle troops at Washington and on the Peninsula. This
Army has done more fighting than all the rest of the Armies
of the country. — Regiments that once numbered a thousand,
have been reduced by battle to fifty or sixty men, — the bones
of the rest are scattered upon twenty fields, — yet the few survivors are pushed forward, without support, and so they will be
as long as a man is left.

This may be right, but I do not see it.

God is over us all, — may he direct all our moves.

Frank A. Haskell.

*   *   *   *   *

□ After crossing the Potomac, the armies returned to the
battlefields of northern Virginia, with the Union army north
and the Confederates south of the Rappahannock River. □

*   *   *   *   *

Near Warrenton Junction, Va.,
July 27, 1863.

Here we are about three miles from Warrenton Junction,
— and for a wonder, we do not expect to move to-day, — a
thing unheard of with us for a long time. Since the morning
of the 15th of June what marches, battles and hardships has
this Army not had! The marching alone is one of the great
things of History, — nearly four hundred miles, with all this
great Army and its trains. What do you think of that?

Then the three days battle of Gettysburgh [sic], and ever
so many hot skirmishes, — the great battle and the great victory of the war so far. — I think the country, by this time,
should accord something but sneers to the Army of the Potomac. I for one am proud to belong to it, and am willing that
with it, my reputation, as a soldier and patriot, may rise to
honor or fall to disgrace, according to desert.

I wish I had time to describe to you the battle of Gettysburgh [*sic*]! I am full of it, — was in it, — saw it — and there had on me the sacred rage of battle as never before. No description can do it approximate justice, for pen and canvas are poor for that great epic. — Still, some time, — it will take many pages, and I shall not soon forget what I saw, — I shall write about it to you.

I may say here, — it may not be vanity to mention it to you — that I personally have received universal commendation for my part in the battle.

Several Generals, — Genl. Gibbon has not written his report yet, — have praised my conduct in the highest terms in their official reports of the battle. — I think I did well there myself.[110]

Genl. Gibbon did command the 2nd Corps during a part of the battle, — but not very long when the fighting was going on. He however put the Corps, both Infantry and Artillery, in the order of battle the same as it actually fought. Enough of these things for the present, — only let me say that when I know that I did more for the country in that battle than some who will be made Major Generals for their conduct there, it gives me a twinge to think I shall get no visible reward.

The Army is now all near here, — what next, I do not know, — we shall see, when the time comes.

---

[110] Winfield Scott Hancock, commander of the Second Corps, commended most strongly the services of Haskell ". . . who, at a critical period of the battle, when the contending forces were but 50 or 60 yards apart, believing that an example was necessary, and ready to sacrifice his life, rode between the contending lines with the view of giving encouragement to ours and leading it forward, he being at that moment the only mounted officer in a similar position." In Gibbon's report, the commander of the 2nd Division, Second Corps, noted that several reports of subordinate commanders had mentioned Haskell's service. Gibbon added that in many battles Haskell had displayed "conspicuous coolness and bravery." He concluded, "It has always been a source of regret to me that our military system offers no plan for rewarding his merit and services as they deserve." *OR*, Ser. 1, Vol. 27, Pt. 1, pp. 376, 418, respectively.

We nearly starve to death here now, — the officers, I mean — for we cannot get half enough to eat. I am almost as thin as I was the first summer of the war, and chiefly because I cannot get enough to eat. You may laugh at this but it is the truth. Oh, if I only could for a few days come up and see you and have you feed me, I think it would be splendid. We expect, though, now to get something soon, as we came here last eve, and the Rail Road is in order to Washington, and brings supplies. My health is excellent, — no return of my old malady of last year yet. Give me a week to rest, and I could do very astonishing things, I have no doubt.

I am sorry to learn that Maria is not well — You must get well, Maria, because if you do not I shall be obliged to come home and take care of you. — This you would not like. My love to you and Martha.

What of Harvey? Why does he not write to me? — I cannot hear of him or about him at all.

The mail will go soon so consider this enough for the present.

Adieu,

Frank —

V

Afterglow

LIKE HASKELL'S WOUNDED GENERAL, John Gibbon, the sorely bled armies in the east convalesced into the early autumn of 1863. During Gibbon's absence, Haskell continued to serve on the headquarters staff of the Second Corps, acting as an aide to General William Hays and to Hays's successor, General Gouverneur K. Warren. In September, when the Confederates sent reinforcements from Virginia to General Braxton Bragg's army in the western theater, Haskell participated in Meade's advance across the Rappahannock against Lee's weakened force. But, after Bragg's Pyrrhic victory at Chickamauga, the United States authorities also reduced the size of the Army of the Potomac by sending two corps to the west. Lee then took the offensive, maneuvering Meade back toward Washington. Haskell, as he describes in the following letters, took part in the battle at Bristoe Station which proved to be the most sizable infantry encounter of the campaign. □

* * * * *

> At Head Quarters 2nd Corps
> Near Culpeper C.H. Va.
> October 9, 1863.

Since I have written, some changes have occurred in the Army of the Potomac. From the preparation for immediate battle, we have come to a state of most profound *do-nothing-ativeness.*

A change has come over the spirit of the dreams of the
powers at Washington — two Corps, the 11th and 12th, have
gone west, — and the battle here has not been fought.

When will it? *Super omnia Deus.*[1] We wait, with as much
patience as may be consonant to the American citizen, but we
think extensively. On the 16th of Sept. we, this Corps, moved
from Culpeper, to Mitchell's Station, a distance of seven or
eight miles, where on the extreme front of the Army, we en-
camped along the Rapid Ann, [Rapidan River] — relieved on
the 5th of this month, we came back here on the 6th, and are
now quietly in camp near, and North of, the distinguished
Culpeper C. H. Genls. Hancock and Gibbon have not yet
returned, — we know not when they will, — and in this state
of mighty repose, were it not for the firm principle established
long ago, to do duty and take the consequences, time would
be irksome. There is nothing to do, but we must be constantly
in readiness to move in a moment. We can have but little to
read, for we cannot get or carry the books, — society, composed of all men of the Army and no women, is not as attractive as you may find in civil life. And so we drag along the
dull hours. — Sleep is a glorious institution, and you have no
idea of the capacity of humanity, when fully perfected in this
direction, for it. — Eating is magnificent, — and then we sometimes dream when peace shall come again, and spread her
white wings over the land. When will it? Will it ever? I cannot see it for years, — and before it thousands of the brave must
go down in the shock of battle, and hundreds of thousands
of poor hearts bleed.

Such is our destiny. — We cannot avert it if we would, —
we will accept it, — we will do the best we can. But as these
things must come, give me rather than this dull inactivity,
the bugle blast for the assault, the shout of the charging line,
and the hiss of the rifled guns. Oh! for one great hour again
of Gettysburg! It was better than a life of this dullness.

---

[1] Above all, God.

I see no prospect of immediate operations by this Army, but still we cannot tell. Conscripts and convalescents are swelling our numbers fast, — and we may soon feel able to advance. I do not know.

I wish to see Genl. Gibbon back here again, so that I can have my place, and, then I shall cheerfully submit to *"every fate"*.

There is one little matter that I wish to mention. — Winter is coming on, and fine good flannel under-clothing is warm, and conducive to health and comfort. — The prices are enormous at Washington. Now could you not get me some and send by express? Mind, I only ask, and I want those that are first class. Can you get them? If you can, then I will tell you what I want, &c. and possibly a package could be sent me that would *do me good*.

Write me a good long letter about matters and things, — tell me of the Wis. politics, — about what they say of drafting, &c. My love to Maria and Martha, but I cannot come home at present.

Frank A. Haskell

*   *   *   *   *

☐ On October 16, 1863, Haskell wrote a brief note, here omitted, to inform his family that he had survived the battle of Bristoe Station. He later wrote the following detailed account of the campaign. ☐

*   *   *   *   *

At Head Quarters 2nd Corps
Two Miles East of Warrenton, Va.
October 31st, 1863.

Since writing last, the Army has been much in motion, and has done some fighting, of which I must tell you a little. On the morning of the 10th inst. it became known that the enemy was attempting to turn the right flank of our Army, and dispositions were at once commenced to be ready to meet him.

Accordingly the 2nd Corps was moved out, on that morning, two and one half miles from Culpeper C. H. on the Sperryville road, and formed in order of battle, facing the West, its left resting on the road mentioned, — the 3d Corps was put in position upon its left, and the rest of the Army was distributed thence to Raccoon Ford on the Rapid Ann River, — the whole Army thus forming a line of more than twelve miles, facing the West and South, and nearly in the shape of a quarter of a circle, with the Cavalry upon the flanks, and well to the front upon the roads coming into our lines. The whole of that day passed with very little fighting, but the left of the Army advanced somewhat and found that the enemy were not in that front, but so much was learned that it became apparent that the Rebel was moving his whole force around our right. Shall we fight a battle here now? — was our query. — We heard that the trains were ordered far to the rear, — except ammunition and the ambulances, — and that the Depot at Culpeper was being broken up, and the sick removed upon the cars. — This looked like falling back, but we could not tell. Late at night I went to bed, but before there had been a show of sleep an order came, that the 2nd Corps would march on the morning of the 11th, at 3 o'clock A.M. back and recross the Rappahannock, and halt at Bealeton Station — Similar orders were distributed to the whole Army, — and these orders were executed accordingly, in perfect order, without confusion, and with little loss of men or material. There was some skirmishing during the day between our rear guard of Cavalry, and the advance of the enemy, but it was unimportant. On that evening our whole army save a little Cavalry at the Rappahannock Station, and all our trains and supplies, could have been found on the left bank of the Rappahannock, in good order and ready for what might occur.

The old 2nd Corps had marched more than twenty miles, but before night went into camp near Bealeton Station, and had a night of perfect rest and repose. This was good.

The morning of the 12th in due time came. — Genl. Meade

had information that a portion of the Rebel Army had pursued our retreat directly, and that the rest of it was marching to cross the [Rappahannock] river at Sulphur Spring and Waterloo Bridge, near Warrenton. — He thought the time had come to strike a good blow upon this Rebel fragment, — accordingly, by his orders, the 6th Corps, Genl. Sedgwick, recrossed the Rappahannock at Rappahannock Station, preceded by Cavalry, ([John] Buford's Division) and followed by the 2nd Corps. About noon on the 12th, — the 5th Corps, Genl. Sykes, crossed the river two miles higher up, and formed on the right of Sedgwick, — the 2nd Corps was in Reserve. — This force moved rapidly forward in the direction of Culpeper, — in order of battle, — found the enemy's outposts some two miles from the river, which our Cavalry attacked and drove in, and found another important fact, — that there was no considerable force of the enemy there, — only a little Cavalry and Infantry for show. — The Cavalry chased these almost to Culpeper before dark, and secured some prisoners — The 5th and 6th Corps went into Camp for the night near Brandy Station, five miles from the river, and the 2nd Corps camped about a mile and a half in their rear. The information to-day gained was important, for it was now clear that the whole force of the enemy was still moving around our right. This was further shown by the fact that late on this day, the 12th, Genl. [David M.] Gregg's Division of Cavalry, which was on the extreme right of our Army, and below Warrenton, on the river, was furiously attacked by the Rebel, with Infantry, Artillery, and Cavalry, and repulsed with a loss of three or four hundred.

I think Gnl. Meade now first formed the plan of falling back on Centreville, — which is a wonderfully strong position — and awaiting the attack of the enemy there. — No time could be lost. — The trains were at once put in motion from around Bealeton for Fairfax C. H. — this was late in the evening of the 12th, — and at 11 o'clock the same evening the 2nd, 5th and 6th Corps, were ordered to return to the left bank

of the Rappahannock at once. — No sleep to-night, — all is
bustle in a few moments, and the retrograde is resumed. During the night or early the next morning, the whole Army was
put in motion. The 1st Corps, Genl. Newton, which was at
Kelly[']s ford, on the extreme left of the Army, and the 6th
Corps, took the direction of Centreville, keeping well to the
South, — the 5th Corps started for Warrenton Junction, —
the 2nd Corps was ordered to Fayetteville, where it arrived
a little after daylight on the morning of the 13th. Here this
Corps halted for some hours. But soon orders came that it was
to follow the 3d Corps, Genl. [William H.] French, in the
direction of Greenwich. The 3d Corps at last passed, with
orders to go into position at Greenwich, and the 2nd Corps
was to follow and take position at Auburn, three or four miles
South of Greenwich. As we marched from Fayetteville towards Greenwich, the enemy was known to be coming towards
us from the direction of Warrenton, but our Cavalry was nearly all out, — [Hugh Judson] Kilpatrick's Division upon the
extreme right, — Gregg's Division in the centre, — and Buford's on the left, between the Infantry and the enemy, and
we could thus get timely notice of his near approach. — The
2nd Corps, as usual, had the fighting place, — it was the one
nearest to the enemy. Very little skirmishing occurred during
the 13th. Towards evening as the head of the 3d Corps was
near Auburn, it met a small force of the enemy's Cavalry,
posted in a piece of woods, but after a very brief skirmish,
the rebels fled. But this delayed us somewhat, and the 3d
Corps was so long in passing, and getting out of the road, with
its Ammunition and ambulance trains, that night overtook
and stopped the 2nd Corps, a half a mile short of Auburn,
the place of its destination. But the night was dark, and the
road narrow, and it was no use to try to go farther so at quite
an early hour the troops of the 2nd Corps were camped, and
had a good chance to get food and rest, which they very much
needed. How do you suppose a Corps looks bivouaced [*sic*]
for the night, and how does it do it? This was what was done

on the eve of the 13th: the Corps consists of about ten thousand men, and has five Batteries of Artillery, and was accompanied with its Ambulances and Ammunition train, in the order: the 1st Division, Genl. Caldwell; then two Batteries, then the 3d Division, Genl. Hays; then the train; then three Batteries; and lastly the 2nd Division, Genl. Webb; the whole extending along the road in the order of march, somewhat more than two miles. At between six and seven o'clock, the Corps halted, its head about a half a mile from Auburn; sentinels are at once thrown out upon the right and left flanks; the trains and the Artillery are parked and guards put over them, and the horses are unhitched, watered and fed with oats, the Infantry stack arms in line, — the two leading Divisions in woods upon the side of the road, and the rear one upon a high open knoll, — and in a twinkling, the whole two miles of the Corps blazes with its thousands of fires, which rail fences and long practice enables [sic] the men to make with the greatest rapidity. Then ten thousand canteens pour water into ten thousand tin cups, and therein are set to boil upon the fire the coffee, and sticks are cut on which to broil slices of pork, and the men take their coffee, and meat and "hard tack", all very tired, but cheerful and uncomplaining, and this done they spread the rubber blanket upon the ground, and on it wrap themselves in the woolen blanket, and soon with feet to the fire they are all asleep. This is all done in a very short space of time, and with no trouble at all to any body. While we were bivouacing [sic] some shots of the enemy were fired upon our flanks, but the men cared nothing for them, as they were known to come from Rebel Cavalry, which our Infantry hold very lightly indeed.

Next morning at three o'clock the drums and bugles sounded the *Reveille,* and some time before five o'clock A.M. the Corps was in motion again; but in the night new orders had come from Genl. Meade, — the 3d Corps was to move on from Greenwich to Manassas Junction, starting at a very early hour; and the 2nd Corps was to turn off to the right at Auburn and march to Catlett's Station, and thence on to Manassas Junction and Centreville Heights, as soon as the preceding Corps, and trains had left the road clear. The 1st Corps was already near Centreville, and the 6th was moving on Chantilly, and it was very desirable that the 2nd and 3d Corps, and the 5th which was near Catlett's should move to Centreville promptly, that our Army might be concentrated and ready to operate as a unit against the advancing Lee, as he should come up from the direction of Warrenton. So were matters on the morning of the 14th. Genl. Warren[2] stayed at his Head Quarters, until the rear of the Corps should move, and his Chief of Staff, Lt. Col. [Charles H.] Morgan, Lt. Mitchell, A.D.C. to Genl. Hancock, and myself were sent forward to conduct the march, and see to the making of proper dispositions.

The road on which we were marching is nearly due North and South in direction, — the road from Auburn to Catlett's runs nearly due East, so that when we started we should move half a mile North to Auburn, then make a right angle to the East. As the Enemy was known to be near us upon the left, it was determined to put the 1st Division in position at Auburn, facing the West, and North-West, there to stay until the rest of the Corps should be well advanced on the road to Catlett's, then this Division would follow and act as rear guard. Before it was fully light on this thick foggy morning the 1st Div. and two batteries were in position at the point indicated; the 3d Division had just crossed Cedar Run, at Auburn and was heading towards Catlett's, and throwing out their advance guard and flankers, and the Ambulances were close up, when the first moment that it was light enough to see[,] the enemy

---

[2] Gouverneur Kemble Warren was a graduate of West Point and a brilliant engineer. Promoted to a major generalcy in 1862, he won fame by preventing the Confederates from seizing strategic Little Round Top at the battle of Gettysburg. After his temporary command of the Second Corps, he headed the Fifth Corps. Summarily relieved during the battle of Five Forks (1865), he was later exonerated. Warner, *Generals in Blue,* 541–42.

upon our left, — that is, in front of the position of the 1st
Div. began to skirmish briskly with Gregg's Cavalry which
covered that flank; his [cavalry] came suddenly upon our cavalry and as usual they supposed it was something very dreadful, and some of them ran, and raised some confusion among
the ambulances. Matters were soon put right. We had seen
some men in front of the 3d Division, on the road to Catlett's
but we thought them some skirmishers of the 1st Div. — when
suddenly, and while the Cavalry were still sharp at their skirmishing in front of the 1st Div. bang, bang, bang, went a Rebel
Battery, seven hundred yards in rear of the 1st Div. and their
shells fell thick and with effect among the masses of that Division. Here was *a pretty kittle* [*sic*] *of fish,* fired at in front
and rear, and the roads full of trains! Whew! It looked a little
skeery. Troops not in position, — and a good many of them
conscripts, and never under fire before. Then the Rebels, by
their battery, which was doing telling work upon the 1st Division, set up their usual damned wolf cry and advanced a
strong line of skirmishers out of the woods in front of the 3d
Div. and formed their Cavalry for a charge. But the 2nd Corps
was not to be easily discomfited.

In the 1st Div. the Infantry were sheltered as soon as possible from the Rebel shells by marching them behind a ridge
of ground. — Rickett's Battery [Capt. R. Bruce Ricketts' Batteries F and G, 1st Pa. Light Arty.] changed front to rear, and
replied to the Rebel guns. — The 3d Div. deployed and moved
rapidly forward upon the Rebel skirmishers, and their Cavalry,
opened fire upon them, — and in about fifteen minutes from
the time the Rebel Battery first opened, the whole force which
had opened upon our rear, — that is the rear of the 1st Div. —
consisting of one battery, and a force about a brigade of Cavalry, were *skedadling* as fast as possible for dear life. They
left over forty prisoners, and a good many dead and wounded
in our hands, including one Colonel and one Lt. Col. mortally
wounded. Our loss here was about fifty killed and wounded,
chiefly in the 1st Div. Our road thus cleared the 2nd and 3d

Divisions, and the trains, moved on towards Catlett's, five miles distant. Genl. Warren came up just as these matters were closing, and of course approved of all that had been done. As the enemy still threatened the front of the 1st Div. Genl. Warren resolved to detain it in position until the other two Divisions were well advanced out of the way, and then to move rapidly after them.

The enemy soon began to display considerable force, both of Infantry and Cavalry in front of the 1st Div. and skirmishing became constant, and at times sharp. At about nine o'clock A.M. so many of the enemy were visible that our two Batteries with the 1st Div. fired occasionally fired [sic] upon them. At last the Rebels got two or three of their Batteries in position, and replied.

From ten to eleven o'clock, a sharp Artillery fire was kept up, and the enemy kept pushing up and showing more and more force, at the same time manifesting an obvious purpose to move around our flanks, and thus to cut us off. By eleven o'clock the road to Catlett's was clear, — the trains even had passed that point, all but sufficient ambulances for the troops, and the 2nd and 3d Divisions were halted there to check the enemy, should he advance along the Railroad from Warrenton [Junction], so the time had now come to move the 1st Div.

Leaving some of Gregg's Cavalry in the same position where it had been posted, at eleven the Division moved rapidly in the direction of Catlett's. Arriving at this latter place at between twelve and one o'clock, P.M. and the Corps thus having become again united, except the 2nd Brig. 2nd Div. which by Genl. Meade's order had been sent with the train as a guard, Genl. Warren pushed on along the Rail Road at once, in the direction of Bristoe Station. At this time the Cavalry was disposed in the same order as in the morning, — the 5th Corps was at Bristoe, to await the arrival of the 2nd Corps to that point, the rest of the Army was across or about to cross, Bull Run, in the neighborhood of Centreville — It was certain that the enemy was pursuing us in force, and was attempting to

pass us upon the right flank, and cut us of [*sic*] at Bristoe. —
All was put in good order, the Corps, both Infantry and Artillery, kept well in hand, and thus we moved on Bristoe
seven miles distant. The march was rapid and in good order.
— The 2nd Div. lead [*sic*], and marched on the South side of
the Rail Road, — and was followed by the 3d Div. on the same
side, and the 1st Div. on the North side of the same Road.

When the rear of the Corps had got in motion Genl. Warren and Staff rode rapidly forward to near the head of the
column, and, arrived at within three miles of Bristoe, we heard
the sound of cannon directly ahead.

This was ominous, — the strictest watch was kept towards
the left, upon which our flankers were thrown well out, — but
after some half a dozen discharges the sound of the guns ceased,
and so we conjectured it to have come from some small party
of the enemy who might be dogging the 5th Corps, and that
it had been driven away. Bristoe is upon Broad Run, on the
right bank, and from this stream back towards Catlett's for
about a thousand yards the ground is open, and rises in swells
and hollows toward the North, — then in the same direction
comes a point of pine thicket woods down to the Rail road,
— then the ground near the road upon the North side is open
again to Kettle Run which is about a mile from Bristoe toward Catlett's. From Kettle Run to Broad Run the Railroad
runs, and there is by it such an embankment made in its construction as of itself to constitute a very good breastwork for
Infantry.[3] When the head of the 2nd Division was within some
five hundred yards of Broad Run, from the woods North of
the road, and at a distance of about a thousand yards both
from the Road and the Run, two lines of Infantry were seen
to advance down over the slope in the direction of a point
about the intersection of Broad Run and the Rail Road. —

---

[3] For a map of this battle which agrees with Haskell's description, see U.S., War Department, *Atlas to Accompany the Official
Records of the Union and Confederate Armies* (Washington, D.C.,
1891–95), plate 45.

One line was behind the other — there was about a brigade in each, — they advanced rapidly. "Who are those people yonder?" — "What does that mean?" — "They are Rebels!" were asked and answered by us all.[4] Now then we are in for it. At the moment it was not certain whether the purpose of this party of Rebels was to attack us immediately, or to push forward and get across the road ahead of us and so cut us of [sic], but we soon caused a development of their designs. Our column of Infantry, by a depression of the ground through which it was marching, was out of the immediate view of the enemy, though they had probably seen it, — one of our Batteries, "B" 1st R. I. Arty. Lt. Brown, alone they could see. — This was near the head of our column, and was soon put into position upon high ground South of the Railroad, and over the heads of our Infantry opened fire with shells upon the enemy. The first shot was fired from our side, and at three o'clock, P.M. Matters soon assumed a look of business. The enemy somewhat staggered by our shells, at once began to make dispositions for immediate attack; and we as promptly prepared the defence. The head of our column was halted within one hundred and fifty yards of Broad Run, closed up, faced to the front, the North, and moved up and took position behind and concealed by the Rail Road embankment, the 1st Brig. 2nd Div. Col. [Francis E.] Heath, Commanding, was on the right, next on the left was the 3d Brigade Col. [James E.] Mallon, Commanding. Then two Brigades of the 3rd Division, the 3d and 2nd, commanded respectively by Gnl. [Joshua T.] Owen

---

[4] Lieutenant General Ambrose Powell Hill's Third Corps, Army of Northern Virginia, was attempting to attack what Hill believed to be the United States Third Corps, which was just finishing crossing Broad Run. Hill overlooked the presence of the Second Corps, the advance of which was mostly concealed by the railroad embankment and which was in a position to take Hill's attackers in the flank. Freeman, *Lee's Lieutenants*, 3: 242–45. Hill was mistaken as to the identity of his original target, which was, as Haskell says, the Fifth Corps. *OR*, Ser. 1, Vol. 29, Pt. 1, pp. 241, 277.

and Col. Smith [Thomas A. Smyth], came up at the double quick and took position on the left of the 2nd Div. and concealed along the Railroad in a similar manner.

While these dispositions were being made, — Brown's Battery mean while being active with shell, and shrapnell [*sic*], the enemy swung forward his line so as to make it parallel with ours, and cautiously advanced to the attack. His line extended from near Broad Run, [for] about a thousand yards to the West, to near the pines that I have mentioned. The Rebel skirmishers advanced and attacked ours, the 1st Minn. Vols., — a Rebel Battery opened from high ground in rear of their line, in the edge of the woods. — The action began to be warm. Rickett's Battery came up and replaced Brown's which crossed Broad Run and opened on the enemy's flank.

Our skirmishers were driven in, — up came the Rebel line of skirmishers and tried to draw our fire from behind the Rail road, — the Infantry were too cool for them, — foiled in this, the Rebel main lines advanced, and as they came over the crest of the rolling ground, at different distances from fifty to one hundred and fifty yards from the Rail road, and attempted to charge, our concealed Infantry of the 2nd and 3d Divisions simultaneously opened fire upon them — they returned the fire, but they fell thick as leaves, stricken by our rain of bullets, — they broke and fled, — again they rallied behind the high ground, — and advanced, — again the Rail road blazed, — the Rebels utterly broken haplessly fled, — our Infantry shouted, and rushed after them firing and shouting as they advanced. Arnold's Battery, "A" 1st R.I. Arty. in the mean time came up and joined with Brown, and Ricketts, and our Artillery and Infantry soon completely swept the field.

The Rebel Battery was last to show resistance, but the Rebel Infantry disposed of, our three Batteries in position made short work of that. Their horses were the larger part of them killed, — one gun was knocked from its carriage, — their men deserted them where they stood and fled. We were now in entire possession of the whole field. The 1st, 2nd, and 3d Bri-

gades of the 1st Division had just come up,[5] but were not
early enough to join in this fight, nor were they needed; but
they did join in the shout that our men gave of victory, which
made the hills and woods ring. At once men were sent to
bring off the captured guns, — the ground was thickly strewn
with the Rebel dead and wounded as they passed, — the men
drew them off, — four guns by hand, and one more they found
four rebel horses uninjured for. The guns were brought in
amidst the shouts of our people.

I may as well here, to announce events in their order, tell
the result of this fight. We lost three hundred and fifty-four
in killed and wounded in the 2nd Corps. We killed and
wounded of the enemy, as I then estimated, — and my estimate
has since been confirmed by their accounts, and the statements
of citizens of the neighborhood, — twelve hundred men. — We
captured six hundred prisoners, — not seven hundred as I
told you, — five guns, — the other of the Battery was dismounted
and could not be taken off, — and two battle flags. The troops
of the Rebels that were encountered here, were Gnl. Heth's
Division, one of the same Divisions that the 2nd Corps punished so terribly on the 3d of July at Gettysburg.[6]

This was one of the most sharp and brilliant little actions
that has occurred for us during the war. But I cannot stop
here to enter into encomium upon any thing. — I must go on
with events. This battle was over in about an hour from the
time the first shot was fired. The movements of the enemy

---

[5] Haskell had ridden back to instruct both the 1st Division and
Arnold's Battery to hasten to the battlefield. Warren commended
his services, together with those of other staff officers. *Ibid.*, pp.
247, 255, 308.

[6] Haskell's reckoning of Union casualties agrees closely with the
official total of 548, but his estimate of Confederate losses is low.
Confederate casualties were at least 1381 and probably as high as
1900 killed, wounded, and captured. Freeman, *Lee's Lieutenants*,
3: 246. Under the command of James J. Pettigrew, who replaced
the wounded Henry Heth, Heth's Division had participated in
"Pickett's Charge" at Gettysburg.

that we saw, and the information obtained from prisoners, were such, as to cause us to adopt the promptest measures for defence, and safety. Our Army was to concentrate at Centreville Heights, — the 2nd Corps was at Bristoe alone, only supported by Gregg's Cavalry, which is not good for much to fight, and only brings some information of what it sees. Prisoners stated, and we became convinced that Heth's Division, which we had routed, was supported by the two other Divisions of A. P. Hill's Rebel Corps, and these soon began to take positions in our front.

During the after-noon they made several shows of attacking us, but our shells quieted them. While these matters were transpiring, our rear guard consisting of the 4th Brigade of the 1st Division, Col. [John R.] Brooke, and the 1st Brigade of the 3d Division, Col. [Samuel S.] Carroll, came up and were formed upon the left of the troops already in position. The Corps was now together, all but the 2nd Brigade of the 2nd Div. which had been detached, as I have mentioned. Our remaining two Batteries which had not joined in the action, and two Horse Batteries of Genl. Gregg, which were with us, were put in position; and we watched as the after-noon wore away. Hill's Corps closed upon our front, but kept out of range of our guns, — they had learned to be respectful during the afternoon. — Ewell's Corps, having taken the same road on which we had marched, came upon our left flank, and partially around to our rear in that direction — These two Corps are all the Infantry of Lee's Army, and we suppose they constitute of [sic] force of at least fifty thousand. Were they not coming rather close to a Corps of less than ten thousand men? Some time before night we were certain that the whole Rebel Army was quietly investing us, in the directions that I have mentioned, but we could not well fall back by day light, or if we did, our prestige of victory would be lost, so Genl. Warren resolved to stay until after dark at all events. He was the more willing to do this, as after the sharp lesson they had learned they were very cautious, and they could not actually know our strength. The 2nd Corps was as furious as a nest of hornets all the afternoon. — Did their skirmishers appear, ours would attack them sharply, in a moment, — and our Batteries gave them shells whenever a line of Infantry advanced in sight. Towards night we were encouraged by the news that the 5th Corps, which had preceded on the march, and was now near Manassas Junction, having moved there from the direction of Bristoe, as they heard the sound of our battle, was, two Divisions of it, returning to our support, and was actually near us.

No fighting of importance occurred after the fight at three o'clock, until almost sundown when the enemy, having silently gotten into position, opened sudenly [sic] with three or four Batteries, upon our position. — We were ready for them. In an instant all our Batteries blazed and thundered, — and from this time until quite dark a splendid Artillery performance ensued. I can scarcely call it a fight, for so far as concerns the guns of the enemy at least, it was a matter of the very smallest harm. — They did hit some horses, — probably a few men, but it looked magnificent. As the sun went down, and darkness came on, the long streams of flame from the guns made a most brilliant spectacle, and their shells, which from the very muzzles of the guns we could trace in their half mile curves, by their burning fuses, were no more than agreeably thrilling, as they would burst near us. We could dodge them, by galloping our horses, more easily than a boy can a snow-ball. Before it was fully dark, — for our Batteries were more numerous, and in better position than theirs — the enemy's fire subsided, and all became quiet, — the fighting of the day was over. — The enemy kindled his camp fires, and so did we upon the field. The 2nd Corps, — the 5th also — had positive orders to cross Bull Run that night, so when it became fully dark, and the 5th Corps, had moved back towards Manassas Junction, — they had come back, you know to support us, — first we put all of our wounded who could be moved into ambulances, and sent them ahead — some twenty had to be left, but men and medicines were left with them — and then off moved the Artillery, followed by the Infantry who moved as silently as shadows towards Centreville. The only sound we heard as we left the field was the groans of the Rebel wounded. Of this class we took away only such as could walk, — in accordance with our plans, we could not care for the rest, and so hundreds of poor fellows, on the field where they had lain since three o'clock, or in ditches whither they had crawled for shelter from the bullets, were making their piteous complaints to the unfriendly darkness alone, with none to help them.

It was sad. I hope their own people found them and cared for them before morning.

The 2nd Corps moved on, — the enemy did not follow, and so far as we know, did not learn of our departure until the next morning.

Before four o'clock the next morning, the Corps was a mile across Bull Run in the direction of Centerville, being the last of the Army to cross that stream, except the Cavalry outposts, and the men were soon bivouaced [sic] and asleep. This was a day of hard work. Within the twenty-four or five hours before this halt, the 2nd Corps had not slept, — had marched fully twenty miles, — and a large portion of the time had been engaged with the enemy. Gnl. Meade, for this day's work, published an order congratulatory to the Corps and its commander. This was the first time our Conscripts had ever been tried, but they behaved throughout the day, on all occasions, admirably. We are very glad of this. On the 15th inst. the Army took up a position on the Heights of Centerville, — the 6th Corps upon the right, near Chantilly, — next on the left, the 1st Corps, which was at the town, and on the Warrenton Pike — next still to the left, the 2nd Corps, which was in front of Blackburn's and Mitchell's fords, — the scene of the battle on the 18th of July, 1861, — and on the extreme left of the Army, the 3d Corps, which extended nearly down to Union Mills, on the Bull Run. — The 5th Corps was in Reserve, in rear of the Army. The outposts of the Infantry were along

Bull Run, on the left bank, up to the mouth of Cub Run, and
thence up the left bank of Cub Run, to the right of the Army.
The Cavalry was as usual upon the flanks and upon the roads
to the front.

You must know that in all this falling back from Culpeper,
the Army did not feel at all that they were being repulsed, —
they were not. — Genl. Meade was maneuvering for a position,
on which to fight — and on the defensive, as the Armies were
about equal, and the Rebel showed a disposition to Attack.
The men felt this, and so they were in capital spirits.

To explain matters a little: Before the 12th of Sept. our
Army was upon the left bank of the Rappahannock, — the
Rebel was between that river and the Rapid Ann. Meade got
information that Longstreet with his Corps had gone to [Brax-
ton] Bragg, — the Cavalry and the 2nd Corps, at the date last
mentioned, moved forward upon Culpeper, cleared the country between the Rappahannock and the Rapid Ann of the
enemy, and learned certainly that Longstreet had left Lee's
Army. The Army of the Potomac is advanced, and preparations were made to attack the enemy South of the Rapid Ann.
— These were somewhat delayed from the fact that many good
troops were away in New York to enforce the draft, and conscripts were being raised, and when these should come in our
Army would be large enough to ensure success. But the time
came when Meade felt strong enough for work. The plan of
the attack had been made, and all was ready, — the next day
operations were to have commenced, when up comes an order
from Washington, sending the 11th and 12th Corps West. —
Equilibrium of the two opposing Armies was thereby restored.
— Meade could not attack with any certainty of success, so he
waited for more conscripts. But in the mean time the enemy
began to grow bold by our apparent timidity, and so on about
the 10th or 11th inst. the Rebel assumed the offensive and
thereafter did what I have described. The Rebel has done
some very rash things, — in this woody, hilly country it is far
best to be on the defensive. — So when the enemy made their

movements against us, Meade thought they would fight him even at Centreville, where he would fight them a defensive battle and whip them badly.

Thither I have shown you that the Army was on the 15th, and the purpose, now I can go on with the events. — On that day we expected that a great battle would soon occur. — The Army was prepared for it. At about noon on that day a large force of the Rebel Cavalry and two of their horse Batteries appeared in front of the 2nd Corps, and opened fire from their guns and dismounted Cavalry, and attempted to force the passage of Bull Run. — They were promptly repulsed. — Then the same Rebel force moved Southward, where the 3d Corps Batteries rapped them, when they continued still to move in the same direction to be repulsed at dark by Buford's Cavalry near Manassas Junction. This was, without doubt, a reconnoitering party of the enemy, but from what he learned from it, I think Gnl. Lee very soon changed his plans. He acted on the offensive no more.

He probably did not dare to. On the 17th and 18th, nothing actually occurred on our side, only the prevalence of nine million rumors of the appearance of the enemy in force upon every point of our line, but truth compels me to narrate that every one of these was without any foundation in fact. On the 18th the Army of the enemy — just what we did not want them to do — commenced to fall back. Meade learned this on that night. What could he do? If the enemy would not come to fight him, he would go to fight the enemy. Accordingly on the 19th the whole Army commenced to move in the direction of the enemy early. The 2nd Corps moved back to Bristoe, — no enemy there, — they had torn up the Railroad and burned the bridges and retired toward Warrenton on the eve before, — then the 2nd Corps marched to Gainesville, thence to Greenwich, thence to Auburn, where we were on the 14th, and there we camped for the night. Some of the enemy were at Warrenton, one Division at least, and some at Rappahannock Station. The next day no enemy was at Warrenton. On the 22nd the

2nd Corps came to this point, having halted at Auburn on the 20th and 21st. Here we are and how long we shall remain, — none can tell. Since the Army came here, — it is now in this vicinity, the whole of it — there has been some skirmishing near Rappahannock Station, but the enemy is understood to be all across the River, possibly the larger portion behind the Rapid Ann. When the Army will resume active operations, I cannot tell. — We could move no farther at the time and halted here, on account of the tearing up of the Railroad over which the supplies came. The road is nearly done again now.[7]

You will see that from the 10th to the 20th of the month the Armies were active, — there was much hard and rapid marching, many sleepless nights, but no very great results.

The successes, in the aggregate, were with us. But this campaign, short and active though it has been, is not one over which either party will dare to boast much, if we look alone to results.

Heigh, ho! — When will the war be over? We expect more active operations this Fall and very likely ere this reaches you, we shall again be on the move.

So far my somewhat brief letter has been of rather a warlike character. — I now propose to make it more peaceful and personal. I am perfectly well and fat. — I have not heard of my promotion yet. — When shall I?

Gnl. Warren is still in command of the 2nd Corps, and when Hancock will be back I cannot tell. Warren is a man of the right sort, and I am getting to like him much. I consider that his management of the Corps in the recent movements has been able and judicious, — it has certainly been eminently successful. Such men as he are required to end this War, — men who will not hesitate to strike when a chance occurs, and who will *hanker* after a chance, and run forward to meet it.

---

[7] This destruction of the transportation system of his more numerous foe was the only real accomplishment of Lee's offensive movement. Boatner, *Civil War Dictionary*, 87.

I do not know when my dear Gnl. Gibbon will be back. — His wound is not yet healed, and it is uncertain when it will be. I wish very much he would come, as I am away from home without him.

On the question of clothes, I think I will not send for any at present. — I do not know when I can go to Washington to get them, — and if I should try to have them sent me here, they would be likely to be lost. — I will wear old clothes for the present. But the time will come some time. I should like to see you all, but God only knows if I ever shall. This war, and the duties of the field are not my normal state I am sure, but I never shall leave it until the war is over. Would to God that some vigor could be shown in the procuring of conscripts to fill the ranks of the Army. Let us all be brave and patient, and all will be well.

I am glad to see that Wisconsin is all right in politics. Politics of all kinds are a curse and a sin, and have ruined the country, but in them are degrees of wickedness and evil.

I do not suppose there is the least chance that I shall come home this Winter. But I tell you I should like to. You may just know how I sometimes get utterly homesick. But what avails it, — I am rather too old for this, so I dry up.

But you will sometimes just consider me there, — sometime of an evening, — bring out a decanter of jolly wine, — and the cigars. You will smoke a little, will you not Maria, just to keep me company? I will not touch the cat, — will not drop any ashes upon the carpet, and will do just as you wish, in all things.

When we get into Winter quarters I shall send for clothes, and shall expect something very nice and warm. I never was so shabby in the world before, as now, in my personal appearance, for I have not had a thing new since I was at home last Winter. I should dislike to have the enemy get hold of me, looking so, but I guess they will not.

Even if you should not read all of this letter, I wish you to keep it, and do not scold about it, for the matters here, are

a part of history, and are true. When I write the history of
the war, I shall want it. — I cannot rely upon the *bosh* of the
papers. I wish you had my account of Gettysburg, but it is
too voluminous to send by mail, and I fear it would so be lost.

I wish you would write me often and tell me all that occurs.
I do not get any papers at all from Madison, and suppose I am
forgotten there. — When Lewis is Governor I intend to make
his acquaintance, — write me about the election.[8]

Much love to each of you and God bless you.

Frank A. Haskell.

*   *   *   *   *

Cleveland, Ohio,
November 16, 1863.

The life of the soldier can never, in time of actual war, be
considered settled or quiet. He must obey orders. To day

---

[8] The Republicans, who in 1863 sought the votes of "War Democrats" by calling themselves the "Union Party," had refused to re-
nominate Governor Edward Salomon. Democrats attributed the
rejection of the German-born War Democrat to residual xenopho-
bia among the Republicans. Certainly Salomon's chief opponent
in the convention was Elisha W. Keyes, who in the 1850's had been
a leader of the nativist Know Nothings, as well as being Haskell's
associate in the militia and in Republican politics. Richard W.
Hantke, "The Life of Elisha Williams Keyes" (unpublished Ph.
D. dissertation, University of Wisconsin, 1942), 81, 88, 152–62.
Keyes, who as Postmaster of Madison headed the "Regency" which
dominated the state's Republican organization, engineered the
gubernatorial nomination of Secretary of State James T. Lewis of
Columbus. Lewis, a lawyer and land speculator, was a War Democrat turned Republican. Klement, *Wisconsin and the Civil War*,
76, 84–85. Haskell may not have been speaking literally in referring
to making Lewis' acquaintance. In 1862, the Secretary of State
had signed the petition for Haskell's promotion. Petition to
Governor L. P. Harvey, February 8, 1862, in Wis., Exec. Dept.,
Applications for Commissions, 1861–65, Series 1/1/5–20, Archives
Div., SHSW. According to Haskell's friend and Lewis' later secretary, Frank H. Firmin, the Secretary of State also had introduced
Haskell to Governor Salomon. Firmin to Harvey M. Haskell, June
15, 1864, in Haskell Mss., Pa. Historical and Museum Commission.

he pitches his tent, upon some fair slope, beneath the shade, with every prospect of months of rest and ease before him; — to-morrow, after the fatigues of the midnight march, and the hurried preparation, he finds himself in the onset of battle, — and so forth.

Having, as I trust, somewhat prepared your minds, by the above elegant remarks, for what follows, I proceed to state that I am here in the city of Cleveland, Ohio, sound, and well, and comfortable, and on duty.

On the day I wrote you last, I believe, the 6th inst.[9] I received notice from Gnl. Gibbon, that he was ordered to duty here to take charge of the Conscripts, and that he desired me to join him here. This was a surprise to me, as his order had been to him. — He is not yet fit for duty in the field, on account of the wound received at Gettysburg. — But I must say that I was not displeased at the prospect of going from the field awhile, now that Winter is coming on, with no great prospect of further military operations for the present, in the Army of the Potomac.

And I thought also, that after the service that I had done, and the battles in which I had participated, I could obey this order without any impeachment upon my patriotism.

So just at evening upon the 6th, having obtained Gnl. Warren's consent to join Gnl. Gibbon, I was just mounting my horse to proceed to Gnl. Meade's Head Quarters, then near Warrenton Junction, for the purpose of getting his order for me to leave the Army, when up came an order for the advance of the whole Army against the enemy at 7 o'clock on the morning of the 7th. We supposed this move meant battle, — my place was then with the Army, under those circumstances, — I wished to stay. — Gnl. Warren said I had better. — So I just staid, — and on that evening instead of packing my things for leaving the Army, the next morning, I got ready to *join the expedition,* at the same time.

---

[9] An inconsequential note, here omitted.

Seven o'clock on the morning of the 7th came frosty, clear
and still, and that hour saw the Army quietly in motion, —
the 2nd, 3d, and two Divisions of the 1st Corps, heading towards Kelly's Ford, on the Rappahannock, at a mean distance
of about fifteen miles away, and the 5th and 6th Corps, towards Rappahannock Station, which is about five miles higher
up the same river. The Cavalry was upon the flanks and in
advance of the Infantry. During the march pains were taken
to conceal the columns as much as possible by woods and high
grounds, from the view of the enemy; and the wind which
arose about nine o'clock and continued to blow quite hard,
from the direction of the enemy, favored this purpose. At
about eleven o'clock the 2nd Corps passed to the left of the
5th and 6th, which had then discovered the outposts of the
enemy near and around Rappahannock Station and on the
left [north] bank of the river. At about two o'clock P.M. we
commenced to hear Artillery firing in the direction of Kelly's
Ford, and soon learned that it was the 3d Corps, Gnl. French,
engaging the enemy at that point. This Corps was at the Ford,
and was followed by the two Divisions of the 1st Corps, then
on the road from Morrisville, and not far off.

At the sound of the guns the 2nd Corps quickened pace,
and soon received an order from Gnl. French, then in temporary command of these three Corps, to take position on the
right of the third Corps, and to support if necessary.

As we neared Kelly's Ford the sound of the firing increased,
and with the sound of the guns, musketry could be heard.
At about three o'clock the 2nd Corps was in position, — the
firing had nearly ceased, at the Ford. The 3d Corps had swept
down to the river, captured the outposts of the enemy on the
left bank, — forded the stream with a brigade, and fought,
routed and captured many of the supports of the outposts.
The number of the enemy captured in this affair was about
four hundred. Their dead and wounded were not numerous.
Our loss here was about forty in killed and wounded.

Two pontoon bridges were soon constructed across the river

and two whole divisions of the 3d Corps marched over and went into position upon the right bank. The ground is open on the right bank of the river at this point for about a thousand yards, and then upon high ground is a line of woods. In these woods the enemy was discovered in line of battle. His skirmishers and those of the 3d Corps kept up some firing until dark, when all became quiet here.

The dispositions here during the night were; two Divisions of the 3d Corps on the right bank of the river, in front of the ford, and one upon the left bank, at the ford ready to cross; — the 2nd Corps upon the left bank, just above the ford; — the two Divisions of the 1st Corps, in rear of the ford, and still along the road from Morrisville.

Towards sundown we heard a good deal of cannon firing at Rappahannock Station. — We guessed what it meant, — and during the evening we heard fully how it had occurred. The 6th Corps, Gnl. Sedgwick, supported by the 5th Corps, had found a small force of the enemy strongly posted at Rappahannock Station, with Artillery in good earth works, over infantry behind rifle pits, — had assaulted them furiously, and after a brief but severe fight, had captured them nearly all. Our loss here was nearly four hundred in killed and wounded. The 5th Wis. was one of the regiments that did magnificently, and lost quite heavily, — I heard, about 75. — I saw the graves of ten (10) from this regiment. Col. Tom. Allen was shot in the left hand.

The enemy's loss was 1700 prisoners, — his killed and wound- were not as numerous as ours, — eight flags, four guns, and a lot of small arms and a pontoon bridge. This was a very brilliant and successful action. The passage of the river at this point was not effected on the 7th, — the enemy still appearing in some force, and strongly fortified upon the other side of the river.[10]

---

[10] Although mostly hearsay, Haskell's account of the battles at Kelly's Ford and Rappahannock Station is accurate. Confederate losses totaled 2023. Freeman, *Lee's Lieutenants*, 3: 264–67. United States losses were 419. Boatner, *Civil War Dictionary*, 681.

We retired early to rest fully expecting a battle to-morrow.

On the morning of the 8th at a very early hour the Division of the 3d Corps which had remained on the left bank of the river, crossed, and the whole of this Corps, as soon as it was light enough to see, advanced to find and attack the enemy.

The 1st and 2nd Corps were in readiness to support the 3d. We waited to hear the sounds of the opening battle, which we expected every moment, but as the 3d Corps advanced, heading towards Brandy Station, it soon became apparent that no enemy was on our immediate front. — He had fallen back in the night. Still showing force opposite the 6th and 5th Corps, the enemy was believed to be in considerable force near Brandy Station; and accordingly, to cut them off if possible, the 5th and 6th Corps were ordered to move down to Kelly's Ford upon the left bank of the river, cross, and uniting with the rest of the Army, to push forward upon Brandy Station. But arriving at that point, the enemy was not there. All along, as the Army advanced between the river, and Brandy Station there appeared abundant evidences that the enemy had left in great haste the night before, — that the retreat had been precipitate, — that they had intended to remain there for the Winter. They had built excellent huts for the men, and roads for hauling supplies.

A good many of their straglers [sic] were picked up, and they all concurred in the statement that the Rebels were in rapid retreat for the Rapid Ann. No battle to day then. Two or three miles beyond Brandy Station, Buford fell in with their rear guard, just at dark, and some skirmishing occurred; and about the same time Kilpatrick found some of them at Stevensburg. But the Rebel Army was South of the Rapid Ann. On the night of the 8th the whole of the Army was near Brandy Station facing towards Culpeper.

Now I could get my order, as there would be no fight, and accordingly on the 9th at the Head Quarters of the Army I received the order to at once join Gnl. Gibbon in Cleveland. Early on the 10th, all then being quiet in the Army, I took leave of the brave 2nd Corps, and the men with whom I have often been in fight, and started for Washington. Though I expect to go back there again, and was coming away but for a time, and to have an easier Winter, I regretted to part with the Army. Arrived at Washington on the evening of the same day and staid there during the 11th and 12th. On the 13th I started for this place, where I arrived at about 10 o'clock A.M. with[out] accident or incident, on the 14th. Found the Gnl. and Mr. Moole,[11] his then Aide, and their wives, and with them am stopping at the "Angier" House. How long we shall stay here we of course do not know — probably during the Winter. The Gnl. has charge of the Conscripts and Recruits at this point, but what there is to do yet I do not know.

So possibly I can come home yet this Winter. — We will see about that at Christmas.

Of course I expect to *suffer* here, but I am too good a soldier to complain about it. Pity me, will you not?

Write me, and direct to me officially at this City. Write me, and when I get settled, and accustomed to the modes and condition of civilization again I will write you.

Frank A. Haskell.

*   *   *   *   *

"La Pierre House", Philadelphia
November 20, 1863.

I must call your attention to the introductory remarks of my last former letter. —

Having paused sufficiently to call them to mind you and I will proceed.

At Cleveland for the Winter? Well, there did not appear much to be done there, — our time was not *all* occupied, — the great consecration of the "Soldiers' Cemetery," at Gettysburg was to occur on the 19th inst. — Genl. Gibbon and I would like again to see those heights and slopes over which the battle had

---

[11] Lt. Edward Moale, 19th U.S. Infantry.

swept on the 2nd and 3d of July, — it could be so arranged that the cost would be nothing. So leaving Lt. Moole to attend to the matters at Cleveland, two o'clock P.M. on the 17th found the General and myself seated in the cars, headed for the old field again, — the same evening we passed Pittsburg [sic], — the early light of the next day came upon us at Harrisburg, — before noon of the 18th we were in the little village of Gettysburg.

We were fortunate enough, by the assistance of a friend we met there, to procure lodgings at the house of a Mr. Wartels, in the village, for the Hotels, such as they were, were already full to overflowing already [sic]. We received very kind treatment while we staid in town, by the family of the resident named.

At Gettysburg again! How different from the time we were there before. The sights and sounds were all changed. Then it was sultry July — now it was sombre November. — The leaves and harvests were then green and luxuriant — now they were yellow and sere, — then the sound of hostile cannon shook the earth — now the voices of women and children filled the air, — but amid all the changes there was no mistaking the prominent features of the horseshoe crest, — "Round Top", "Cemetery Hill" and the slopes and ridges were all there, and we knew them well. We obtained horses, and during the afternoon of the 18th and the 19th we rode all over the field — a thing of the greatest interest to us, I assure you, — but I shall omit the description for a fitter place and time, — the *appendix* to my account of the battle.

The President and some of his Cabinet came that evening — Mr. Everett[12] was already there — and we joined in the celebration on the 19th, the Gnl. and I representing the "Army of the Potomac."

---

[12] Edward Everett of Massachusetts. A politician and orator, he was intended to be the principal speaker at the dedication of the cemetery. Boatner, *Civil War Dictionary*, 268.

We had the flag of the "Iron Brigade",[13] — the most magnificent flag I ever saw. It is of very heavy blue silk, with yellow silk fringe. In the centre, of most superb embroidery, in many colored silk, is the coat of Arms of the Union. — In the upper corner next the staff, in yellow, "2nd Wis. Vols", in the other upper corner "6th Wis. Vols." — in the lower corner next the staff, "19th Ind. Vols." — in the other lower corner, "7th Wis. Vols"; and between these latter names, "24th Mich. Vols." This last Regiment hardly deserves a place upon the flag, I should think.[14] Then at different places upon the flag are beautifully embroidered, "Gainesville", "Bull Run", "Antietam", "South Mountain", "Fredericksburg", "Gettysburg". That Brigade is known to everybody, and the flag was much noticed.

We had little interest in the ceremonies, and I shall not attempt to describe them.[15] You may think strange of my notions of this matter, — but I will tell you what they are. Of course as our brave men who fell at Gettysburg were buried hastily in all parts of the field — many of them where they fell — without this collection of their bones, the places of their graves would soon be unknown, and the plow would have obliterated them. But what so appropriate for the soldier's rest as the spot where he died nobly fighting the enemies of the country, — where perhaps the shout of victory went up with his spirit to Heaven — where his companions in arms, his survivors, had lovingly wrapped him in his blanket, and wet with brave men's

---

[13] The flag was commissioned by citizens of Indiana, Michigan, and Wisconsin living in Washington and was presented to the remnant of the Iron Brigade in September, 1863. After the war, it became part of the War Museum at the Wisconsin Capitol. Nolan, *Iron Brigade,* 265–66, 369.

[14] This regiment was not assigned to the Brigade until October 8, 1862. Nolan, *Iron Brigade,* 159.

[15] Gibbon later claimed that they had listened to part of Everett's long oration and had then gone to the battlefield where he and Haskell had described events to a small party. "We then returned in time to hear Mr. Lincoln's touching address." Gibbon, *Personal Recollections,* 184.

tears, had covered him with the earth his blood had consecrated.
Wherever the body of a Union soldier was so buried upon all
that broad field, — what if the mound had been leveled with
the plow, — and the mark of lath were gone, — would be a holy
spot, and tradition would point it out for a thousand years.
"Tread lightly on this field, for on every spot may be a patriot's grave."

But no, — these things were not to be. The skeletons of
these brave men must be handled like the bones of so many
horses, for a price, and wedged in rows like herrings in a box,
on a spot where there was no fighting — where none of them
fell!

It may be all right, but I do not see it. Had the thing to be
done, if some place had been selected where hard fighting occurred, it would have been better; but as it is now, this field,
before so thick with all that could appeal to the patriotism
or touch the sensibility of Americans, has been stripped of all
signs that would affect the sense, — of the best of all that which
would kindle sentiment, — but we have instead a common,
badly arranged grave yard, in which names, and graves, if desig-
nated at all, are as likely to be wrong as right. But read the
newspapers. — Every body says this is splendid, this making
the "Soldiers' Cemetery," and I suppose it is.

But there is another thing that I must mention in this letter,
— we are not likely to spend the Winter at Cleveland — for on
the morning of the 19th the General received notice of an order putting him on duty at Philadelphia. Whew. — He likes
this best — I cannot say that I do, for now there is a doubt about
seeing you at Christmas, but I have to submit, — so we tele-
graphed to Moole at Cleveland to bring on our baggage, and at
nine P.M. on the 19th we started for this place, where we arrived at 9 A.M. this morning [sic], having been joined at Harrisburg, by Moole and his wife, and Mrs. Gibbon, who were on
their way from Cleveland. We stop at the "La Pierre House",
a most excellent Hotel, where we can be vastly comfortable,
and I pay the nice little sum of two dollars per day for board,

as a permanent arrangement. But even at these rates I can get along much cheaper than in the field, — for I keep no servant here, and for fuel and quarters I get near forty dollars per month from the government, which I would not in the field.

I of course cannot tell you much of the "Quaker City" yet, but I think we shall have a good time. You will of course write me here.

I shall have to write Maria and Martha a chapter some day upon the women here, for they are handsome, and dress with the greatest elegance.

With love to you all.

                                        Frank A. Haskell.

                    *   *   *   *   *

                    Headquarters Rendezvous for Drafted Men.
                    Philadelphia, Pa Dec. 23, 1863.[16]

I cannot come home for the holy days. I should like to see you all, but my duties will detain me here. It is very uncertain if I can get a leave of absence during the Winter. — So you will not be disappointed if you do not see me at all, — until "this cruel war is over," — and the end of that is not yet. — A merry Christmas to you all. — I hope you may enjoy it to your heart's content, — be happy in all things, — in health, in the good things to eat and to drink, in fun, and humor, and contentment, — and that war's desolation may not reach you, — nor the sound, except softened and subdued by thousands of miles of distance. Not but that you should think sometimes, in the midst of all your happiness of the soldiers in the field who fight the country's battles, and of those who are wounded and suffering in hospitals, — and give them something to comfort and cheer them from your abundance.

As for me, I shall probably sit alone at the "La Pierre", or look out of the windows upon the sea of Christmas, not in envy if not partaking, not lonesome if alone, happy, if for no

---

[16] A printed heading except for part of the date.

other reason than that I have no reason to be otherwise.

You will not regard this a letter, — only the announcement that I cannot come home. — O, there is one thing that I wish to ask about. — I sent you a quite long account of our battle at Bristoe Station, Oct. 14, — and you have not written me a word as to whether you received it or not. Please do so, in your next. — State whether you have or have not, received it.

With much love for you all
I remain yours,

Frank A. Haskell.

*   *   *   *   *

Philadelphia, Pa.
Jan. 17, 1864.

Dear Brother:[17] — Yours of the 11th inst. is at hand. You say, if I desire promotion, &c. *by all means come home at once.* In this connection I may be allowed to remark, that whatever of reputation I have, I have gained, not by being away from my place, but by being always in it. To seek office for myself, — to importune those personally who have the granting of commissions, — to urge before them my claims and my disappointments, is a thing so uncongenial to my sense of propriety, so repugnant to all my instincts, and so different from my habits, that I do not think any thing will ever induce me to do it again, or to do it at all. These vile wretches who have disgraced our arms, — prolonged the war by their blunders — and shed the fruitless blood of many thousands of men, have themselves sought and obtained the high offices which they now desecrate. — Would you have me imitate such? I hope not. — I am on duty here; and could not if I would, and would not if I could, go home to get promotion. Promotion must come

---

[17] The addressee is Harrison S. Haskell. See H.S. Haskell to Gov. James T. Lewis, January 27, 1864, in Wis., Exec. Dept., Applications for Commissions, 1861–65, Series 1/1/5–20, Archives Div., SHSW.

to me, because I deserve it, and not because I ask for it, — or
it comes not at all..

I desire promotion — am ambitious — as much as any man:
— but I value my own self respect, above all promotions and
the gratification of all ambitions, — and this I shall endeavor
to preserve at all hazards. I think I deserve the colonelcy of
a regiment, — that of the 6th would please me, above any
other, — for I helped to make that regiment. — There have
been those of high position in the regiment, and in other
regiments, who have said that I made the 6th. But the colonelcy
of any good regiment would suit me — or any regiment — for
I could make it good. Gnls. Hancock and Gibbon have given
me to understand that any thing they could do for me, by
recommendation or otherwise, for such a place, they would be
glad to do. I do not know what Gov. Lewis thinks of me. —
If you can find out, and the recommendations of these Gnls.
and Gnl. Meade would help me get a colonelcy, I can get them
and send them to you. — If such recommendations would be of
no avail, I should prefer not to send, or get them. Possibly
the Governor will not feel at liberty to brake [sic] the rule of
his predecessors, and that the Larebees, the Utleys, the Sand-
ers, the Sweets, the Jussens, the Hobarts, and so forth will go
on receiving commissions to the end, — remote — of the war.
— God deliver the country from such, and from the Wash-
burns and Schurzs![18]

I would like you to see, or to write to the Governor, and
learn his views. — I shall until the end of the war be unwilling
to take a less commission than that of Colonel of a regiment.
— I do not think I could be induced to. By-and-by I shall

---

[18] These men — all of them politically appointed officers from
Wisconsin — are Col. Charles H. Larrabee, 24th Wisconsin Infantry; Col. William L. Utley, 22nd Wisconsin Infantry; Cols.
Benjamin J. Sweet and Harrison C. Hobart, both of the 21st Wisconsin Infantry; Lt. Col. Edmund Jussen, 23rd Wisconsin Infantry;
Maj. Gen. Cadwallader C. Washburn, originally of the 2nd Wisconsin Cavalry; and Brig. Gen. Carl Schurz, then a divisional commander in the Army of the Cumberland.

probably get a Staff promotion, but I do not know.

I should be willing to write to the Governor, and tell him that I thought I was fit to be a Colonel, but farther, I should be unwilling personally to do any thing for my promotion.

This making offices and officers public prostitutes is a thing that has made, and is making, so much evil and mischief in the country, that I cannot be a party to the crime.

A Colonelcy would be desirable for the rank it would give me, — with that, — if I should live, — I might be the wearer of a star before the war was over. — In this connection let me say that a gentleman has told me that a General who knew me told him — I suppose the Gnl. was Hancock — that had I been at West Point, I should have been a Major General before this, and that I ought to be a Brigadier now.

Gnl. Cutler[19] is here, — he tells me that Salomon's refusing to promote me, lost him the re-nomination, — if this is so, it is good. — He says he has had the pleasure of assuring the Ex-Dutchman, from Judea, of the fact, by letter.

This then is about what I would like: for you to ascertain if Gov. Lewis will, when there is a chance, make me a Colonel, and to let me know if you desire the recommendations of Generals in the field, who know me.

If I can get a Colonelcy, well; — if not, then I shall do as I have done, attend right along to my duties, on the field or elsewhere as long as I am able, — and let results, and promotions go as they will, — and thank Heaven that I am not a politician.

There is one thing, however, about the 6th, — 1st, I do not think Bragg[20] will be promoted, — 2nd, if he is I do not think a Colonel of the 6th can be mustered into the service, — the regiment is not large enough.

---

[19] Lysander Cutler, Haskell's regimental commander in the 6th Wisconsin, was promoted to brigadier general in late 1862.

[20] Edward S. Bragg, who had succeeded Cutler as colonel of the 6th Wisconsin, was promoted to brigadier general on July 2, 1864, and commanded the Iron Brigade. Nolan, *Iron Brigade*, 197, 275.

Let me hear from this matter again. I should like to know about the re-nomination of Salomon, too.

Truly yours.

Frank A. Haskell.

La Pierre House

*   *   *   *   *

"La Pierre House"

Philadelphia, Pa.

February 2, 1864.

I have written to Harvey today,[21] but since writing, Gnl. Gibbon has handed me his and General Meade's recommendations to the Governor for my promotion to the Colonelcy of the 10th or 19th Wis.

These recommendations I have forwarded to Firmin,[22] to hand to the Governor.

They are good recommendations, and I think should have weight, for not many could get such.

Advance my interest, with the Governor, if you can.

Frank A. Haskell.

to H. S.

---

[21] Not found. This note to Harrison S. Haskell is the last by Frank A. Haskell in the Haskell Papers, SHSW.

[22] For identification of Frank H. Firmin, see the first and concluding chapters.

VI

Ambition Fulfilled

FOR FRANK HASKELL, the gray winter days of early 1864 were bright with promise. After two years of waiting, his ambition for promotion was to be fulfilled. He had the warm endorsements of his superiors. The former commander of the 6th Wisconsin, General Lysander Cutler, asserted that Haskell ". . .contributed more than any one officer to bring the Regiment to the condition which has gained it so much credit." The old general went so far as to say, "If he had his deserts, he would now lead a Brigade instead of being a first Lieut." General Gibbon, despite his feelings about political appointment of officers, urged the promotion of his staff officer to a colonelcy. In an appeal to state pride, the ex-chief of the Iron Brigade concluded, ". . .I have such faith in Wis. troops and such a regard for their welfare that I would not recommend an undeserving officer to command them." Even the commander of the Army of the Potomac, General George G. Meade, endorsed Lieutenant Haskell for a colonel's commission because of his "gallantry and good conduct" at Fredericksburg and Gettysburg. Haskell possessed, as usual, the confidence of the army leaders.

The key which at this time opened the door for Haskell's promotion was not military but political. At the end of Governor Edward Salomon's term in January, 1864, James T. Lewis assumed the governorship with its appointive power. Lewis, who had practiced law in Columbus, Wisconsin, since

241

1845, almost certainly knew Harrison S. Haskell, one of the few other pioneer lawyers there, and perhaps had met Frank Haskell as well. Certainly Harrison Haskell pled his brother's cause with assurance. He sent the Governor Frank Haskell's military recommendations and also his brother's letter of January 17, with its strictures on politically appointed Wisconsin officers. He attributed the lieutenant's failure to win higher rank to Salomon's obstruction and to his brother's being on staff duty, outside the usual line of promotion. Harrison Haskell asked, "Has Wisconsin Honors and promotions for all her sons else, and none for him?"[1] The Governor's private and military secretary, who acknowledged this letter, was Frank H. Firmin, the Madison lawyer and Haskell's prewar companion. Firmin later acknowledged that he had come "to love & admire" Haskell. With his own secretary joining in the cry for promotion, Governor Lewis on February 9 offered Haskell the first available colonelcy, that of the new 36th Wisconsin Infantry Regiment.[2]

By the latter part of the month, Frank Haskell was back in Madison, ready to recruit and train his regiment. The veteran's appearance reflected his 35 years. His sunken eyes sometimes had a look of weariness, and his hair had receded to bare the top of his head. He wore the long sideburns which had become fashionable during the war and he had grown an arching mustache something like that of his former commander,

---

[1] The quotations are, respectively, from L. Cutler to J. T. Lewis, January 3, 1864, John Gibbon to Gov. of Wis., February 2, 1864, with endorsement by [George G. Meade — signature clipped off], and H.S. Haskell to Lewis, January 27, 1864. See also H.S. Haskell to Lewis, January 30, 1864. All these letters are in Wis., Exec. Dept., Applications for Commissions, 1861–65, Ser. 1/1/5–20, Archives Div. SHSW. For Lewis, see DWB, 229–30.

[2] Frank H. Firmin to H.S. Haskell, February 6, 1864, and to Frank A. Haskell, February 9, 1864, in Wis., Exec. Dept., Letters Sent Books, General, 1861–64, Vol. 11, pp. 468, 485, Ser. 1/1/11, Archives Div., SHSW. The quoted words are in Firmin to Harvey M. Haskell, June 15, 1864, in the Haskell Mss., Pa. Historical and Museum Commission.

John Gibbon.[3] A journalist felt that Haskell's years of conflict had even added to "the soldierly zest and spirit that have always characterized him."[4] With his civilian background, military tastes, and practical education in the field, he was well prepared to instruct inexperienced officers, lead men who would never be professional soldiers, maneuver his regiment competently, and, if necessary, inspire it with a display of raw courage. He had all the attributes of a successful Civil War colonel.[5]

Just as Camp Randall, trampled by countless recruits and even war prisoners, was no longer the green fairgrounds of old, so the men whom Haskell collected at the Madison encampment were not the eager young bachelors who had filled the ranks in 1861. Addressing Haskell's potential recruits, a local editor urged, "Hurry up your enlistments, boys, or the draft will soon be after you."[6] Among those who responded to this coercive appeal were many married men, concerned about the support of their families and much interested in the sizable bounties then being given for enlistments. Colonel Haskell, having been mustered into Federal service with his men on March 23, tried to make this half-willing material into a fighting regiment before the spring campaign. He drilled the men and did his best to keep them from "taking frenches." To stop unauthorized absences, he combined stern orders with fatherly promises to do his best to grant furloughs to all. In personal speeches at the barracks, he held out the hope that they might be kept at Madison for a time or sent to Minnesota to guard against hostile Indians.[7] Alternately threatening and

[3] Portrait in Lathem, "Chronicler of Gettysburg," in *Dartmouth Alumni Magazine* (May, 1958), 22.

[4] Madison *Wisconsin Daily State Journal*, February 23, 1864.

[5] For a good discussion of a colonel's attributes, see T. Harry Williams, "Badger Colonels and the Civil War Officer," in *Wisconsin Magazine of History*, 47: 38–39 (Autumn, 1963).

[6] Madison *Daily Patriot*, March 1, 1864.

[7] Haskell's file in U.S., War Dept., A.G.O., Compiled Services Records for 36th Wisconsin, National Archives. For attitudes of

cajoling, Haskell, as one recruit put it, "brought us to strict discipline as soon as circumstances would permit."[8]

Haskell and the 36th Wisconsin had little enough time for training before they had to respond to the Army of the Potomac's insatiable demand for manpower. On May 10, 1864, they left by rail for Washington, where the men were kept within a guarded fence. Control of new regiments, like all else, had become part of a vast system. The troops grumbled about Haskell, both as a stern disciplinarian and as a hardened veteran supposedly eager to hurry them into battle. They knew how scant was their preparation — they had received their rifles only days before leaving Madison — and they feared that "it is his intention to rush us right into the thickest of it without having had a chance to try our arms. . . ."[9] Haskell, on the contrary, worried about his fate as their commander. To a college friend whom he met on the street, he predicted that he would fall in his next battle. "You see, I have a green regiment. . .," he explained. "I cannot get behind the lines as I might do in the case of seasoned troops. I shall be obliged always to lead," he gloomily predicted, "and of course I shall be shot."[10]

On May 16, troubled by such grim thoughts, Haskell and

---

enlisted men towards bounties, "French leaves," and Haskell, see David Coon to wife, February 28, April 6, 30, 1864, in the David Coon Letters, SHSW, and John Black to Jane Black, February 25, March 17, 1864, in the John Black Letters, SHSW.

[8] James M. Aubrey, *The Thirty-Sixth Wisconsin Volunteer Infantry. . ., An Authentic Record of the Regiment from Its Organization to Its Muster Out. . ., With Reminiscences from the Author's Private Journal* (n.p. [1900]), 37. Unless otherwise indicated, the subsequent discussion of the unit's movements rests on this source.

[9] Black to Black, May 14, 1864, Black Letters, SHSW; quotation from Coon to wife, May 15, 1864, SHSW.

[10] Recollection by Daniel Hall quoted in Lathem, "Chronicler of Gettysburg," 22. In Civil War tactics, a colonel's normal place was thirty paces to the rear of a regiment moving into battle. Williams, "Badger Colonels," 45.

his men started for the front. The Army of the Potomac, still
headed by Meade but under the immediate supervision of the
new supreme commander, Ulysses S. Grant, had already fought
a bloody stand-off with Lee in the Wilderness of northern
Virginia. Haskell's regiment was in reserve during the next
indecisive bloodletting at Spotsylvania, south of the old Chancellorsville battlefield. The 36th Wisconsin was assigned to
Winfield Scott Hancock's Second Corps and, at the request of
both Haskell and Gibbon, Hancock put the regiment in the
latter's 2nd Division. Gibbon intended to give his friend
command of a brigade at an early opportunity.[11] On May 31,
as Grant continued his turning movement to the south, Haskell's regiment was in its first actual battle, at Bethesda Church.
Admonishing some of his men against attempting to dodge
enemy fire, Haskell told them that the musket balls were already passed by the time they heard them. Just then a shot went
through his hat and he unconsciously ducked. Raising his hat
immediately, he coolly remarked, "Excuse me, gentlemen."[12]
Colonel Haskell was doing his best to inspire his green troops.

He and his men soon had desperate need for courage. After a
month of flanking operations, Grant decided upon a frontal
assault on Lee's formidable entrenchments near Cold Harbor.
Very early on the morning of June 3, Haskell led his regiment
in this Federal repetition of the horrors of Pickett's Charge.
When his brigade commander fell, Haskell succeeded him. At
last he was exercising all the powers of a general. The heavy
Confederate fire pinned down the Union troops, but Gibbon
sent word to push on. Haskell's men stood up and a storm of
lead thinned their ranks. He shouted to them to lie down.
As he stood almost alone, leaning on his sword, a musket ball
smashed into his temple. During one of the war's bloodiest
disasters, Frank Haskell fulfilled his ambition to command —
and within three hours was dead.[13]

[11] Gibbon, *Personal Recollections*, 234.
[12] Aubrey, *Thirty-Sixth Wisconsin*, 58–59.
[13] [Reuben Gold Thwaites], preface to Frank Aretas Haskell,

"This sad event has cast a gloom over all of us. . . ," General Gibbon told Haskell's older brother. Gibbon and General Hancock repeatedly displayed their sorrow over the death of the subordinate who had become their friend. Later they named for him a fort in the Union entrenchments at Petersburg. Newspaper editors and Wisconsin spokesmen registered their shock. The Madison city council and the bar of that city adopted resolutions of regret. Most of those who mourned Haskell stressed his honor, his courage, his intelligence and his cultivated tastes.[14] So too did his formal eulogist. On June 12 an Episcopal clergyman, the Reverend A. J. M. Hudson, conducted his funeral at Portage, the home of Harrison and Harvey Haskell. The minister described Frank Haskell as the culmination of a line of martyrs beginning with St. Stephen. Having read some of Haskell's letters, he paraphrased them in describing the dead man's war record. He told of how Haskell had rallied the troops at Gettysburg and cried out, "That one act is fame enough for any man." Finally, he predicted the erection of a marble shaft over Haskell's grave. There, said he, "other generations of freedom's children . . . will proudly read

The Battle of Gettysburg (2nd ed., Madison, 1910), xv–xx; Harvey M. Haskell to Betsey Ann Haskell, June 25, 1864, in the Dartmouth Archives. From May 26 to June 7, 1864, the 36th Wisconsin lost 400 killed or wounded. By percentage of its enrollment killed in action, the unit finally ranked seventeenth among all Union regiments. "Letters from a Soldier," in *Wisconsin Then and Now,* 12: 4 (May, 1966), which contains excerpts from the Coon Letters cited above.
[14] The quotation is from General Gibbon to H. S. Haskell, [June, 1864], in *Columbus Democrat* (Wisconsin), May 29, 1895. See also Francis A. Walker, *History of the Second Army Corps in the Army of the Potomac* (New York, 1886), 512–13, 608; Madison *Wisconsin State Journal,* June 4, 6, 8, 11, 1864; Madison *Daily Patriot,* June 4, 1864; copy of the resolutions of the Madison City Council in the Haskell Mss., Pa. Historical and Museum Commission; H. M. Haskell to Betsey Ann Haskell, June 25, 1864, in the Dartmouth Archives.

the record of thy life, will drop a tear of tenderness and reverently whisper 'The Grave of Frank A. Haskell'."[15]

Haskell's eulogist overestimated posterity's remembrance of his subject's heroic deeds. True, Haskell's brothers raised a modest shaft over his grave in Portage's Silver Lake Cemetery; but it would be nearly a century before his government would supplement it with even the uniform block of stone used for soldiers' burial places. Some of his comrades remembered him — the Columbus post of the Grand Army of the Republic bore his name, and the painter of a picture of the battle of Gettysburg included him as one small figure on a mammoth canvas. All of these memorials to his deeds might have been enough to make known the name of Frank Haskell to an occasional curious schoolboy or antiquarian. If there had been nothing more, Haskell would probably be remembered as much — or as little — as Rufus Dawes or Lysander Cutler.[16]

While Haskell's military renown faded like the old uniforms of his surviving comrades, his reputation as an author began to rise. Most of his letters, carefully preserved at Portage by Harrison S. Haskell, ultimately went to the State Historical Society of Wisconsin, where they long remained unpublished. But Haskell's description of Gettysburg, the longest and all-around best of his war papers, made his name known to successive generations of readers. Soon after its author's death, his brothers submitted it to Andrew Jackson Turner, editor of the Portage *Wisconsin State Register,* who rejected it as being too long for newspaper publication. Harvey Haskell took the Gettysburg manuscript to western Pennsylvania, either when he moved there in the 1860's or after Harrison Haskell's

---

[15] Portage *Wisconsin State Register,* June 18, 1864.
[16] Notes by Andrew T. Weaver about Haskell's grave; Frederick Stare, "Frank A. Haskell," a typewritten sketch in the Weaver materials in Mss. Div., SHSW; P. F. Rothermel's painting of Gettysburg and accompanying description in the Pa. State Museum, Harrisburg.

death in 1879. In about 1881 he published a slightly edited version of it as a pamphlet for private circulation. One of Frank Haskell's Dartmouth classmates, Daniel Hall, then edited the pamphlet's contents for inclusion in a history of the Class of 1854 published in 1898. Hall omitted some of Haskell's critical statements, notably those concerning the still-living Daniel Sickles. In 1908, the Massachusetts Commandery of the Military Order of the Loyal Legion reprinted the Dartmouth edition. In the same year, the Wisconsin History Commission, which included the historian Frederick Jackson Turner, son of the Portage editor who had originally considered the Gettysburg narrative for publication, reissued the text of Harvey Haskell's pamphlet. Since the Wisconsin edition numbered 2500 copies, Haskell's work began to reach a wider audience.[17]

Some of Haskell's readers resented his harsh comments on individuals and units. General Alexander S. Webb, commander of the "Philadelphia Brigade" which Haskell had helped to rally during Pickett's Charge, had not disagreed with the pamphlet edition of the letter which he had first read in 1881. But, when he saw the Massachusetts Commandery edition circulating more widely Haskell's description of his men's

---

[17] The history of the earlier publication of the narrative is in [Thwaites], Preface to Haskell, *Battle of Gettysburg*, xxi–xxiii. But, because of a misinterpretation of Andrew Jackson Turner's inscription on the copy of the original pamphlet in the Portage Public Library (from which the Commission reprinted its edition), Thwaites asserts that A. J. Turner himself published or printed the pamphlet about fifteen years after its author's death. Letters by C. C. Britt of Portage to Lyman Copeland Draper, June 13 and 29, 1887, pasted inside the copy of the pamphlet in SHSW, indicate that the pamphlet, which lacked a formal title page, was probably printed in Pennsylvania. The date of 1881 is supplied on the basis of the fact that Harvey Haskell was then distributing complimentary copies. For this, see Alexander S. Webb to H. M. Haskell, November 3, 1881, and W. G. Mitchell to Haskell, November 11, 1881, in Haskell Mss., Pa. Historical and Museum Commission.

near-rout, he called on the Philadelphia Brigade Association to issue a reply. In it, a committee of the Association offered little or no specific evidence to refute Haskell's assertions. Instead, they pictured the writer as an immature young man, so swept by passion as to be incapable of accurate observation. And they fired at him barrages of abuse. They ridiculed Haskell's story of "his wild 'Buffalo Bill' ride" between the contending forces and even questioned his account of the wounding of his horse "with enough of Confederate lead to have warranted Haskell in organizing a Company to mine the lead in 'Dick's' body." They mocked Haskell as both "the Napoleon of Gettysburg" and "this Wellington of Lee's Waterloo." They demanded from the publishers retractions of Haskell's "raving distracted, ridiculous utterances," of his "incoherent, disconnected trash."[18]

Haskell's words outlived the angry veterans. In 1910, the Wisconsin History Commission proceeded with plans to issue a second edition of 2500 copies to satisfy the demand for the Haskell book.[19] During the same year, it allowed Charles W. Eliot to reprint its version in his popular set of *Harvard Classics*. In 1937, the *Titusville Herald* (Pennsylvania) republished the Wisconsin History Commission's edition; and twenty years later (Boston, [1957]) Bruce Catton edited it for yet another appearance. Then James B. Stevenson, editor of the *Titusville Herald*, discovered that the Pennsylvania Historical

---

[18] For Webb's initial reaction, see Webb to H. M. Haskell, November 3, 1881, in *ibid.* His letter of September 7, 1909, denouncing Haskell's essay is in "Reply of the Philadelphia Brigade Association to the Foolish and Absurd Narrative of Lieutenant Frank A. Haskell. . . ," a typescript of the pamphlet which was published in 1910. This document, together with related correspondence between the Association and Governor James O. Davidson, is in Wis., Exec. Dept., Civil War Memorials Correspondence, Ser. 1/1/5–12, Archives Div., SHSW.

[19] The Commission first learned at this time of the existence of the other Haskell letters. Entry for January 20, 1910, in the minute book, Wis. History Comm. Papers, SHSW.

and Museum Commission, of which he was also Chairman, had the manuscript of Haskell's letter. Comparing it with Harvey Haskell's pamphlet and making a few corrections, he published the narrative in 1963 in his newspaper. Thus, through the early 1960's, Haskell's account of Gettysburg appeared in nine printings and reached thousands of readers.

Even these numerous editions were not the full measure of Frank Haskell's renown. Many who never saw his book nevertheless heard of him and read at least some of his words. Most of the many popular and scholarly books on Gettysburg paraphrased and quoted Haskell. Compilers of anthologies and even of phonograph records included excerpts from his essay.[20] The name of Frank Haskell became inseparably associated with the battle. With the aid of twentieth-century editors, authors, and publishers, this nineteenth-century soldier fulfilled his wish for fame. No lofty marble shaft testified to it. Obelisks of printed pages, columns of words by and about him: these were the enduring monuments to Haskell of Gettysburg. □

---

[20] For examples, besides the works previously cited, see Earl Schenck Miers, *Gettysburg* (New Brunswick, New Jersey, 1948); Fairfax Davis Downey, *The Guns at Gettysburg* (New York, 1958); Glenn Tucker, *High Tide at Gettysburg: The Campaign in Pennsylvania* (Indianapolis, 1958); Charlton Laird, ed., *Pickett at Gettysburg (Casebooks for Objective Writing,* Boston, 1965); *The Civil War, Its Music and Sounds,* Vol. 1, a Mercury record and accompanying pamphlet with a print of the battle by John B. Bachelder which shows Haskell.

INDEX

Abbott, Henry L., captain, 166, 169
Adams, Charles P., lieutenant colonel, 125
Allen, Thomas S., colonel, 37, 81, 230
"The American Character," essay by Haskell, 11
Anderson, Richard H., general, 114
Antietam, Md., battle of: 89, 136, 150, 172, 187, 234; described, 42, 47–49; Haskell rallies troops at, 56
Armistead, Lewis A., general, 171, 187
Army of the Cumberland, 238
Army of Northern Virginia, 217
Army of the Potomac: 18, 29, 42, 51, 52, 79, 87, 111, 128, 135, 146, 159, 173, 181, 184, 201, 206, 223, 228, 233, 245; condition of, 54, 57–58; Haskell praises, 85, 92, 183, 187, 202–203; morale of, 91–93
Army of Virginia, 23, 24
Arnold, Mrs., friend of Haskell family, 60
Arnold, William A., captain, 107, 124, 160, 218
Artillery: employment of, 30–38 *passim*, 108, 114–115, 118–119, 124, 143, 144, 148–157, 160, 161, 214, 217–221
Artillery units. *See* respective states; United States
Atwood, Julius, P., lieutenant colonel, 10, 12, 15, 16, 18, 20

Bachellé, Werner Von, captain, 49
Barksdale, William, general, 187
Barlow, Francis C., general, 96
Batteries. *See* respective states; United States
Bethesda Church, Va., battle of, 245
Biddle, James C., major, 144
"Billy." *See* Haskell, Frank A., horses
Birney, David Bell, general, 121, 132
Bivouacking, described, 211–212
Black Hat Brigade. *See* Iron Brigade
Bragg, Braxton, general, 206, 223
Bragg, Edward S., promotions from major through general, 20, 37, 66, 239
Brandy Station, Va., battle of, 87

Brawner Farm. *See* Gainesville, Va., battle of
Bristoe Campaign, 206, 208–225. *See also* Kelly's Ford, Va., battle of
Bristoe Station, Va., battle of: 206, 237; described, 216–221
Brooke, John R., colonel, 220
Brooks, William T. H., general, 61
Brown, T. Fred, lieutenant, 107, 124, 125, 127, 155, 217, 218
Buford, John, general, 95, 210, 211, 224, 231
Bull Run, Va., second battle of, 29, 136, 150, 172, 185, 234; Iron Brigade in, 45
Burial, soldiers': Haskell's views on, 195–197, 199, 234–235
Burns, John, 97
Burnside, Ambrose E., general: 51, 52, 87, 132; at South Mountain, 31, 32, 34, 35, 46
Butterfield, Daniel, general, 132

Caldwell, John C., general, 106, 118, 121, 140, 174, 212
Callis, John B., lieutenant colonel, 97
Camp Randall, Madison, Wis., 16, 17, 18, 243
Campbell, Joseph B., captain, 27, 28, 32, 45
Carroll, Samuel S., colonel, 130, 220
Catton, Bruce, 249
Cavalry: Union, reviewed, 57; Haskell disparages, 94, 115, 181, 214; employment of, 107–108, 210, 224
Cedar Mountain, Va., battle of, 23, 24
Chancellorsville, Va., battle of: 93, 98, 172, 185; described, 52, 61–86 *passim;* Hooker blamed for defeat, 91, 201
Charleston, S.C., attack on, 58
Chickamauga, Ga., battle of, 206
Cold Harbor, Va., battle of, 245
Collins, Alexander Lynn, 10, 11
Colquitt, Alfred H., general, 36, 37
Columbus, Wis.: Haskell's years at, 4–5
Colvill, William, Jr., colonel, 125

253

Colwell, Wilson, captain, 37

Committee on the Conduct of the War, 84

Confederates: Haskell's dislike for, 54–55, 71, 197–198; bravery of, 115, 184–185, 196

Conscription: conscripts, 208, 214, 222; administration of, 223, 228, 232, 235, 236; and enlistments, 243

Corps (Army of the Potomac):

—First, 30, 31, 51, 61, 65, 66, 68, 100, 112, 115, 138, 140, 177, 180, 181, 187, 195, 200, 200, 211, 213, 222, 229, 230, 231; on first day, Gettysburg, 95–97, 98, 99, 101; subsequent disposition of, 104, 106, 109; on second day, Gettysburg, 123, 127, 129

—Second, 55, 57, 61, 80, 89, 93, 102, 103, 110, 111, 113, 132, 135, 143, 147, 177, 180, 181, 185, 190, 192, 199, 204, 206, 207, 209–225 passim, 229, 230, 231, 232, 245; on first day, Gettysburg, 98–100; subsequent disposition of, 106–107, 109; on second day, Gettysburg, 117–118, 120–121, 122–127, 130; early on third day, Gettysburg, 136–137, 138–139, 140–142; and Pickett's Charge, 148–176; Haskell praises, 186–187

—Third, 57, 61, 63, 80, 99, 102, 111, 113, 114, 132, 139, 140, 177, 180, 181, 187, 209–224 passim, 229, 230, 231; disposition of, Gettysburg, 107, 109; on second day, Gettysburg, 116–123, 124, 127

—Fifth, 57, 61, 63, 140, 177, 180, 181, 210–212 passim, 229, 230, 231; disposition of, Gettysburg, 107; on second day, Gettysburg, 118–127 passim

—Sixth, 57, 61, 66, 68, 70–79, 81, 108, 118, 122, 127, 140, 141, 177, 180, 181, 210, 211, 213, 222, 229, 230, 231

—Ninth, 30, 31

—Eleventh, 55, 61, 63, 65, 85, 112, 113, 115, 177, 180, 181, 207, 223; alleged misconduct of, Chancellorsville, 80–81; on first day, Gettysburg, 95–97, 99, 101; subsequent disposition of, 104, 106, 109; on second day, Gettysburg, 129, 130; alleged misconduct of, Gettysburg, 184, 185

—Twelfth, 61, 63, 99, 102, 112, 115, 132, 140, 177, 180, 181, 190, 195, 200, 207, 223; disposition of, Gettysburg, 106, 109; on second day, Gettysburg, 123, 127, 129, 130; on third day, Gettysburg, 137–138

Couch, Darius N., general, 56, 57, 63, 98

Cross, Edward E., colonel, 125

Cushing, Alonzo, lieutenant, 107, 124, 150, 152, 160, 161, 162, 164

Cutler, Lysander, colonel: 18, 19, 21, 37, 66, 68, 247; described, 16; urges Haskell's promotion, 20, 50, 239, 241

Dartmouth College: 2, 248; Haskell at, 1, 7–9

Davis, Nelson H., lieutenant colonel, 106

Dawes, Rufus R., captain: 247; relationship with Haskell, 16–17, 19, 20–21

Dean, Charles K., adjutant, 24

Delaplaine, George P., 13, 15

Devereux, Arthur F., colonel, 166, 169

"Dick." See Haskell, Frank A., horses

Doubleday, Abner, general: 26, 28, 47, 95, 97, 123, 140, 142; Haskell's criticism of, 39–40, 165

Downie, Mark W., major, 126

Dudley, William W., lieutenant colonel, 97

Early, Jubal A., general, 73, 76, 114

Eliot, Charles W., 249

Ellsworth, E. Elmer, 13–14

Everett, Edward, 233, 234

Ewell, Richard S., general, 114, 115, 129, 137, 176, 195, 220

Fairchild, Charles, 193

Fairchild, Lucius, colonel, 37, 66, 97, 193

Falling Waters, W. Va., battle of, 181, 202

Farrell, Wilson B., captain, 147, 167

Finnicum, Mark, major, 68

Firmin, Frank H.: 11, 12; and Haskell's promotion, 227, 240, 242

Fitzhugh's Crossing, Va., battle of, 66–68. See also Chancellorsville, Va., battle of

Fort Haskell, near Petersburg, Va., 246

Franklin, William B., general, 61

Fredericksburg, Va., battle of: 56, 68, 69, 71, 100, 136, 150, 172, 183, 185, 187, 234; Haskell in, 51

Fredericksburg, Va., "second battle of" (1863): 136, 187; described, 68–75, 80. See also Chancellorsville, Va., battle of

French, William H., general, 181, 211, 229

INDEX

Gainesville, Va., battle of: 234; described, 23, 25–28, 43–45
Garnett, Richard B., general, 171, 187
Geary, John W., general, 123, 137
George, Haskell's servant. See Hamlin, George
German-Americans: Haskell's scorn for troops, 80, 81, 85, 96, 97, 129, 130, 184. See also Salomon, Edward
Gettysburg, Pa.: civilian reactions in, 194, 197–198; appearance after battle, 197–198
Gettysburg, Pa., battle of: 207, 227, 228, 234, 246–250 passim, 249; preceding campaign, 87, 91–94; Pickett's Charge, 89, 157–176, 186–187, 219, 245, 248; first day of, 95–102; disposition of forces in, 103–116; second day of, 116–131; Union war council, 131–135; third day of, 138–176; casualties, 177–178; aftermath, 179–184, 202; characteristics of, 185–186; post-battle descriptions of field, 193–199, 233
Gettysburg, Pa., National Cemetery: consecration of, 232–235
Gibbon, John, general: 68, 79, 93, 100, 101, 103, 106, 117, 121, 125, 135, 136, 143, 148, 165, 173, 174, 187, 188, 189, 190, 199, 204, 206, 207, 208, 231, 243; commands Iron Brigade, 19; influence on Haskell, 19, 20, 22; described, 21, 134; at South Mountain, 29–38; Haskell's affection for, 49, 226; wounds, 51, 88, 89, 191–193; divisional commands, 55–56, 147; corps commands, 98–99, 122, 132; at Fredericksburg, "second battle of," 69–75; luncheon at Gettysburg, 144–147; philosophy on danger, 155; at Pickett's Charge, 157, 159, 160, 161; at Cleveland, Ohio, 228, 232; at Gettysburg National Cemetery, 232–235; at Philadelphia, Pa., 235; backs Haskell's promotion, 238, 240, 241; and Haskell's death, 245, 246
Gordon, Alexander, Jr., captain, 68
Gorman, Willis A., general, 36
Governor's Guard, Madison, Wis.: 37; Haskell's membership in, 12–15
Grand Army of the Republic post: named for Haskell, 247
Grant, Ulysses S., general, 187, 245
Gregg, David M., general, 210, 211, 214, 215, 220
Groveton. See Gainesville, Va., battle of

Guppy, Joshua J., colonel, 5, 21

Hall, Daniel, 248
Hall, Norman J., colonel, 161; at Pickett's Charge, 165–167, 169
Hamlin, George, 136, 146
Hancock, Winfield Scott, general: 110, 117, 125, 135, 140, 143, 165, 171–175 passim, 188, 190, 204, 207, 213, 225, 245; wound, 89, 191–192; commands, 122, 132, 147; at first day, Gettysburg, 98–99, 101–102; described, 101, 133; Gettysburg luncheon, 145, 146; backs Haskell's promotion, 238, 239; and Haskell's death, 246
Harrow, William, general, 89, 106, 161, 165, 167, 175, 193
Harvey, Louis P., governor, 19, 20
Haskell, Frank A.: described, 1, 6, 9, 242–243; education, 1, 6–9; early life, 2–6; religion, 4, 246; and women, 5–6, 85–86; shortens first name, 8; affection for relatives, 7, 17, 49–50, 82; lawyer, 9–11; essay on "The American Character," 11; in militia, 12–15; in politics, 14; and training of 6th Wisconsin, 16–18; hopes for promotion, 19–21, 50, 227, 237–242, 245; staff assignments, 22, 64–65, 85, 89, 99, 206, 228, 232, 235; war letters, 24, 42, 77–78, 83; illness, 43; horses, 49, 88, 125–136, 188–189, 249; Gettysburg essay, preparation, 87–90 passim, 199–200, 203–204, 227; wound, 88, 189, 193; text of Gettysburg essay, 90–202; publication history of Gettysburg essay, 90, 247–250; praised for Gettysburg role, 166, 167, 191, 199, 204; views on history, 200–202; colonel of 36th Wisconsin, 242; death, 245; funeral, 246–247
Haskell, Franklin A. See Haskell, Frank A.
Haskell, Harrison S.: influence on Frank Haskell, 2–6 passim; seeks brother's promotion, 56, 237, 240, 242
Haskell, Harvey M.: edits Gettysburg essay, 90, 247–248, 250
Hatch, John P., general, 25, 26, 27, 30
Hays, Alexander, general, 106, 114, 165, 212
Hays, William, general, 89, 181, 206
Hazard, John G., captain, 107, 149
Heath, Francis E., colonel, 118, 217
Heth, Henry, general, 114, 158, 219, 220

Hickory Guards, 15
Hill, Ambrose P., general, 114, 115, 120, 217, 220
Hill, Daniel H., general, 37
Hobart, Harrison C., colonel, 238
Hood, John B., general, 114
Hooker, Joseph, general: 30, 31, 32, 34. 46, 47, 48, 52, 63, 64, 65, 74, 76, 79, 80, 81, 87, 94; blamed for Chancellorsville defeat, 82–86, 91, 98, 200
Howard, Oliver Otis, general: 55, 63, 65, 81, 95, 101, 104, 130, 132, 181, 187, 201; described, 133, 134
Hudson, A. J. M., 246
Hunt, Henry J., general, 157
Huston, James, lieutenant colonel, 120, 125

Indiana infantry regiments, 19, 24, 27, 28, 31–41 passim, 43, 97, 234
Infantry regiments. See respective states
Iron Brigade: 23, 81, 239, 241; creation of, 19, 21; at Gainesville, 25–28, 43–45; named Black Hat Brigade, 29; at South Mountain, 29–38, 46–47; at Antietam, 42, 47–48, 56; at Second Bull Run, 45; at Fitzhugh's Crossing, 66–69; at Gettysburg, 97, 98; flag described, 234

Jackson, Thomas Jonathan, general, 23, 25, 80, 128, 137, 195
Jews, hostile references to, 50, 239
"Joe." See Haskell, Frank A., horses
Johnson, Edward, general, 114
Jussen, Edmund, lieutenant colonel, 5, 21, 238

Kelly's Ford, Va., battle of, 229–231
Kemper, James L., general, 171, 187
Key, Philip Barton, 84, 117, 188
Keyes, Elisha W., 12, 13, 227
Kilpatrick, Hugh Judson, general, 211, 231
King, Rufus, general: 19, 24, 25, 43, 47, 66; backs Haskell's promotion, 50
Know Nothings, 227

Larrabee, Charles H., colonel, 238
Lawe, Ransom, 68
Leclerq, Agnes, 85
Lee, Fitzhugh, general, 114
Lee, Robert E., general, 23, 29, 51, 65, 76, 82, 87, 156, 176, 180, 184, 197, 206, 213, 220, 223, 224, 245

Lewis, James T., governor: Haskell's ties to, 227; and Haskell's promotion, 238–242 passim
Lincoln, Abraham: 94, 233, 234; Haskell's sarcasm about, 57–58, 85, 188
Lincoln, Mary Todd, 57, 58
"Listen to the Mocking Bird," song, 59, 65
Longstreet, James, general, 76, 77, 79, 114, 115, 120, 190, 223
Looting, at Gettysburg, 197–198
Lyman, Theodore, colonel, 101

McClellan, George B., general: 18, 23, 29, 31, 35, 38, 39, 46, 51, 57, 83, 84, 179; Haskell praises, 22, 43, 45, 49, 50
McDowell, Irvin, general: 23, 25; criticized, 45
McLaws, Lafayette, general, 114
Macy, George N., lieutenant colonel, 166
Madison, Wis.: appearance in 1850's, 9–10; city council and bar, on Haskell's death, 246
Madison Institute, 11
Madison Regency, 227
Mallon, James E., colonel, 166, 169, 217
Manassas, First, 172
Manassas, Second. See Bull Run, Va., second battle of
Mansfield, John, major, 97
Massachusetts infantry regiments, 120, 124, 125, 143, 166, 167, 199
Meade, George, captain, 173, 174
Meade, George G., general: 30, 39, 57, 63, 98–103 passim, 106, 107, 110, 112, 117, 123, 137, 140, 144, 152, 160, 161, 167, 176, 180, 183, 188, 190, 201, 206, 209, 215, 222, 228, 245; takes command of army, 93–94; war councils of, 131–135, 181; described, 132, 134, 142–143; luncheon at Gettysburg, 146–147; at Pickett's Charge, 173–174; generalship praised, 179; plans for Bristoe campaign, 210, 212–213, 223–224; backs Haskell's promotion, 238, 240, 241
Medical service, 111, 128, 190–191
Meredith, Solomon, general, 27
Michigan infantry regiments, 67, 167, 234
Military Order of the Loyal Legion: Massachusetts commandery publishes Gettysburg essay, 248
Miller, W. D. W., lieutenant, 125

Minnesota infantry regiment: 147, 167, 199, 218; Haskell praises, 125–126
Mississippi infantry regiments, 98
Mitchell, W. G., lieutenant, 171, 213
Moale, Edward, lieutenant, 232, 233, 235
Morgan, Charles H., lieutenant colonel, 175, 213

National Cemetery. See Gettysburg, Pa., National Cemetery
Newspapers: Haskell's hostility toward, 45, 60, 83–84
Newton, John, general: 104, 132, 146, 181, 211; described, 133
New York artillery battery, 107
New York infantry regiments, 28, 85, 120, 124, 125, 167
North Carolina infantry regiment, 98
Noyes, David K., captain, 47

Oakley, Frank W., lieutenant, 24
O'Connor, Edgar, colonel, 27
Orton, Harlow S., 10
Orton, Myron H., 10
Owen, Joshua T., general, 217

Parsons, William L., captain, 33
Patrick, Marsena, general, 26
Pender, William D., general, 114
Peninsular Campaign, Va., 23, 172
Pennsylvania Historical and Museum Commission, 249, 250
Pennsylvania infantry regiments, 28, 130, 165, 169
Pennsylvania light artillery battery, 214
Pettigrew, James J., general, 158, 171, 181, 186, 219
Philadelphia, Pa.: conditions at, 235, 236
Philadelphia Brigade: focus of Pickett's Charge, 161–170; protests Gettysburg essay, 248–249
Pickets, stationing of, 39–41
Pickett, George E., general, 114, 158, 170, 175, 185, 186, 187, 199
Pickett's Charge. See Gettysburg, Pa., battle of, Pickett's Charge
Pleasonton, Alfred, general: 132, 146, 181; described, 133–134
Plummer, Thomas W., captain, 68
Politics: in Madison, 14; and Haskell's promotion, 19–21, 56, 237–242; Haskell's hostility toward politicians, 22, 83–84, 179–180, 200–201, 202; in Wis., 208, 226, 227
Pope John, general, 29, 45

Portage Wisconsin State Register, and Haskell letters, 24, 42, 247
Prisoners, at Gettysburg, 171–172, 173, 175–176
Provost guards, 111, 147, 190

Randall, Alexander W., governor, 15
Rappahannock Bridge. Va., battle of, 229–231
Regiments. See respective states; United States
Reno, Jesse L., general, 30–34 passim, 46
Republicans, 14, 227. See also Politics
Revere, Paul J., colonel, 125
Reynolds, John F., general: 25, 66, 67, 95, 98, 100, 104, 110, 185; described, 100
Rhode Island artillery battery, 107, 217, 218
Richardson, Israel B., general, 40, 41
Rice, Edmund, major, 166
Ricketts, James B., general, 30, 39
Ricketts, R. Bruce, captain, 214, 218
Robinson, John C., general, 95
Rodes, Robert E., general, 114
Ropes, Henry, lieutenant, 143
Rorty, James McKay, captain, 107, 124, 161
Rothermel, P. F.: includes Haskell in painting, 247
Ryan, William W., lieutenant, 68

Salem Church, Va., battle of, 73–75
Salm-Salm, Agnes, princess, 85
Salm-Salm, Felix, prince, 85
Salomon, Edward, governor: denies Haskell's promotion, 20–21, 50, 241, 242; not renominated, 227, 239, 240
Sanborn, Edwin David, 1
Sapler. See Suplee, Andrew C., captain
Schurz, Carl, general, 80, 96, 238
Second Bull Run or Manassas. See Bull Run, Va., second battle of
Second Fredericksburg. See Fredericksburg, Va., "second battle of" (1863); Chancellorsville, Va., battle of
Sedgwick, John, general: 55, 57, 66, 79, 80, 81, 108, 181, 187, 210, 230; at Second Fredericksburg, 68, 70–73; at Salem Church, 73–78; described, 132–133
Sharpsburg. See Antietam, Md., battle of
Sickles, Daniel E., general: 57, 63, 93, 102, 107, 123, 140, 143, 188, 201, 248; Haskell's contempt for, 84–85, 184; advances at Gettysburg, 116–121

Sigel, Franz, general, 55, 184
Signal officers, 68, 114, 160
Slocum, Henry W., general: 63, 99, 102, 106, 123, 132, 137, 181; described, 133, 134
Smyth, Thomas A., colonel, 218
Soldiers' Cemetery. *See* Gettysburg, Pa., National Cemetery
South Mountain, Md., battle of: 172, 234; described, 29–38, 46–47
Spotsylvania, Va., battle of, 245
Stannard, George J., general, 140, 142, 160
Steele, Amos E., Jr., lieutenant colonel, 167
Steinwehr, Adolph W. A. F. Von, general, 101
Stevens, George H., liuetenant colonel, 97
Stevenson, James B., 249
Stewart, James, lieutenant, 33, 34, 35
Stone, Charles P., general, 55
Stuart, James Ewell Brown, general, 114
Sumner, Edwin V., general, 56, 187
Suplee, Andrew C., captain, 169
Sweet, Benjamin J., lieutenant colonel, 20, 238
Sykes, George, 107, 132, 181, 210; described, 133, 134

Tenney, Daniel K., 15
Thoman, Max, lieutenant colonel, 125
Thwaites, Reuben Gold, 248
Titusville Herald (Pa.), 249, 250
Topping, William C., lieutenant, 68
Tunbridge, Vt.: Haskell's boyhood home at, 2
Turner, Andrew Jackson, 247, 248
Turner, Frederick Jackson, 248
Turner's Gap. *See* South Mountain, Md., battle of

Union Party, 227
United States artillery regiments, 21, 27, 28, 32–38 *passim,* 45, 107

United States Sanitary Commission: nurses, 86
Utley, William L., colonel, 238

Vicksburg, Miss., battle of, 187
Vilas, William F., 20

Wade, Jennie, 198
Wadsworth, James S., general, 66, 95, 138, 181
War Democrats, 227
Ward, George H., colonel, 120, 125
Warren, Gouverneur K., general: 132, 206, 213, 215, 216, 219, 220, 228; Haskell praises, 225
Wartels, Mr., Gettysburg citizen, 233
Washburn, Cadwallader C., general, 238
Webb, Alexander S., general: 161, 165–168 *passim,* 212; rallies troops, 162, 164, 169; reacts to Gettysburg essay, 164, 248–249
Wessels, Francis, captain, 150, 157
Wilderness, Va., battle of the, 245
Williams, Alpheus S., general, 123, 132, 137
Williamsport, Md., 89
Winkler, Frederick C., general, 96
Winner, Septimus, 59
Wisconsin History Commission: publishes Gettysburg essay, 248, 249
Wisconsin infantry regiments: *1st,* 15; *2nd,* 19, 24, 27, 28, 31–38 *passim,* 43, 48, 97, 234, 238; *3rd,* 24, 81; *5th,* 81, 230; *6th,* 16–20 *passim,* 24–28 *passim,* 31–38 *passim,* 43, 47, 48, 51, 67–68, 98, 129, 234, 238, 239, 241; *7th,* 19, 24, 28, 31–38 *passim,* 43, 97, 234; *10th* and *19th,* 240; *21st* and *22nd,* 238; *23rd,* 21, 238; *24th,* 238; *36th,* 242–246 *passim*
Wood, J.P., captain, 64, 85
Woodruff, George A., lieutenant, 107, 124, 151, 157, 160, 161, 199

Zook, Samuel K., general, 125